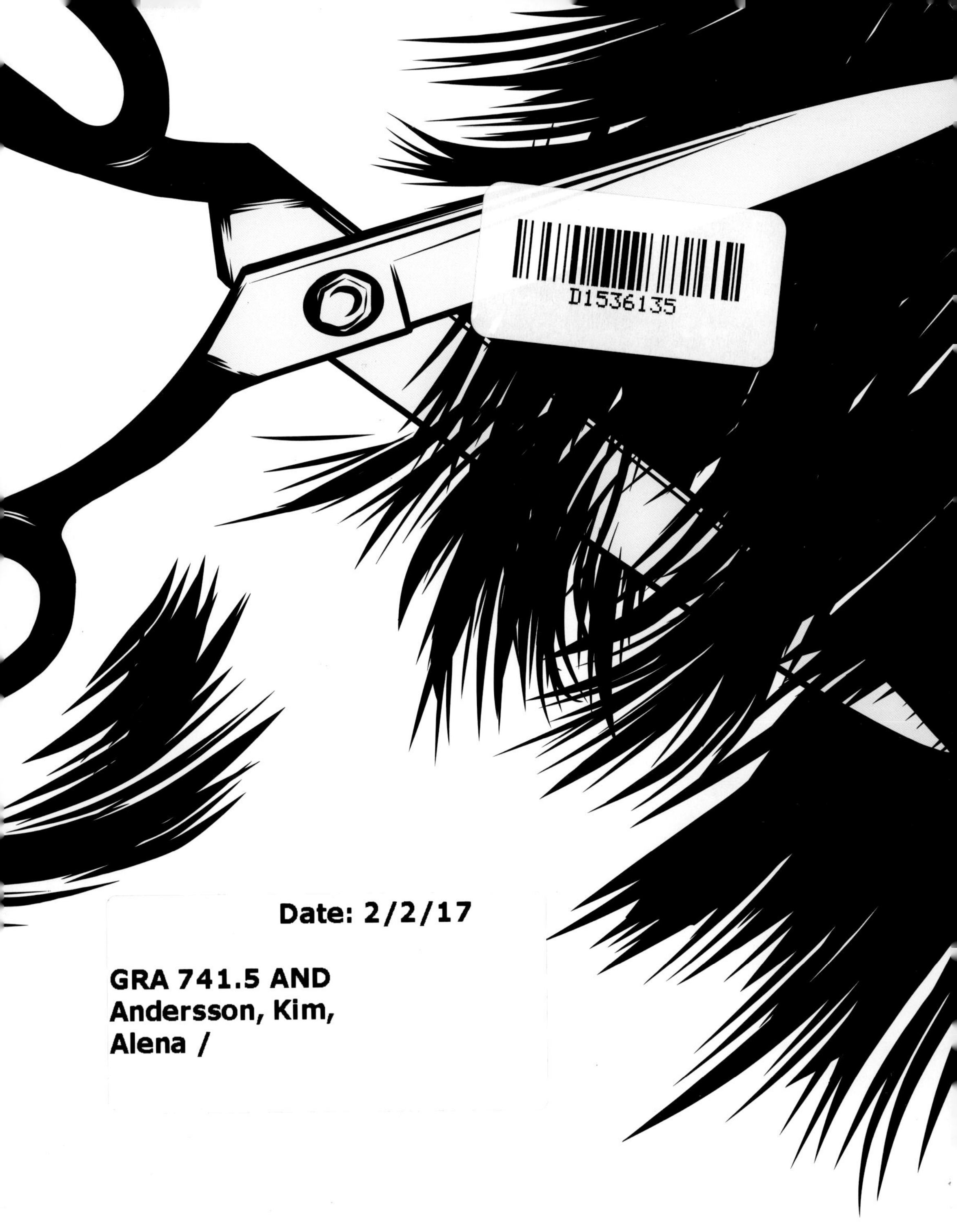



DARK HORSE BOOKS
PRESENTS

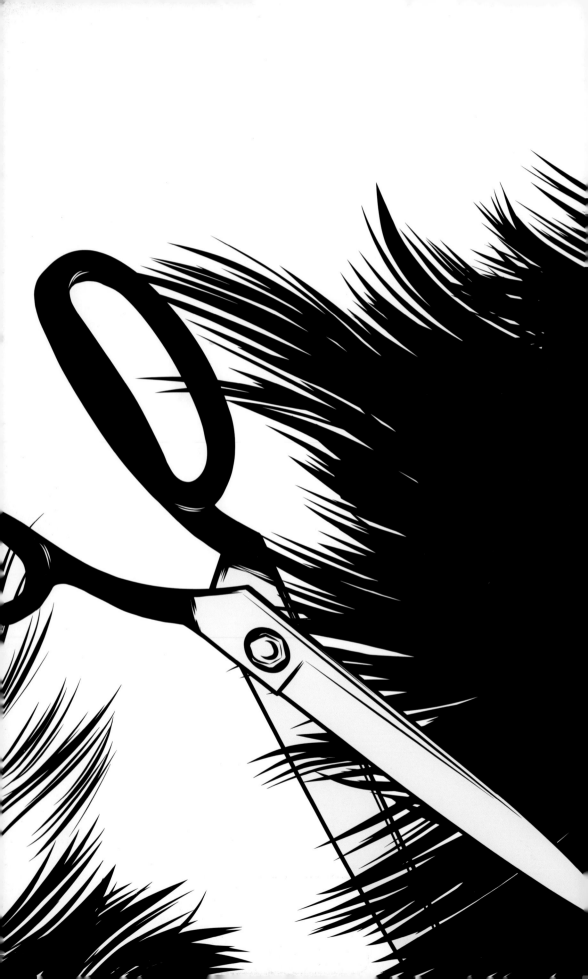

A graphic novel by
KIM W. ANDERSSON

Dialogue written in collaboration with C/M Edenborg

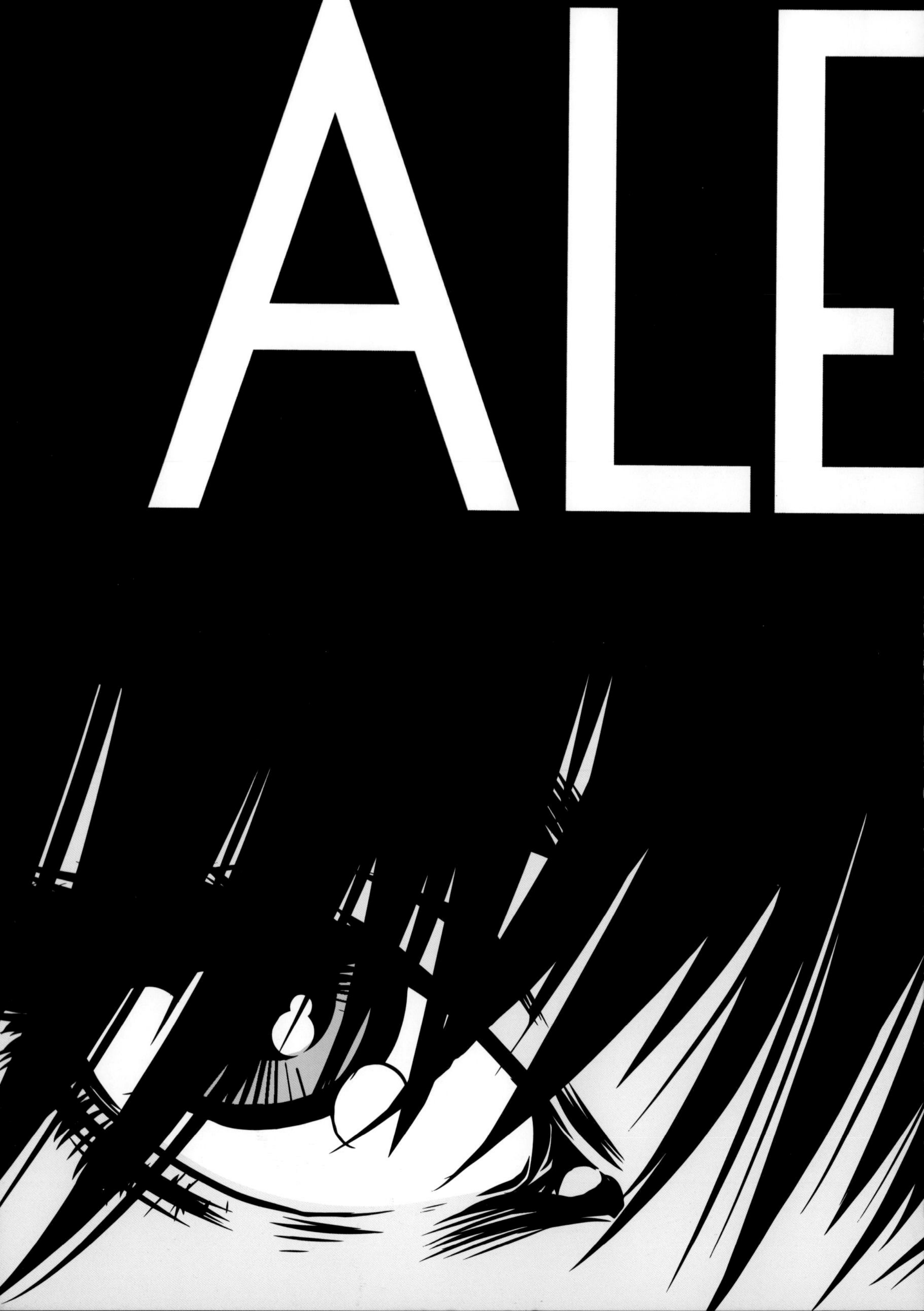
ALE

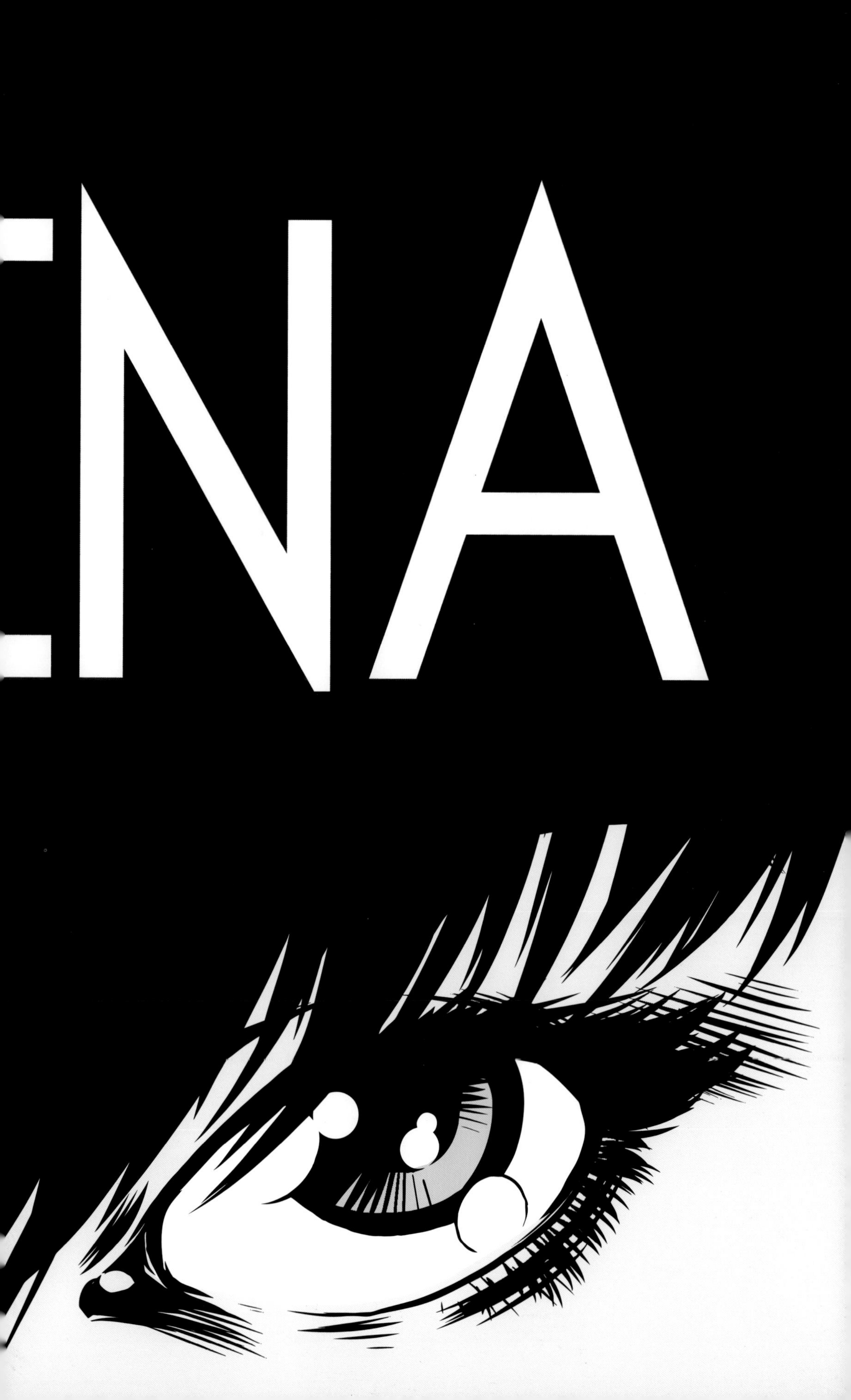
NA

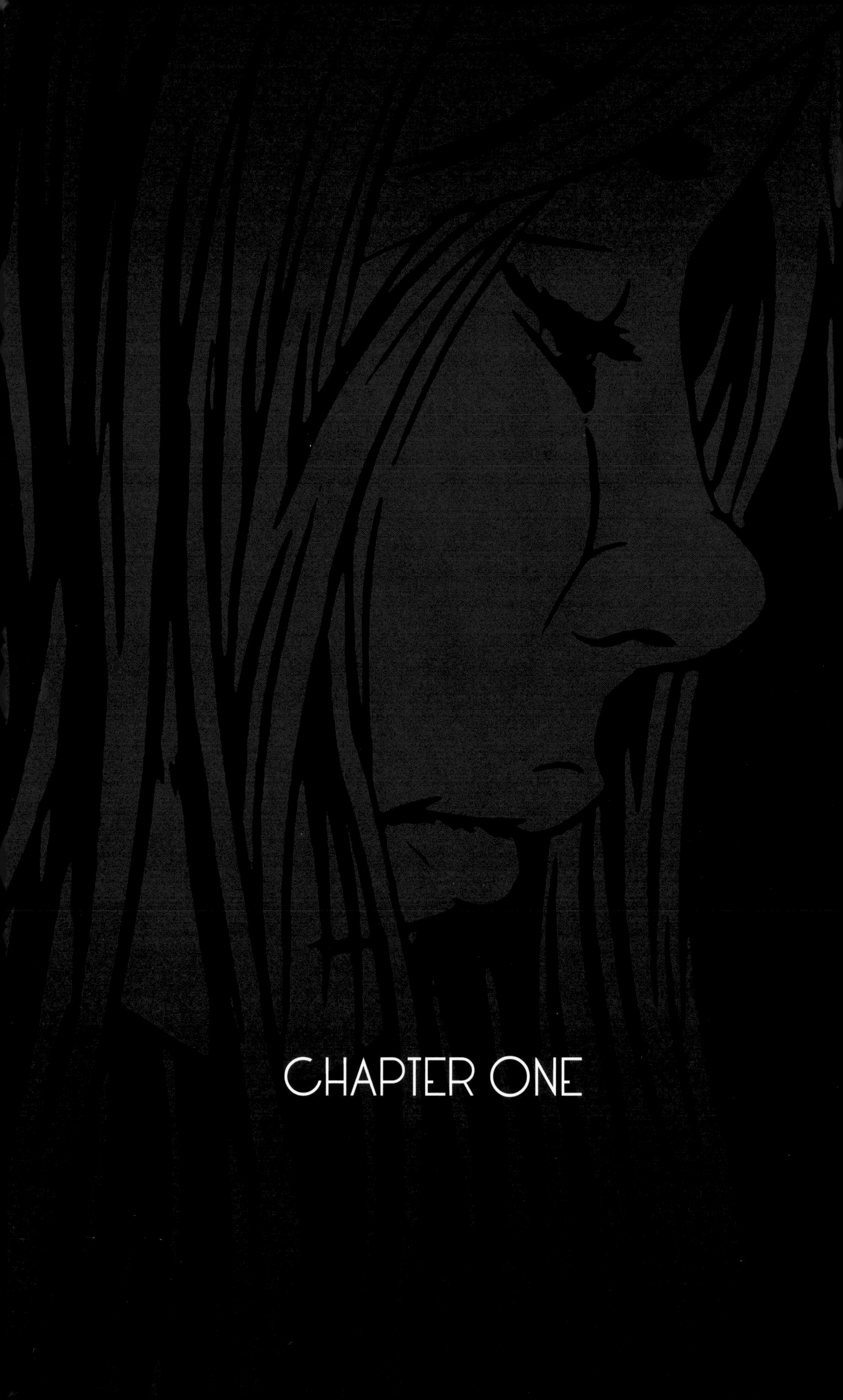

# CHAPTER ONE

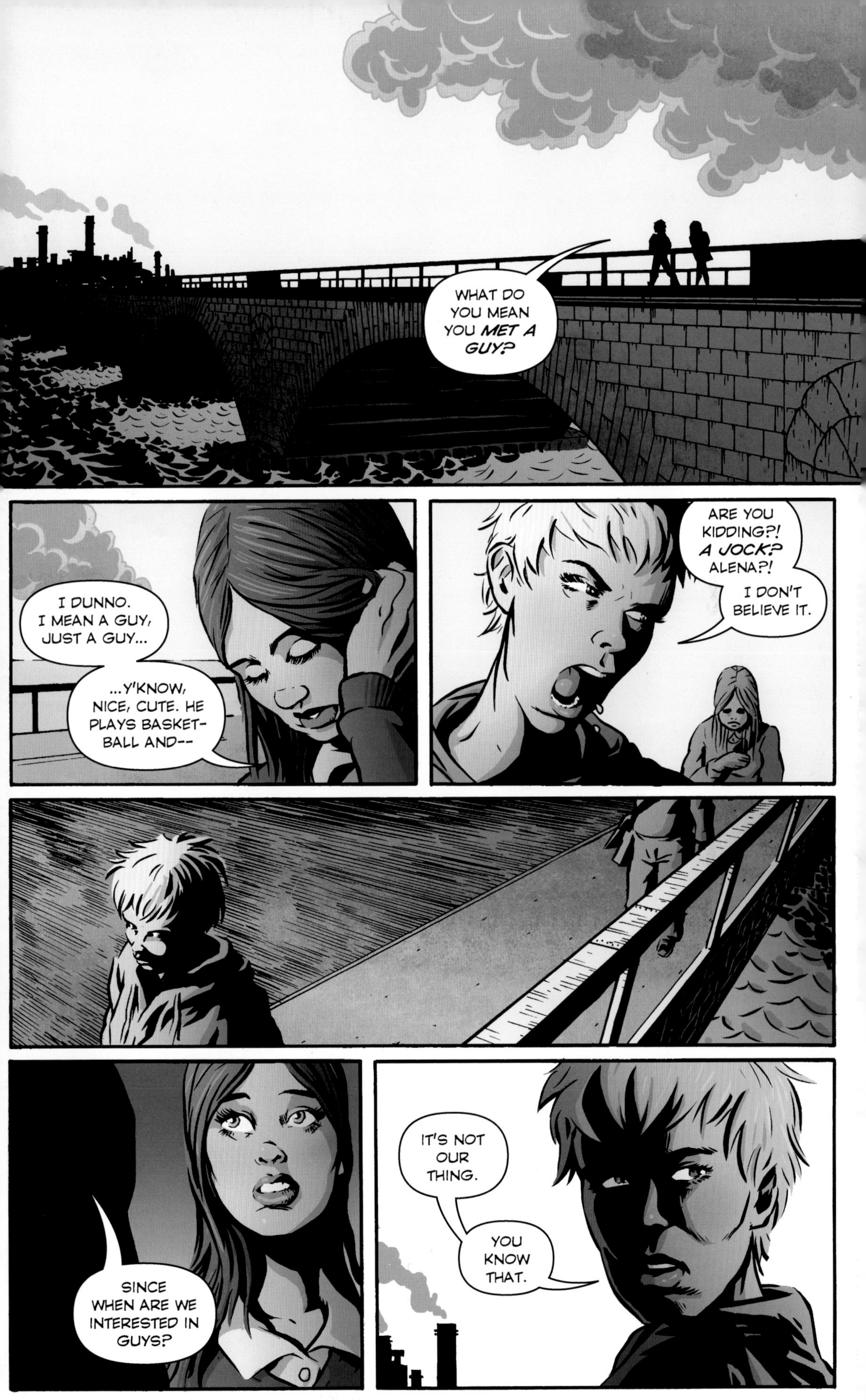
WHAT DO YOU MEAN YOU MET A GUY?
I DUNNO. I MEAN A GUY, JUST A GUY...
...Y'KNOW, NICE, CUTE. HE PLAYS BASKET-BALL AND--
ARE YOU KIDDING?! A JOCK? ALENA?!
I DON'T BELIEVE IT.
SINCE WHEN ARE WE INTERESTED IN GUYS?
IT'S NOT OUR THING.
YOU KNOW THAT.

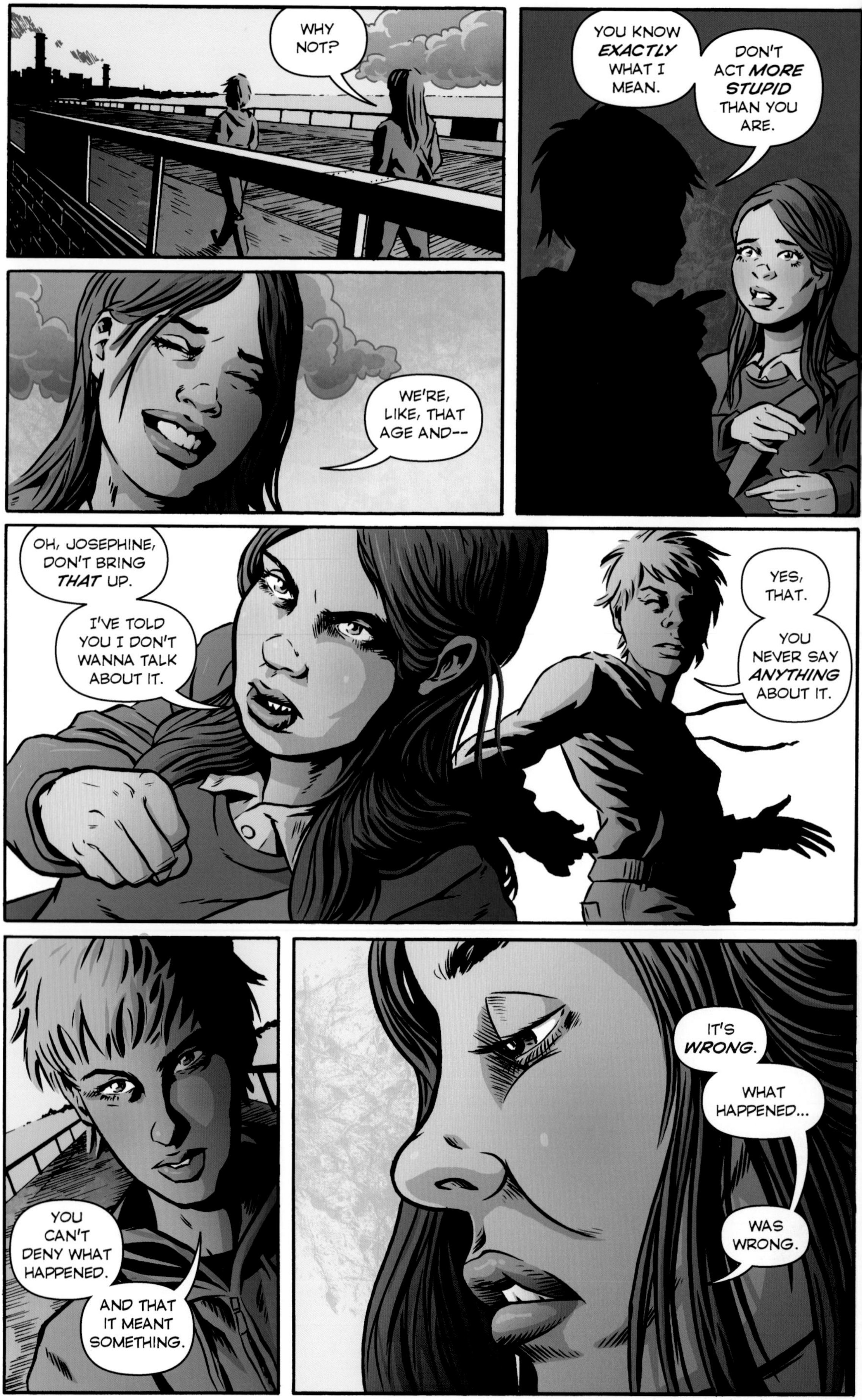
WHY NOT?
YOU KNOW EXACTLY WHAT I MEAN.
DON'T ACT MORE STUPID THAN YOU ARE.
WE'RE, LIKE, THAT AGE AND--
OH, JOSEPHINE, DON'T BRING THAT UP.
I'VE TOLD YOU I DON'T WANNA TALK ABOUT IT.
YES, THAT.
YOU NEVER SAY ANYTHING ABOUT IT.
YOU CAN'T DENY WHAT HAPPENED.
AND THAT IT MEANT SOMETHING.
IT'S WRONG.
WHAT HAPPENED...
WAS WRONG.

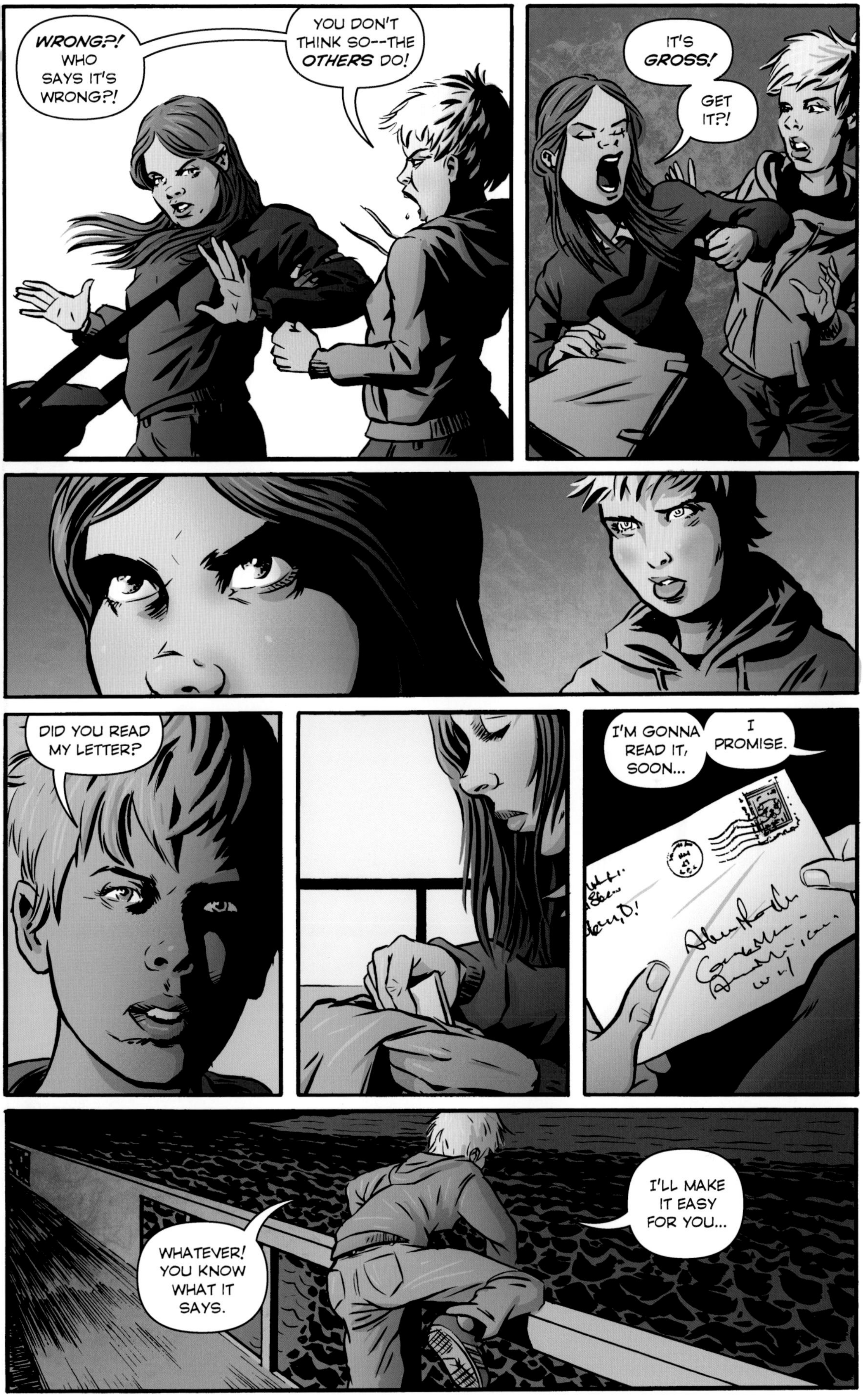

WRONG?! WHO SAYS IT'S WRONG?!
YOU DON'T THINK SO--THE OTHERS DO!
IT'S GROSS!
GET IT?!
DID YOU READ MY LETTER?
I'M GONNA READ IT, SOON...
I PROMISE.
WHATEVER! YOU KNOW WHAT IT SAYS.
I'LL MAKE IT EASY FOR YOU...

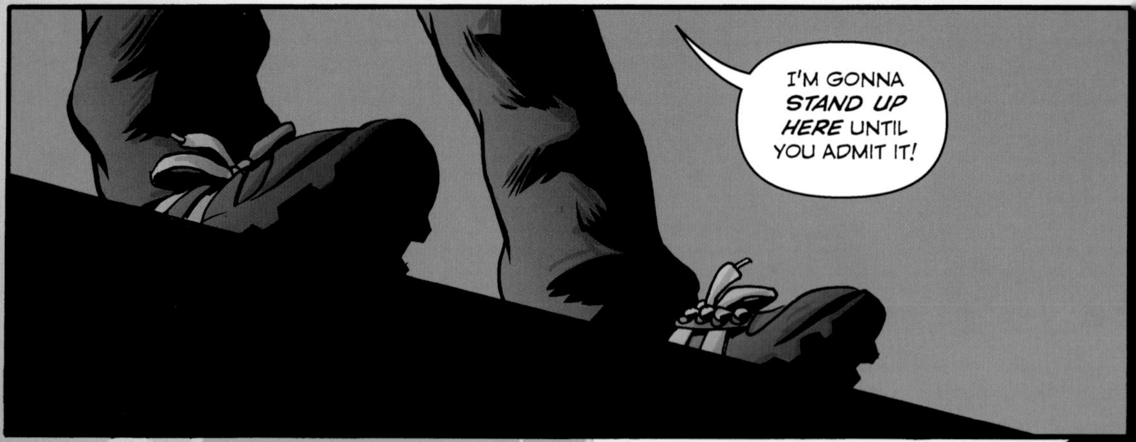
I'M GONNA STAND UP HERE UNTIL YOU ADMIT IT!

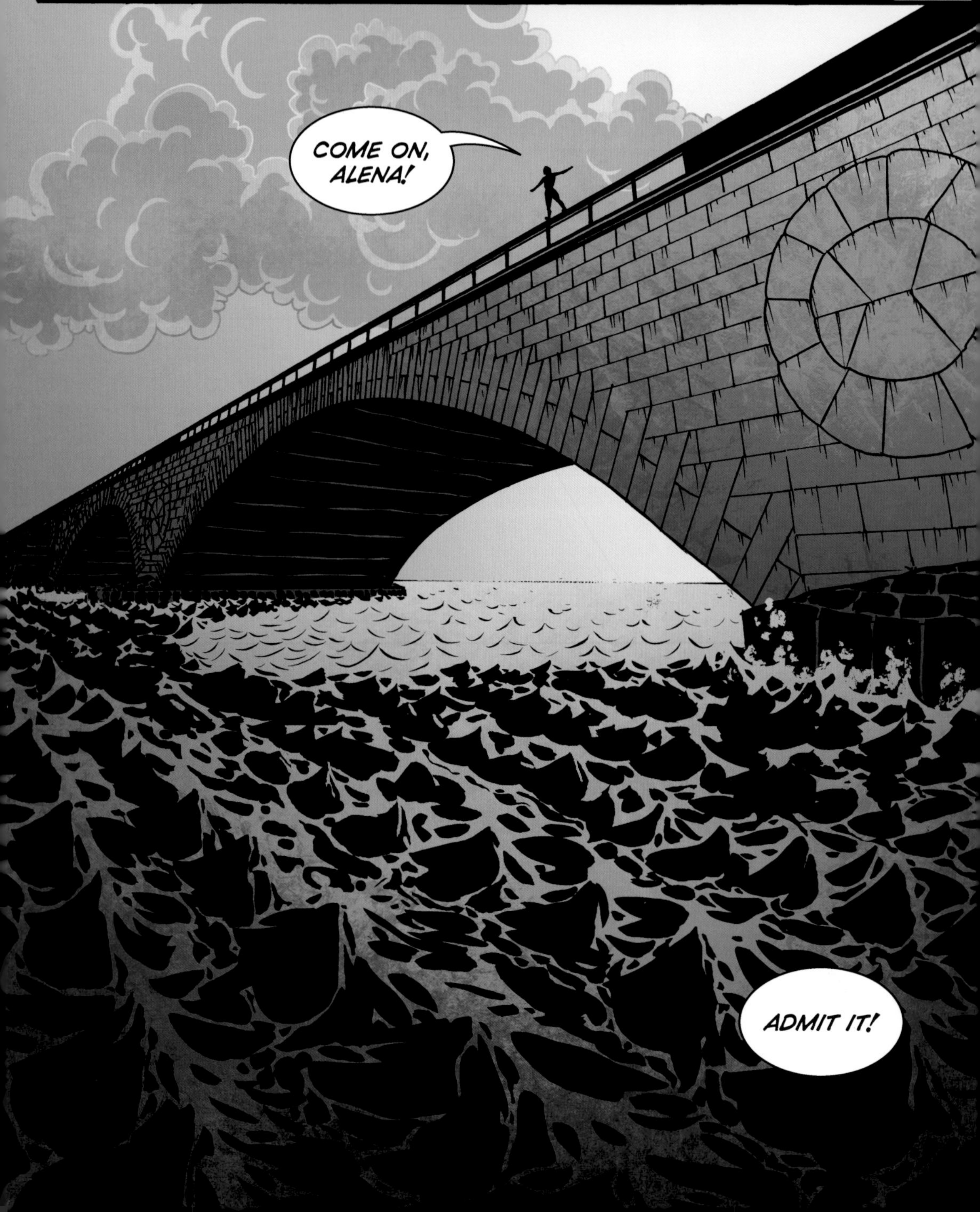
COME ON, ALENA!
ADMIT IT!

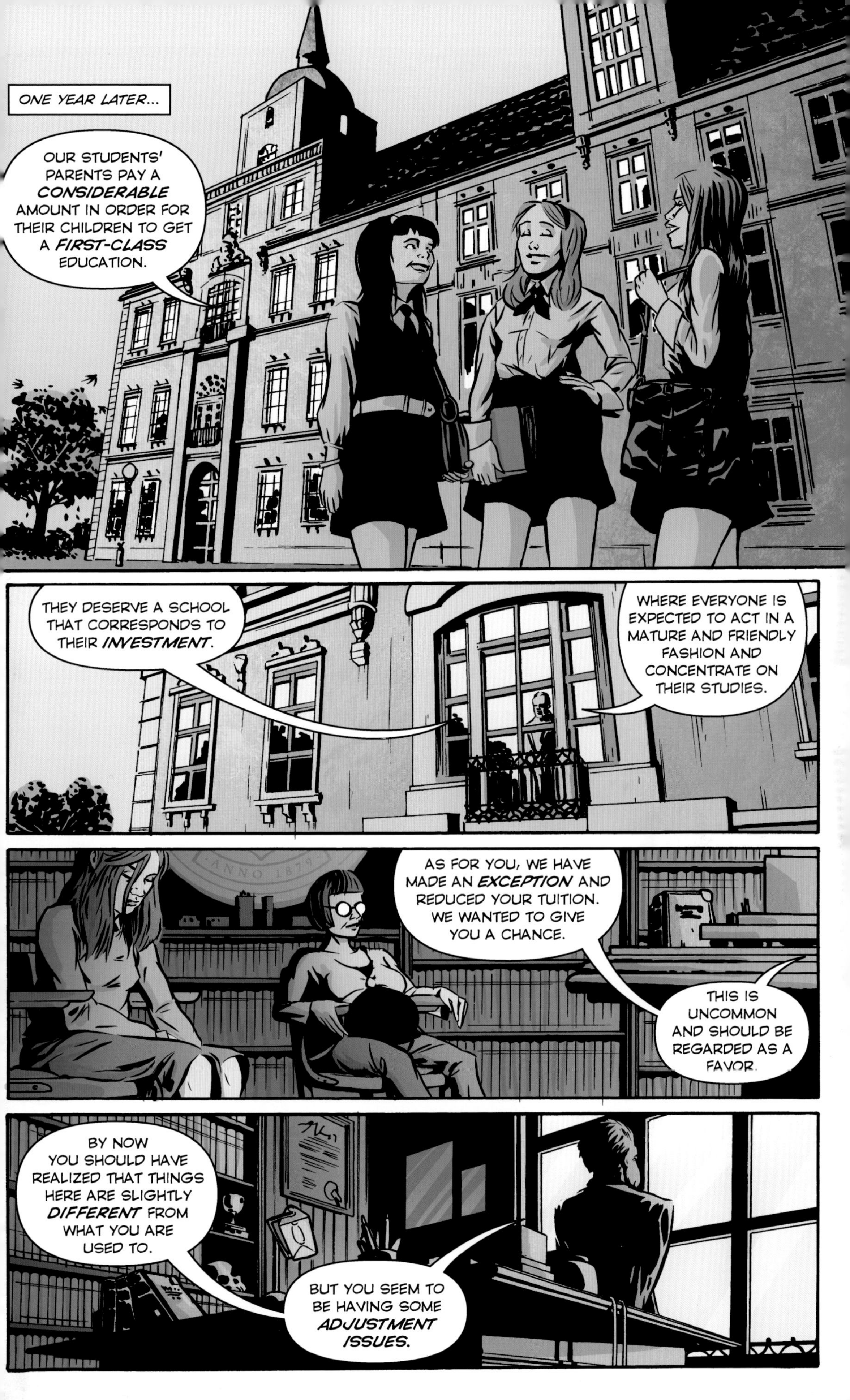
ONE YEAR LATER...
OUR STUDENTS' PARENTS PAY A CONSIDERABLE AMOUNT IN ORDER FOR THEIR CHILDREN TO GET A FIRST-CLASS EDUCATION.
THEY DESERVE A SCHOOL THAT CORRESPONDS TO THEIR INVESTMENT.
WHERE EVERYONE IS EXPECTED TO ACT IN A MATURE AND FRIENDLY FASHION AND CONCENTRATE ON THEIR STUDIES.
AS FOR YOU, WE HAVE MADE AN EXCEPTION AND REDUCED YOUR TUITION. WE WANTED TO GIVE YOU A CHANCE.
THIS IS UNCOMMON AND SHOULD BE REGARDED AS A FAVOR.
BY NOW YOU SHOULD HAVE REALIZED THAT THINGS HERE ARE SLIGHTLY DIFFERENT FROM WHAT YOU ARE USED TO.
BUT YOU SEEM TO BE HAVING SOME ADJUSTMENT ISSUES.

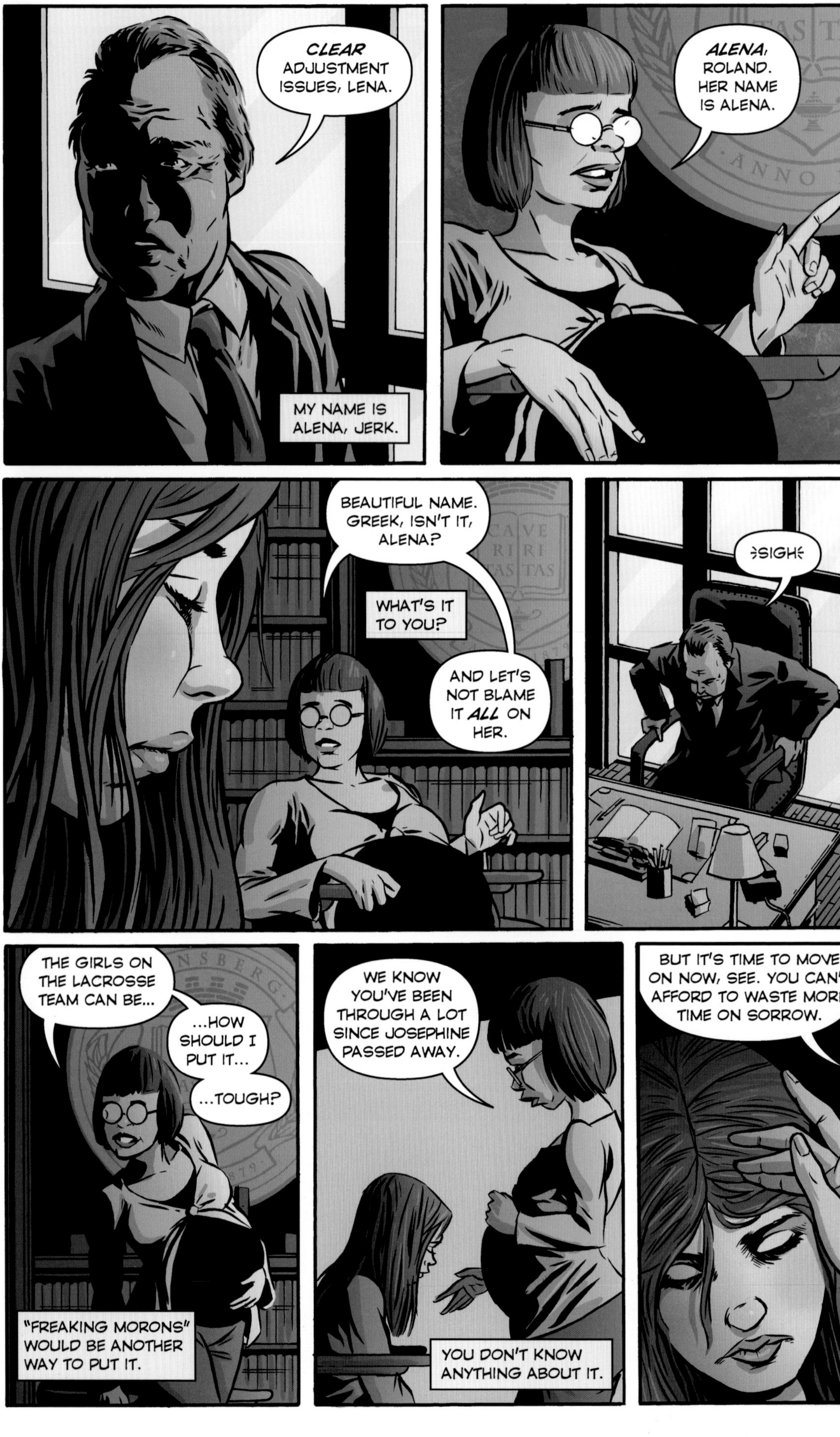
CLEAR ADJUSTMENT ISSUES, LENA.
MY NAME IS ALENA, JERK.
ALENA, ROLAND. HER NAME IS ALENA.
BEAUTIFUL NAME. GREEK, ISN'T IT, ALENA?
WHAT'S IT TO YOU?
AND LET'S NOT BLAME IT ALL ON HER.
SIGH
THE GIRLS ON THE LACROSSE TEAM CAN BE...
...HOW SHOULD I PUT IT...
...TOUGH?
"FREAKING MORONS" WOULD BE ANOTHER WAY TO PUT IT.
WE KNOW YOU'VE BEEN THROUGH A LOT SINCE JOSEPHINE PASSED AWAY.
YOU DON'T KNOW ANYTHING ABOUT IT.
BUT IT'S TIME TO MOVE ON NOW, SEE. YOU CAN'T AFFORD TO WASTE MORE TIME ON SORROW.

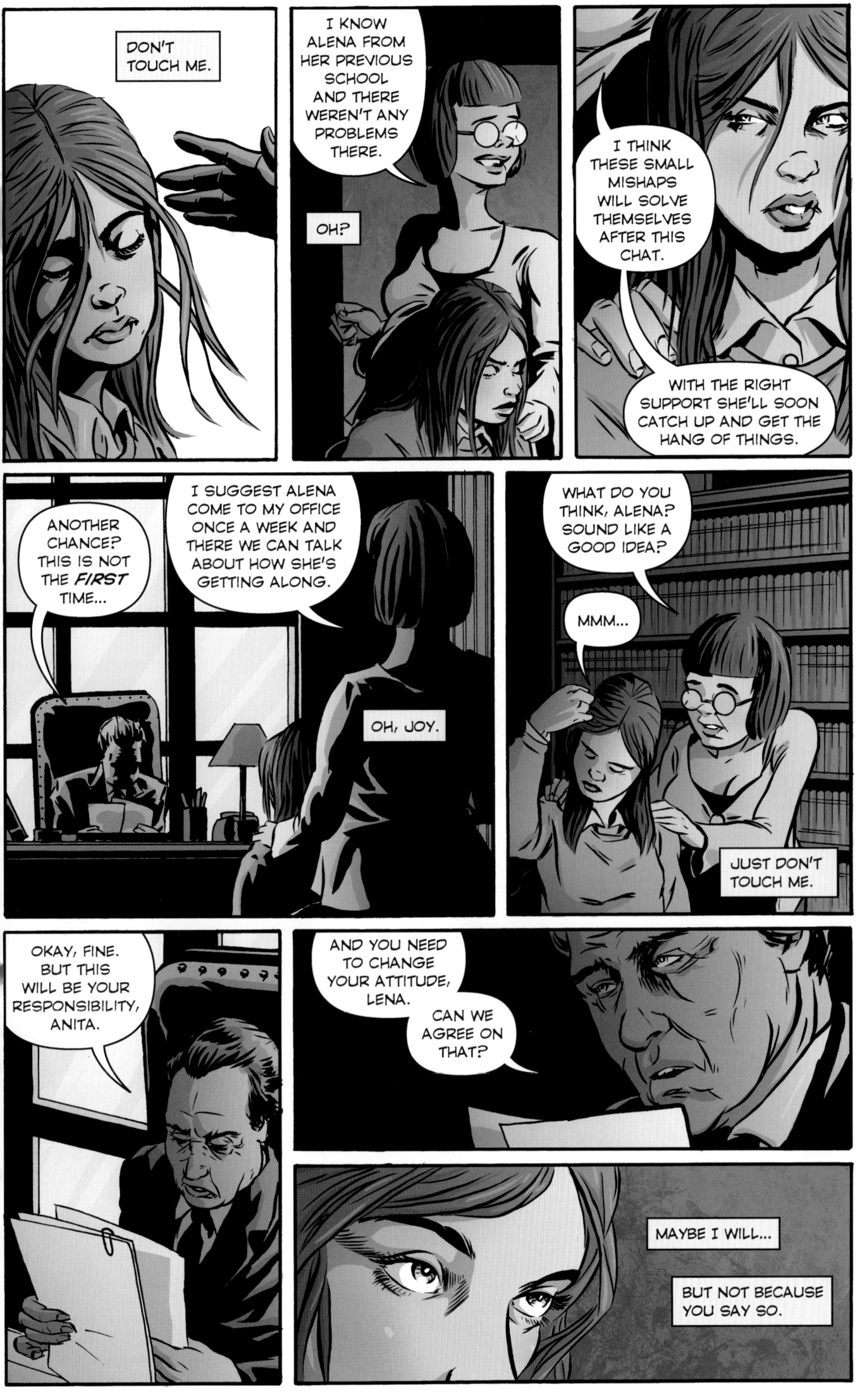
DON'T TOUCH ME.
I KNOW ALENA FROM HER PREVIOUS SCHOOL AND THERE WEREN'T ANY PROBLEMS THERE.
OH?
I THINK THESE SMALL MISHAPS WILL SOLVE THEMSELVES AFTER THIS CHAT.
WITH THE RIGHT SUPPORT SHE'LL SOON CATCH UP AND GET THE HANG OF THINGS.
ANOTHER CHANCE? THIS IS NOT THE *FIRST* TIME...
I SUGGEST ALENA COME TO MY OFFICE ONCE A WEEK AND THERE WE CAN TALK ABOUT HOW SHE'S GETTING ALONG.
OH, JOY.
WHAT DO YOU THINK, ALENA? SOUND LIKE A GOOD IDEA?
MMM...
JUST DON'T TOUCH ME.
OKAY, FINE. BUT THIS WILL BE YOUR RESPONSIBILITY, ANITA.
AND YOU NEED TO CHANGE YOUR ATTITUDE, LENA.
CAN WE AGREE ON THAT?
MAYBE I WILL...
BUT NOT BECAUSE YOU SAY SO.

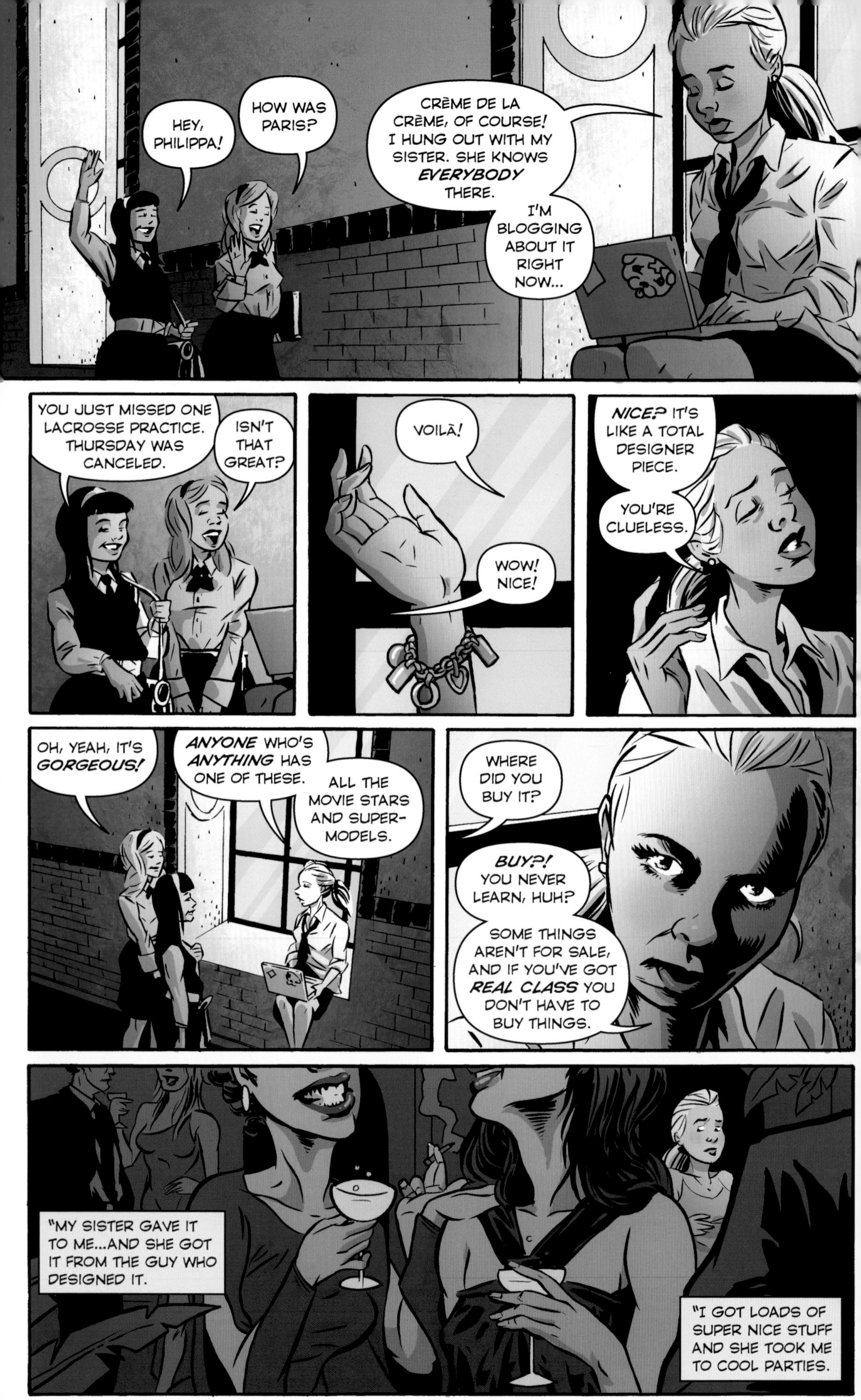

HEY, PHILIPPA!
HOW WAS PARIS?
CRÈME DE LA CRÈME, OF COURSE! I HUNG OUT WITH MY SISTER. SHE KNOWS *EVERYBODY* THERE.
I'M BLOGGING ABOUT IT RIGHT NOW...
YOU JUST MISSED ONE LACROSSE PRACTICE. THURSDAY WAS CANCELED.
ISN'T THAT GREAT?
VOILÀ!
WOW! NICE!
*NICE?* IT'S LIKE A TOTAL DESIGNER PIECE.
YOU'RE CLUELESS.
OH, YEAH, IT'S *GORGEOUS!*
*ANYONE* WHO'S *ANYTHING* HAS ONE OF THESE.
ALL THE MOVIE STARS AND SUPER-MODELS.
WHERE DID YOU BUY IT?
*BUY?!* YOU NEVER LEARN, HUH?
SOME THINGS AREN'T FOR SALE, AND IF YOU'VE GOT *REAL CLASS* YOU DON'T HAVE TO BUY THINGS.
"MY SISTER GAVE IT TO ME...AND SHE GOT IT FROM THE GUY WHO DESIGNED IT.
"I GOT LOADS OF SUPER NICE STUFF AND SHE TOOK ME TO COOL PARTIES.

"THIS ONE GUY ASKED ME IF I WAS A MODEL. HE'S, LIKE, SCOUTED ALL THE SUPERMODELS.

"HE SAID I COULD MAKE IT BIG. HE SAID I'VE GOT 'IT.'

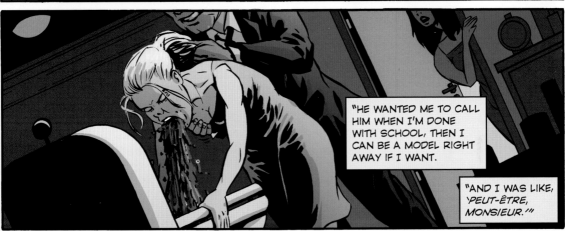

"HE WANTED ME TO CALL HIM WHEN I'M DONE WITH SCHOOL, THEN I CAN BE A MODEL RIGHT AWAY IF I WANT.

"AND I WAS LIKE, 'PEUT-ÊTRE, MONSIEUR.'"

WOW, THAT'S SOO COOL!

I'M GOING THERE WITH MY PARENTS ON SPRING BREAK.

WELL, ENJOY SPENDING TIME WITH YOUR PARENTS.

MAYBE YOU GUYS'LL END UP AT SOME *AWESOME* PARTIES.

HEY, FABIAN! CHECK OUT MY BRACELET!

NICE.

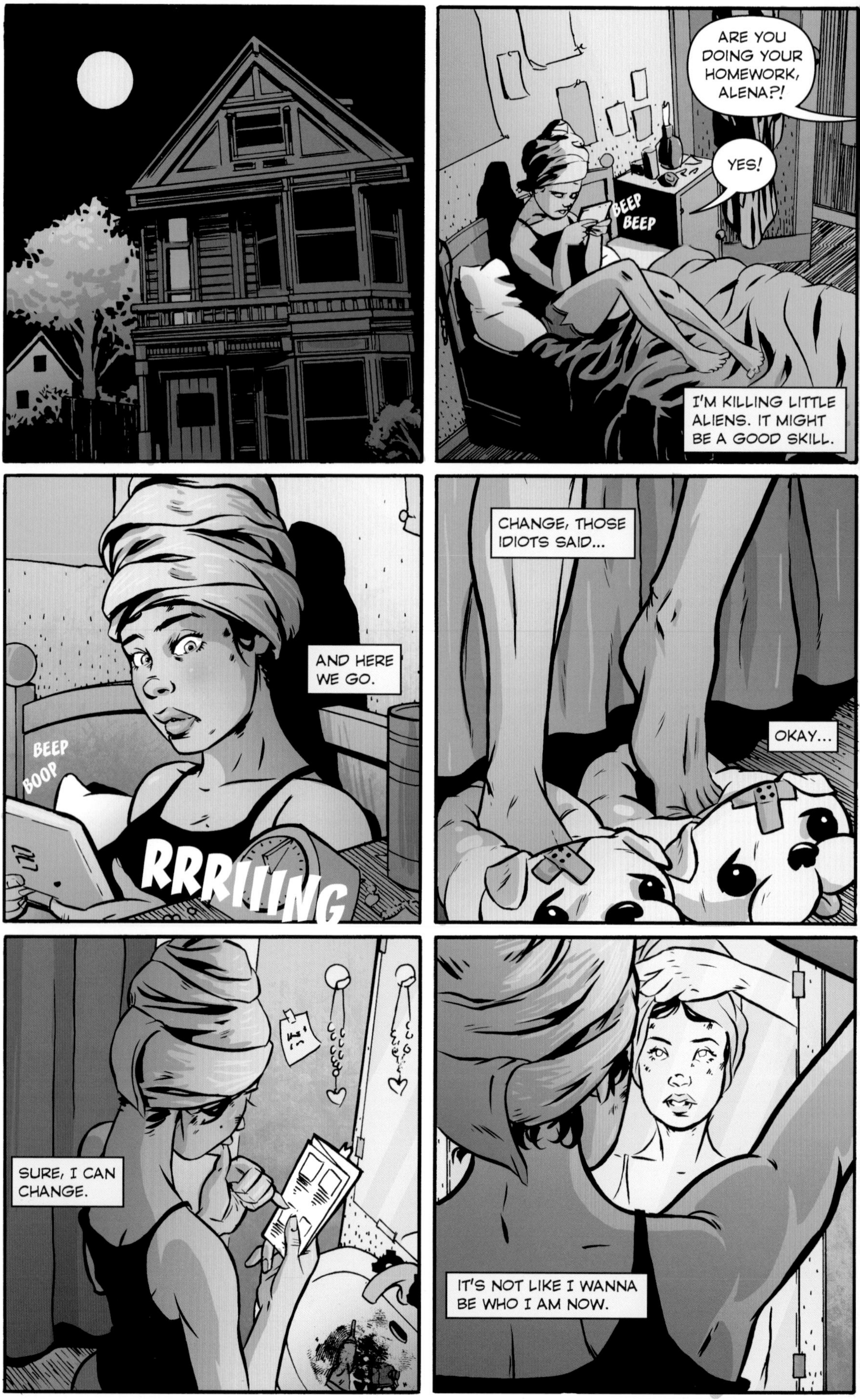
ARE YOU DOING YOUR HOMEWORK, ALENA?!
YES!
BEEP BEEP
I'M KILLING LITTLE ALIENS. IT MIGHT BE A GOOD SKILL.
AND HERE WE GO.
BEEP BOOP
RRRIIING
CHANGE, THOSE IDIOTS SAID...
OKAY...
SURE, I CAN CHANGE.
IT'S NOT LIKE I WANNA BE WHO I AM NOW.

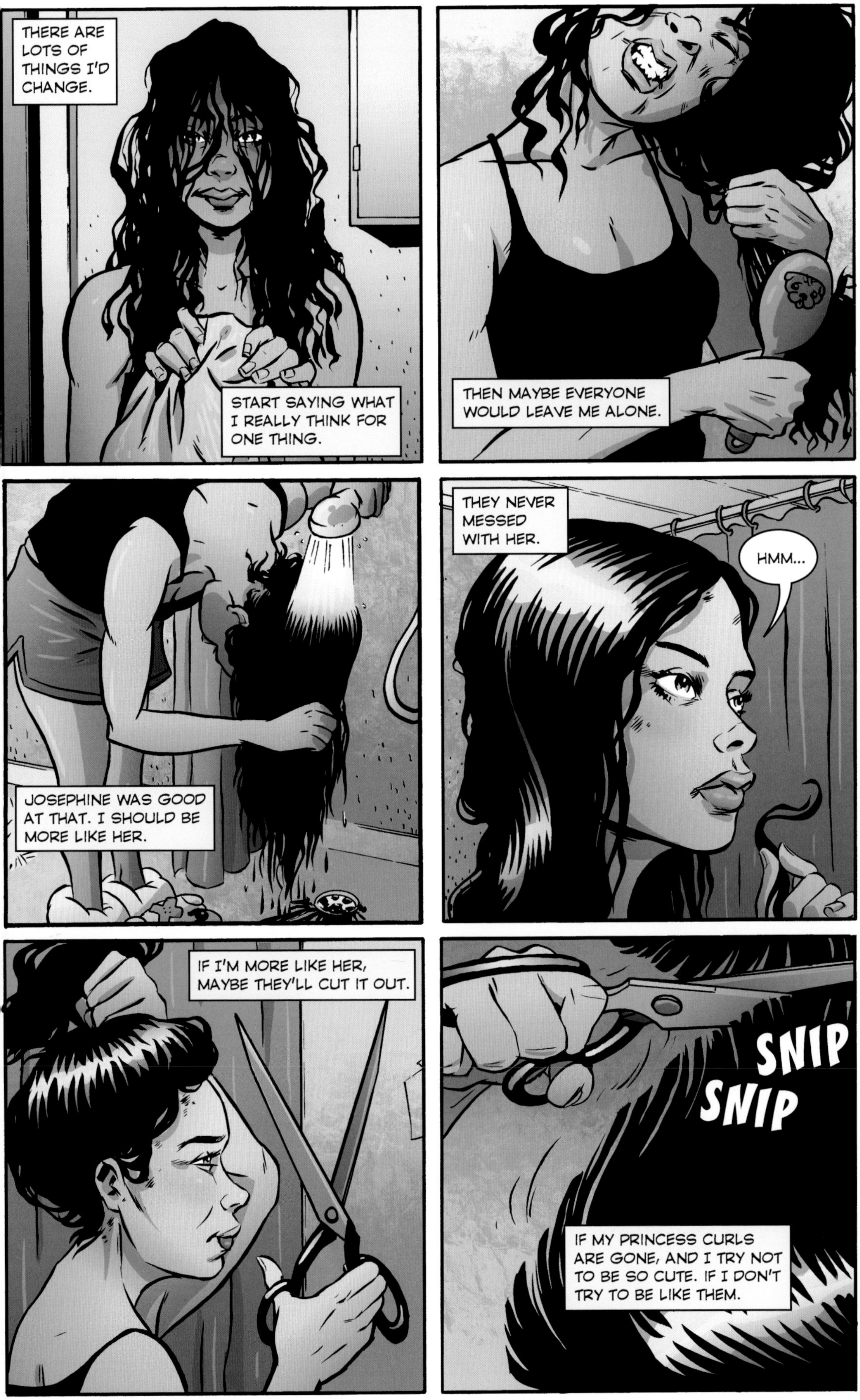
THERE ARE LOTS OF THINGS I'D CHANGE.
START SAYING WHAT I REALLY THINK FOR ONE THING.
THEN MAYBE EVERYONE WOULD LEAVE ME ALONE.
JOSEPHINE WAS GOOD AT THAT. I SHOULD BE MORE LIKE HER.
THEY NEVER MESSED WITH HER.
HMM...
IF I'M MORE LIKE HER, MAYBE THEY'LL CUT IT OUT.
SNIP
SNIP
IF MY PRINCESS CURLS ARE GONE, AND I TRY NOT TO BE SO CUTE. IF I DON'T TRY TO BE LIKE THEM.

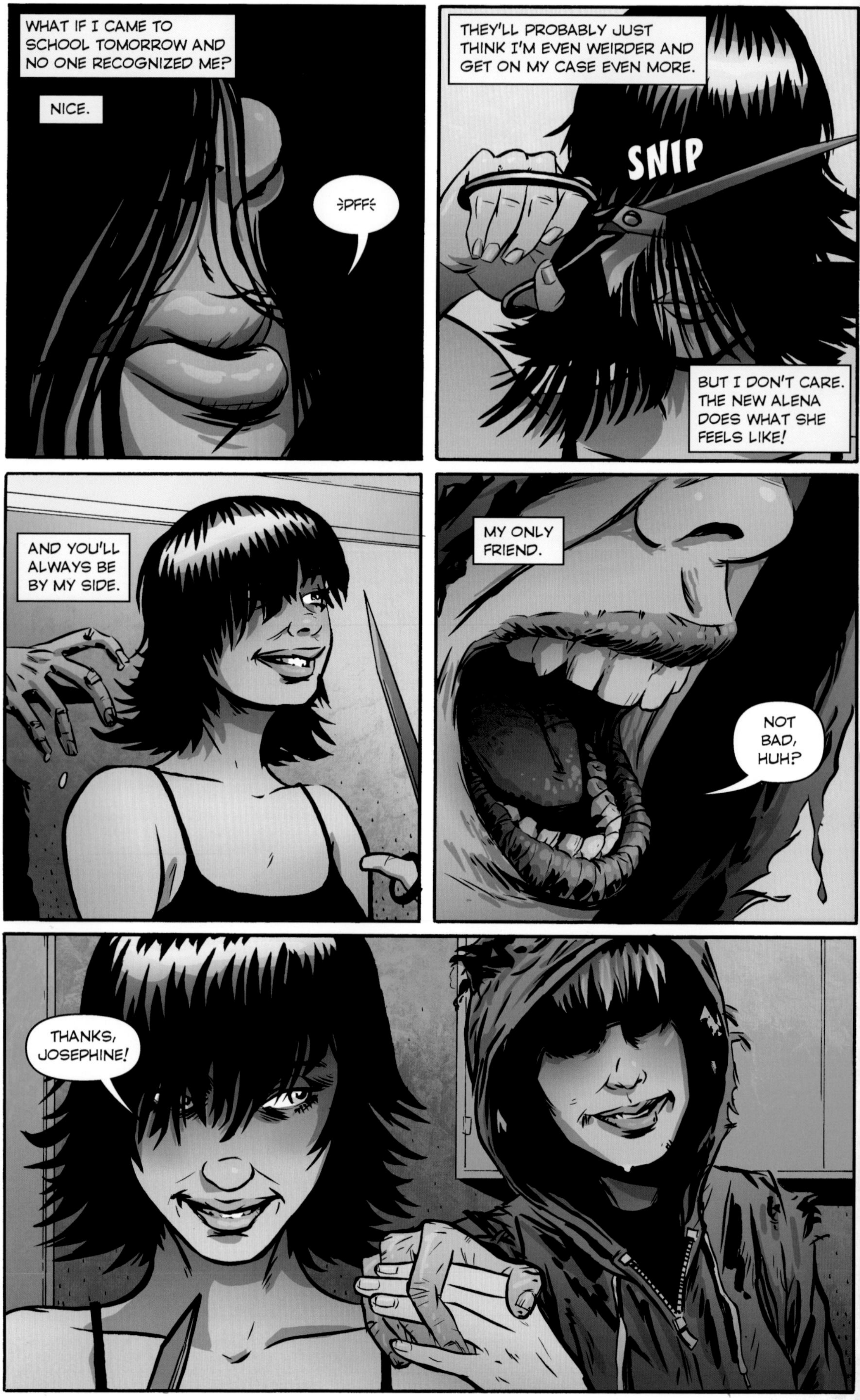
WHAT IF I CAME TO SCHOOL TOMORROW AND NO ONE RECOGNIZED ME?
NICE.
PFF
THEY'LL PROBABLY JUST THINK I'M EVEN WEIRDER AND GET ON MY CASE EVEN MORE.
SNIP
BUT I DON'T CARE. THE NEW ALENA DOES WHAT SHE FEELS LIKE!
AND YOU'LL ALWAYS BE BY MY SIDE.
MY ONLY FRIEND.
NOT BAD, HUH?
THANKS, JOSEPHINE!

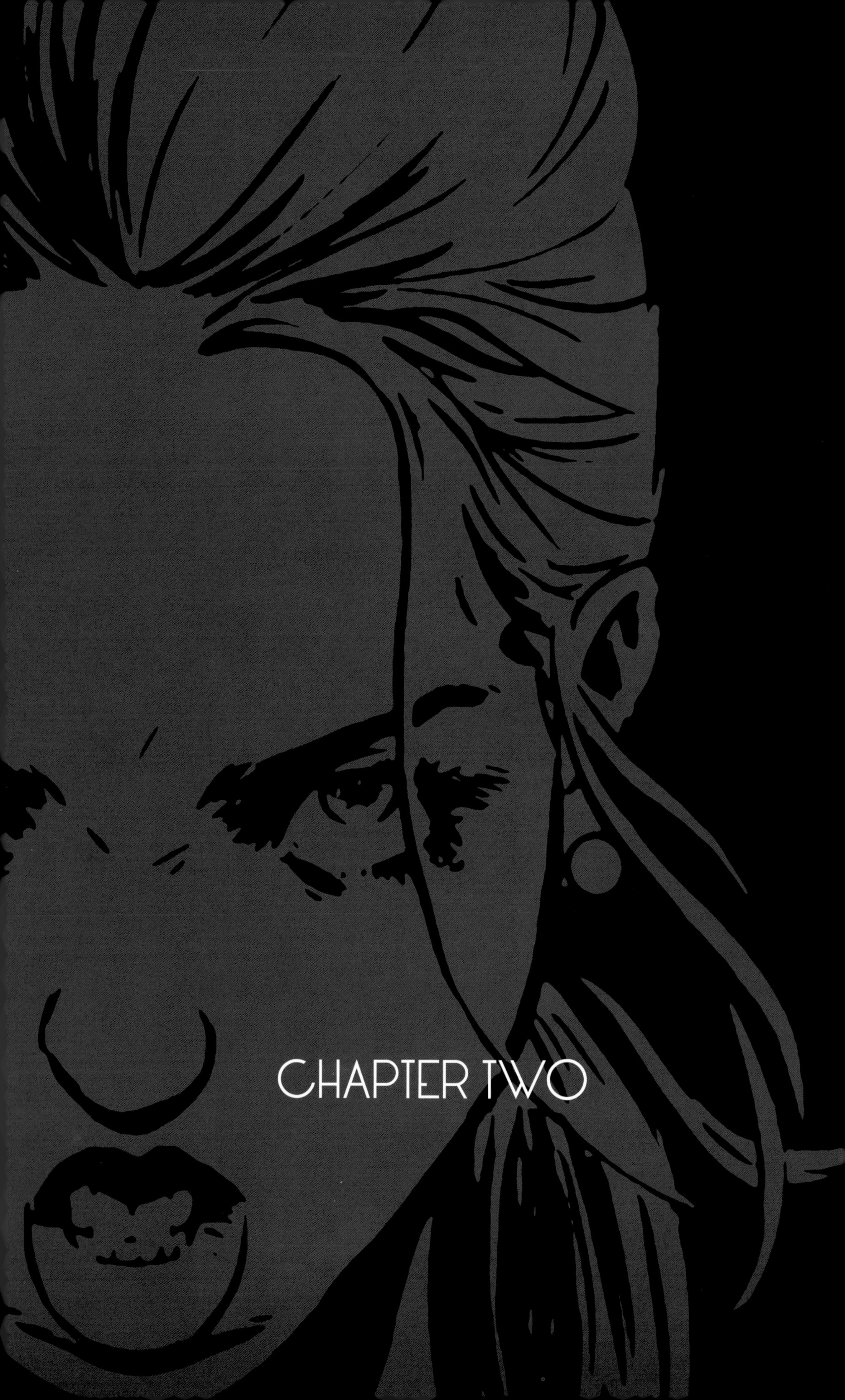

# CHAPTER TWO

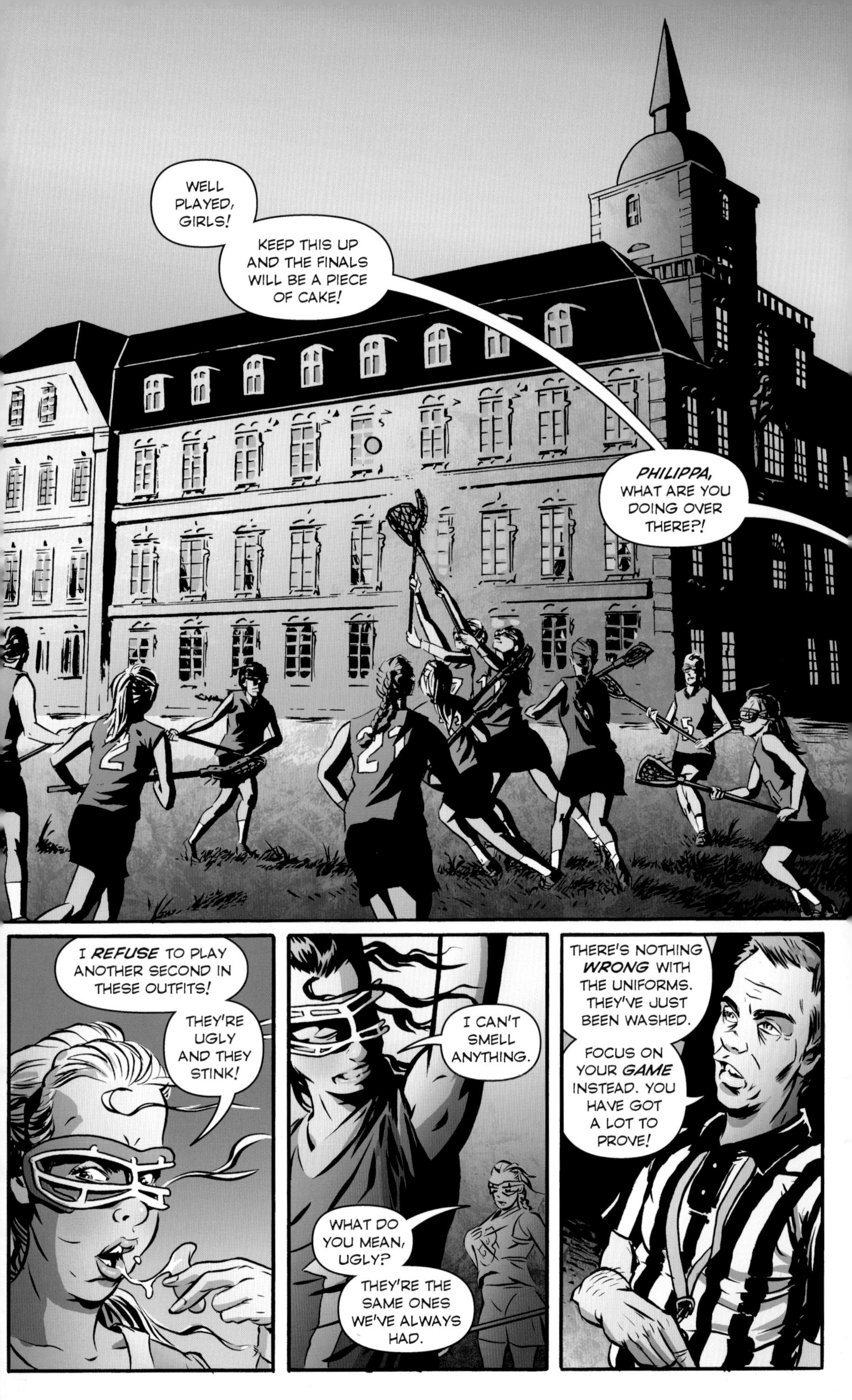
WELL PLAYED, GIRLS!
KEEP THIS UP AND THE FINALS WILL BE A PIECE OF CAKE!
PHILIPPA, WHAT ARE YOU DOING OVER THERE?!
I REFUSE TO PLAY ANOTHER SECOND IN THESE OUTFITS!
THEY'RE UGLY AND THEY STINK!
I CAN'T SMELL ANYTHING.
WHAT DO YOU MEAN, UGLY?
THEY'RE THE SAME ONES WE'VE ALWAYS HAD.
THERE'S NOTHING WRONG WITH THE UNIFORMS. THEY'VE JUST BEEN WASHED.
FOCUS ON YOUR GAME INSTEAD. YOU HAVE GOT A LOT TO PROVE!

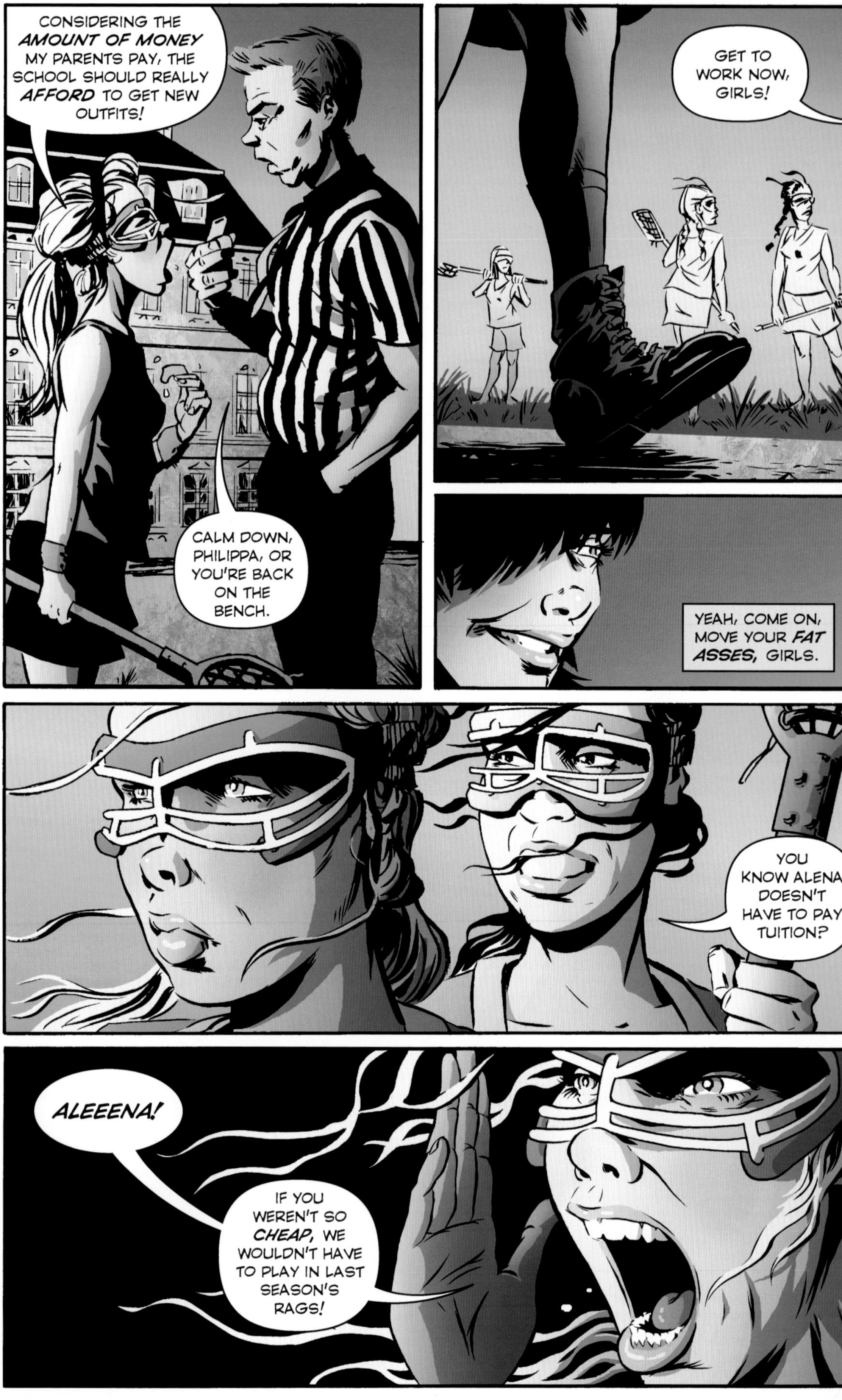
CONSIDERING THE AMOUNT OF MONEY MY PARENTS PAY, THE SCHOOL SHOULD REALLY AFFORD TO GET NEW OUTFITS!
CALM DOWN, PHILIPPA, OR YOU'RE BACK ON THE BENCH.
GET TO WORK NOW, GIRLS!
YEAH, COME ON, MOVE YOUR FAT ASSES, GIRLS.
YOU KNOW ALENA DOESN'T HAVE TO PAY TUITION?
ALEEENA!
IF YOU WEREN'T SO CHEAP, WE WOULDN'T HAVE TO PLAY IN LAST SEASON'S RAGS!

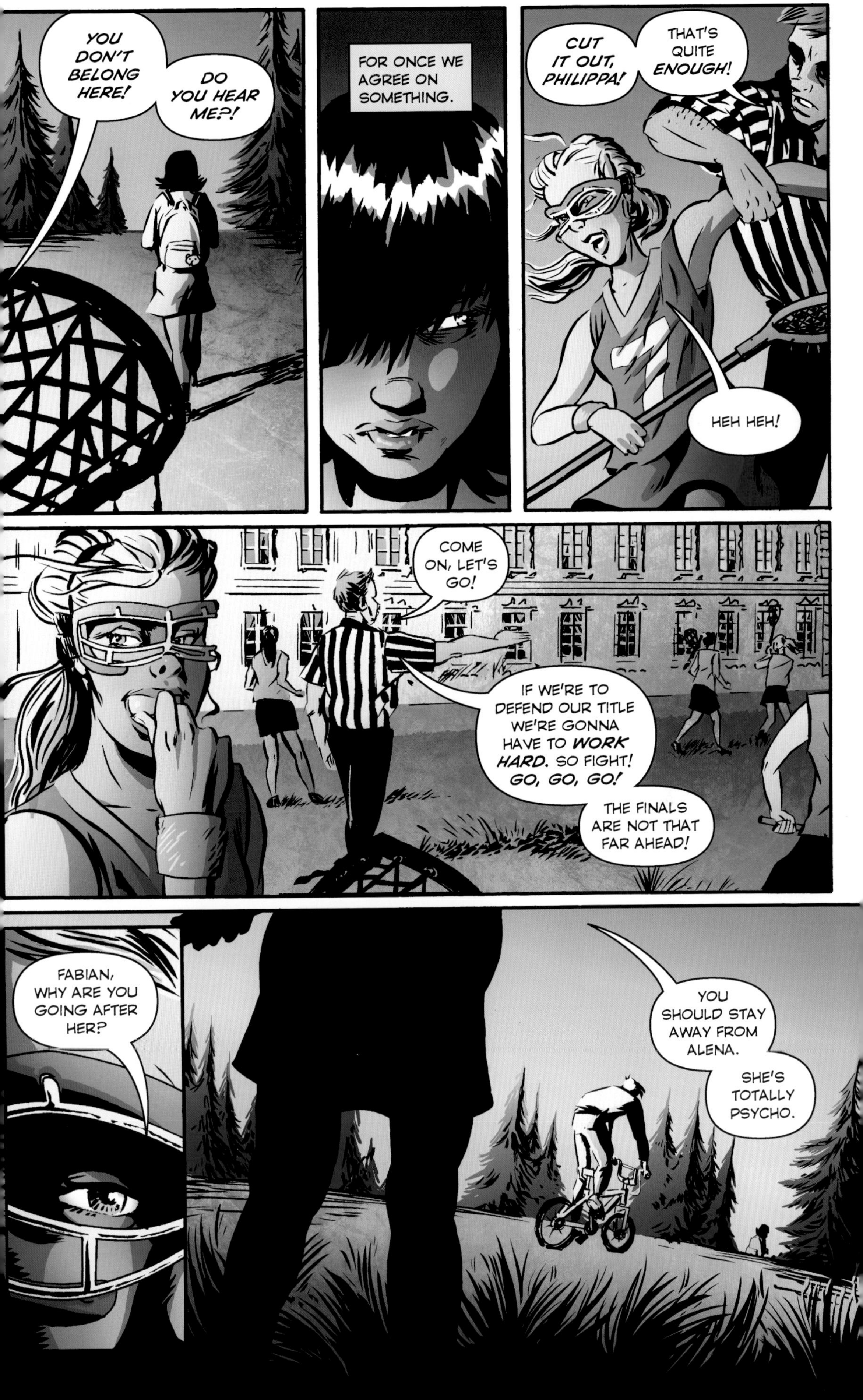
YOU DON'T BELONG HERE!
DO YOU HEAR ME?!
FOR ONCE WE AGREE ON SOMETHING.
CUT IT OUT, PHILIPPA!
THAT'S QUITE ENOUGH!
HEH HEH!
COME ON, LET'S GO!
IF WE'RE TO DEFEND OUR TITLE WE'RE GONNA HAVE TO WORK HARD. SO FIGHT! GO, GO, GO!
THE FINALS ARE NOT THAT FAR AHEAD!
FABIAN, WHY ARE YOU GOING AFTER HER?
YOU SHOULD STAY AWAY FROM ALENA.
SHE'S TOTALLY PSYCHO.

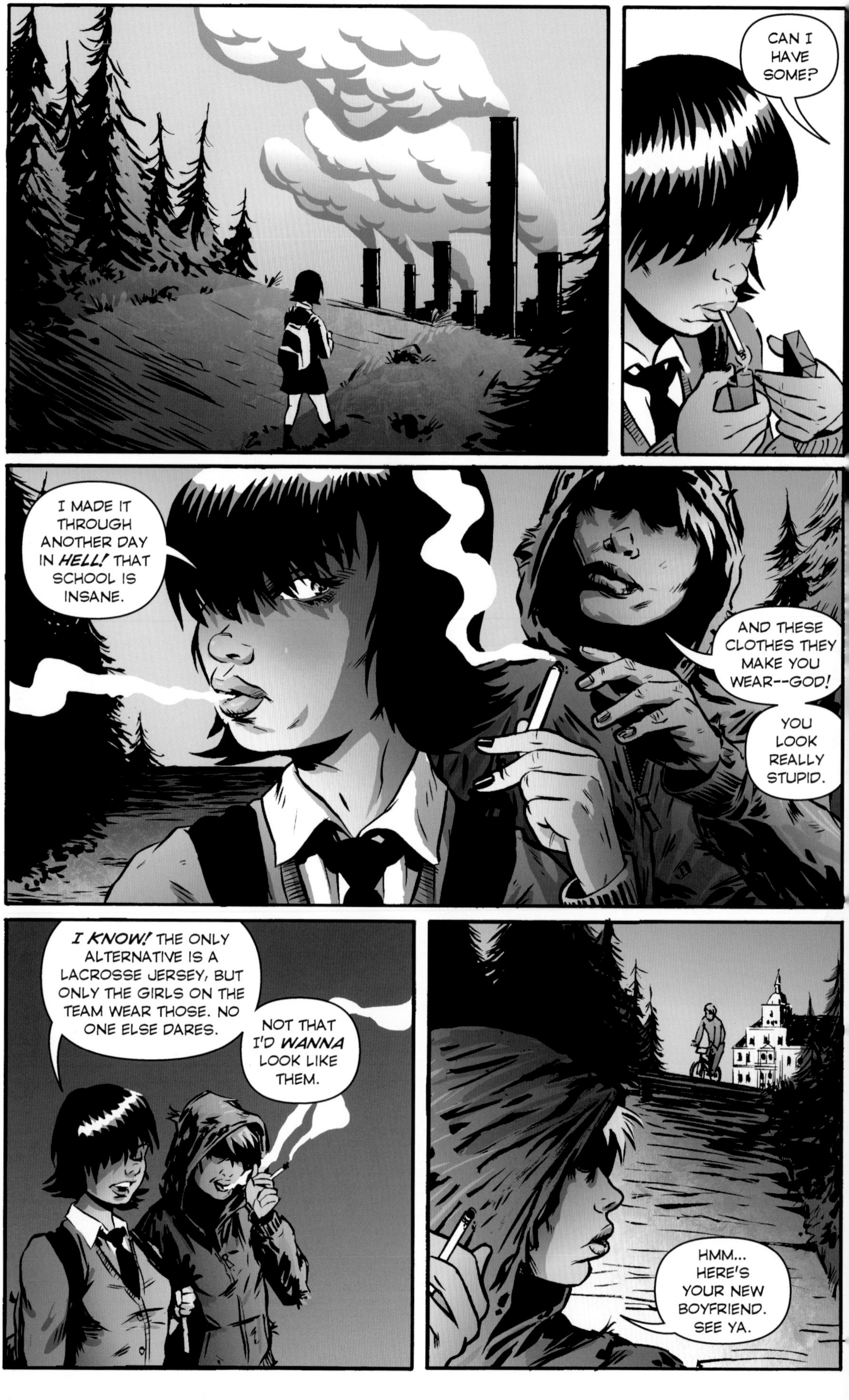
CAN I HAVE SOME?
I MADE IT THROUGH ANOTHER DAY IN HELL! THAT SCHOOL IS INSANE.
AND THESE CLOTHES THEY MAKE YOU WEAR--GOD!
YOU LOOK REALLY STUPID.
I KNOW! THE ONLY ALTERNATIVE IS A LACROSSE JERSEY, BUT ONLY THE GIRLS ON THE TEAM WEAR THOSE. NO ONE ELSE DARES.
NOT THAT I'D WANNA LOOK LIKE THEM.
HMM... HERE'S YOUR NEW BOYFRIEND. SEE YA.

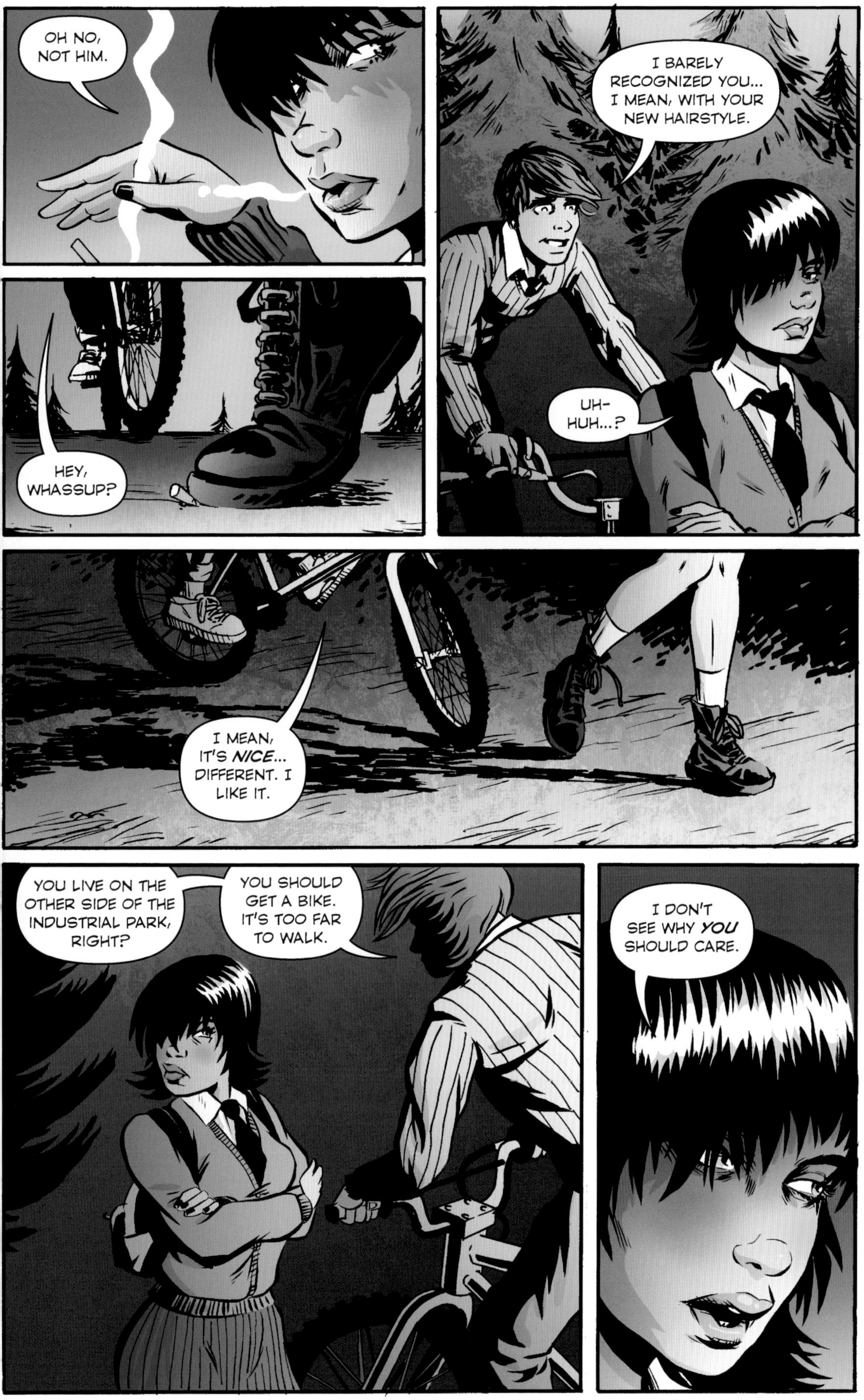
OH NO, NOT HIM.
HEY, WHASSUP?
I BARELY RECOGNIZED YOU... I MEAN, WITH YOUR NEW HAIRSTYLE.
UH-HUH...?
I MEAN, IT'S *NICE*... DIFFERENT. I LIKE IT.
YOU LIVE ON THE OTHER SIDE OF THE INDUSTRIAL PARK, RIGHT?
YOU SHOULD GET A BIKE. IT'S TOO FAR TO WALK.
I DON'T SEE WHY *YOU* SHOULD CARE.

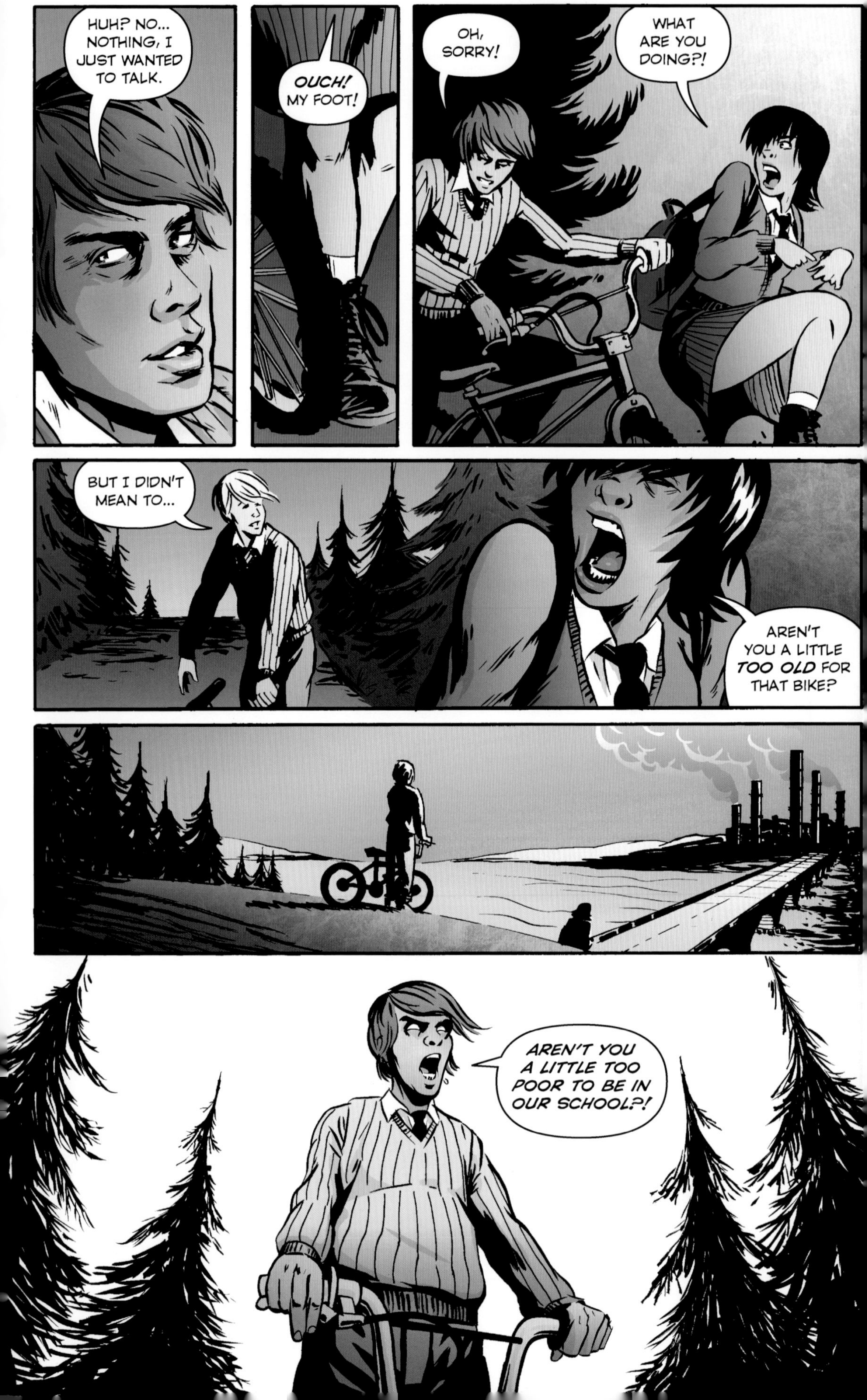
HUH? NO... NOTHING, I JUST WANTED TO TALK.
OUCH! MY FOOT!
OH, SORRY!
WHAT ARE YOU DOING?!
BUT I DIDN'T MEAN TO...
AREN'T YOU A LITTLE TOO OLD FOR THAT BIKE?
AREN'T YOU A LITTLE TOO POOR TO BE IN OUR SCHOOL?!

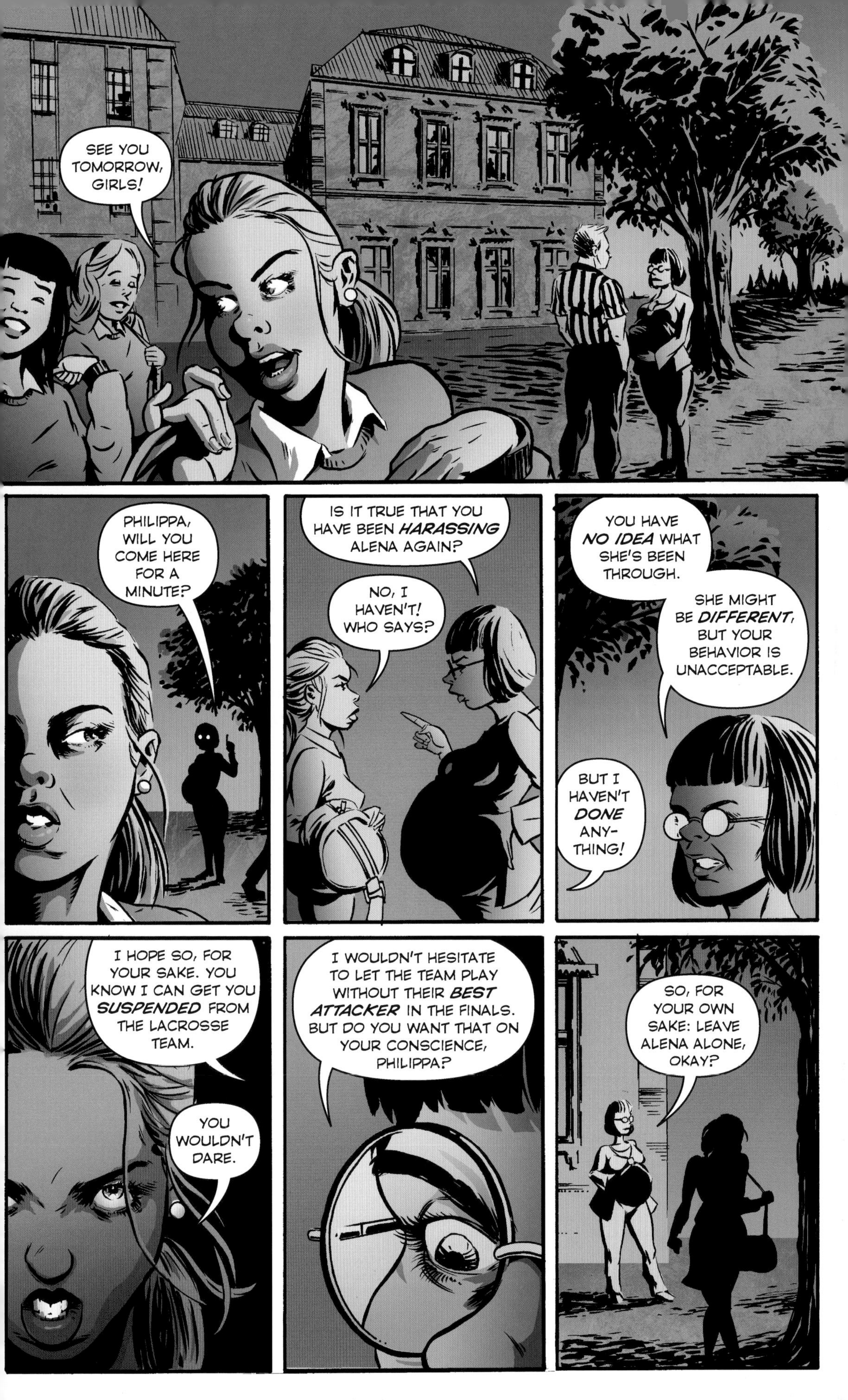
SEE YOU TOMORROW, GIRLS!
PHILIPPA, WILL YOU COME HERE FOR A MINUTE?
IS IT TRUE THAT YOU HAVE BEEN HARASSING ALENA AGAIN?
NO, I HAVEN'T! WHO SAYS?
YOU HAVE NO IDEA WHAT SHE'S BEEN THROUGH.
SHE MIGHT BE DIFFERENT, BUT YOUR BEHAVIOR IS UNACCEPTABLE.
BUT I HAVEN'T DONE ANY-THING!
I HOPE SO, FOR YOUR SAKE. YOU KNOW I CAN GET YOU SUSPENDED FROM THE LACROSSE TEAM.
YOU WOULDN'T DARE.
I WOULDN'T HESITATE TO LET THE TEAM PLAY WITHOUT THEIR BEST ATTACKER IN THE FINALS. BUT DO YOU WANT THAT ON YOUR CONSCIENCE, PHILIPPA?
SO, FOR YOUR OWN SAKE: LEAVE ALENA ALONE, OKAY?

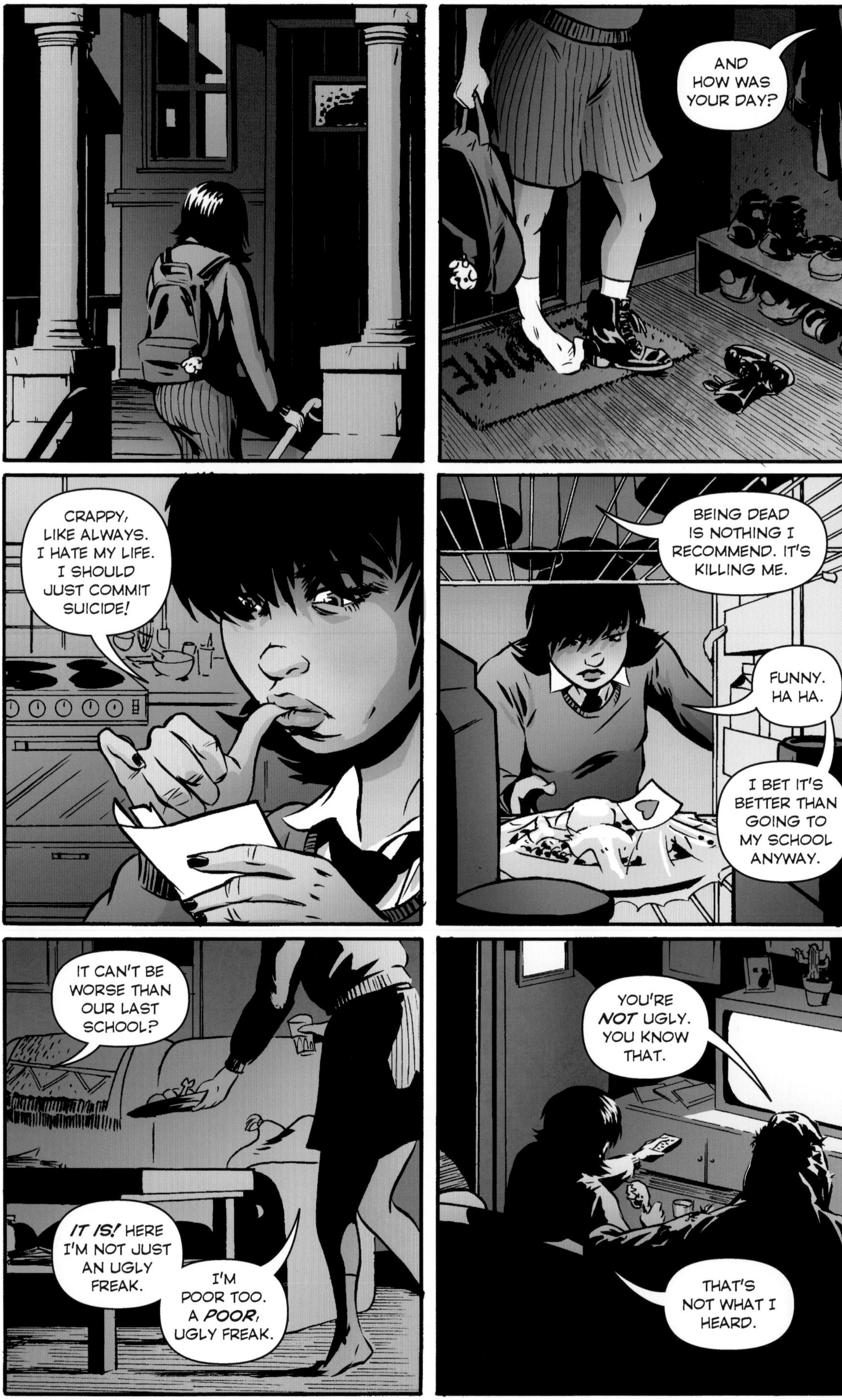
AND HOW WAS YOUR DAY?
CRAPPY, LIKE ALWAYS. I HATE MY LIFE. I SHOULD JUST COMMIT SUICIDE!
BEING DEAD IS NOTHING I RECOMMEND. IT'S KILLING ME.
FUNNY. HA HA.
I BET IT'S BETTER THAN GOING TO MY SCHOOL ANYWAY.
IT CAN'T BE WORSE THAN OUR LAST SCHOOL?
IT IS! HERE I'M NOT JUST AN UGLY FREAK.
I'M POOR TOO. A POOR, UGLY FREAK.
YOU'RE NOT UGLY. YOU KNOW THAT.
THAT'S NOT WHAT I HEARD.

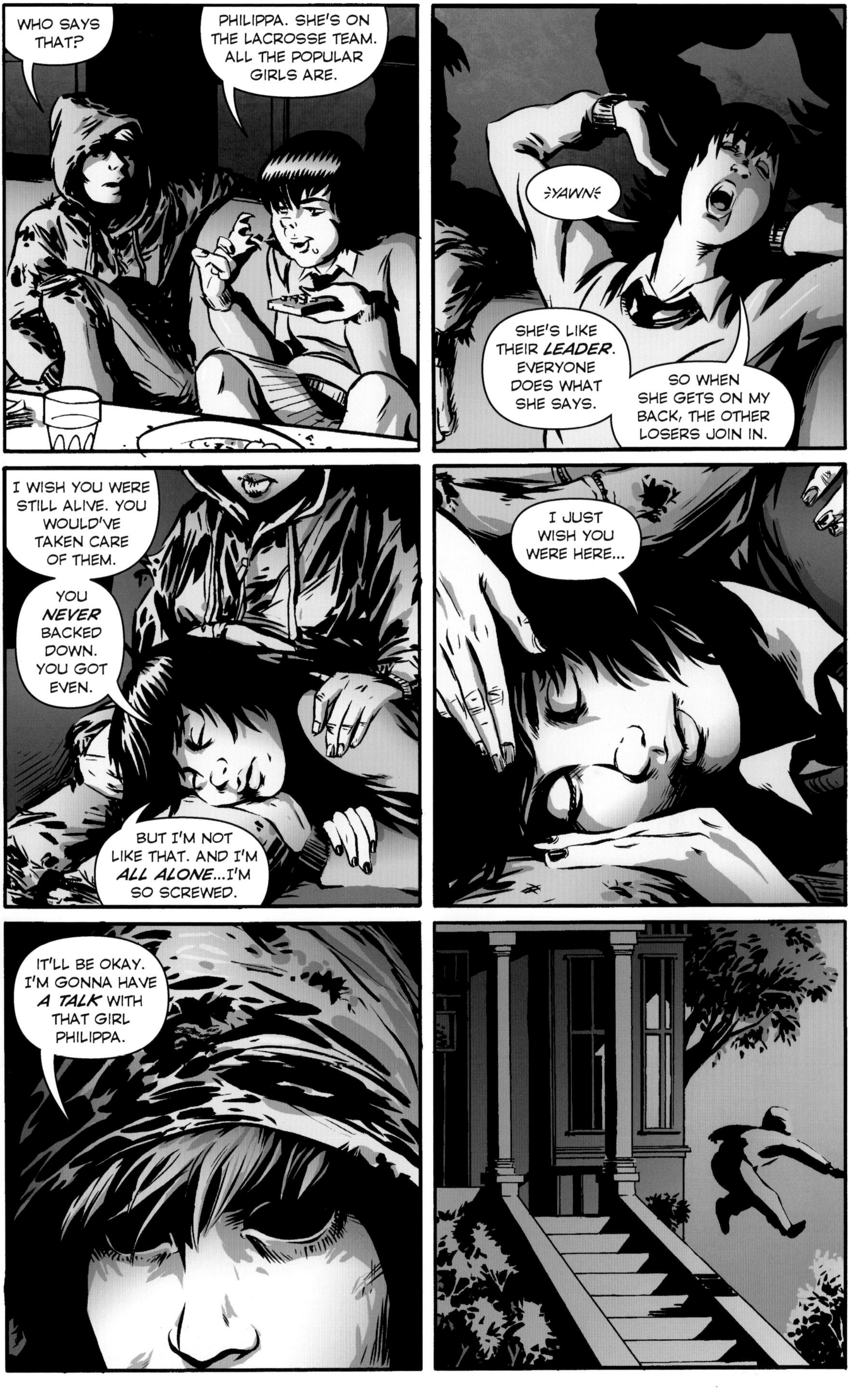
WHO SAYS THAT?
PHILIPPA. SHE'S ON THE LACROSSE TEAM. ALL THE POPULAR GIRLS ARE.
YAWN
SHE'S LIKE THEIR LEADER. EVERYONE DOES WHAT SHE SAYS.
SO WHEN SHE GETS ON MY BACK, THE OTHER LOSERS JOIN IN.
I WISH YOU WERE STILL ALIVE. YOU WOULD'VE TAKEN CARE OF THEM.
YOU NEVER BACKED DOWN. YOU GOT EVEN.
BUT I'M NOT LIKE THAT. AND I'M ALL ALONE...I'M SO SCREWED.
I JUST WISH YOU WERE HERE...
IT'LL BE OKAY. I'M GONNA HAVE A TALK WITH THAT GIRL PHILIPPA.

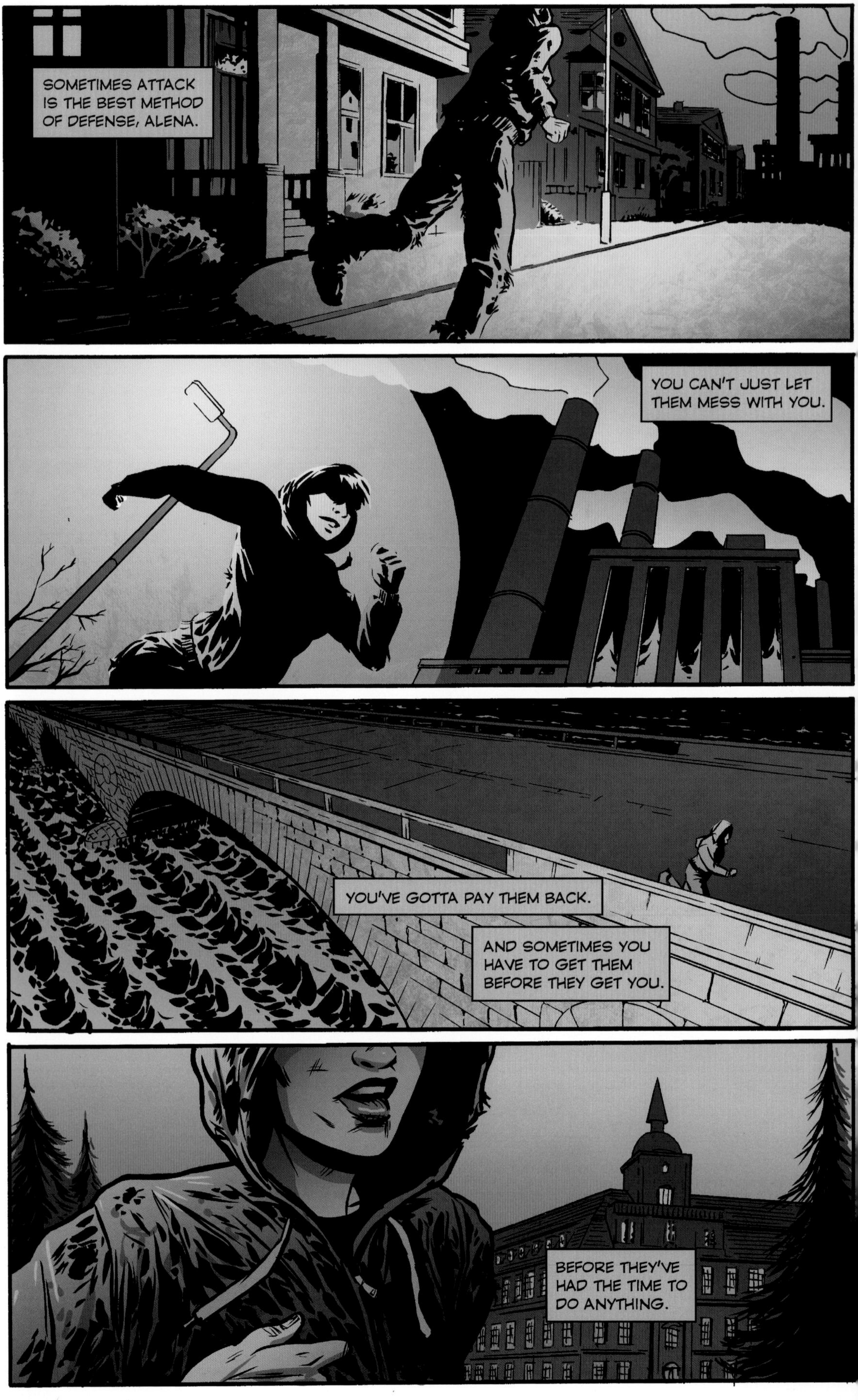
SOMETIMES ATTACK IS THE BEST METHOD OF DEFENSE, ALENA.
YOU CAN'T JUST LET THEM MESS WITH YOU.
YOU'VE GOTTA PAY THEM BACK.
AND SOMETIMES YOU HAVE TO GET THEM BEFORE THEY GET YOU.
BEFORE THEY'VE HAD THE TIME TO DO ANYTHING.

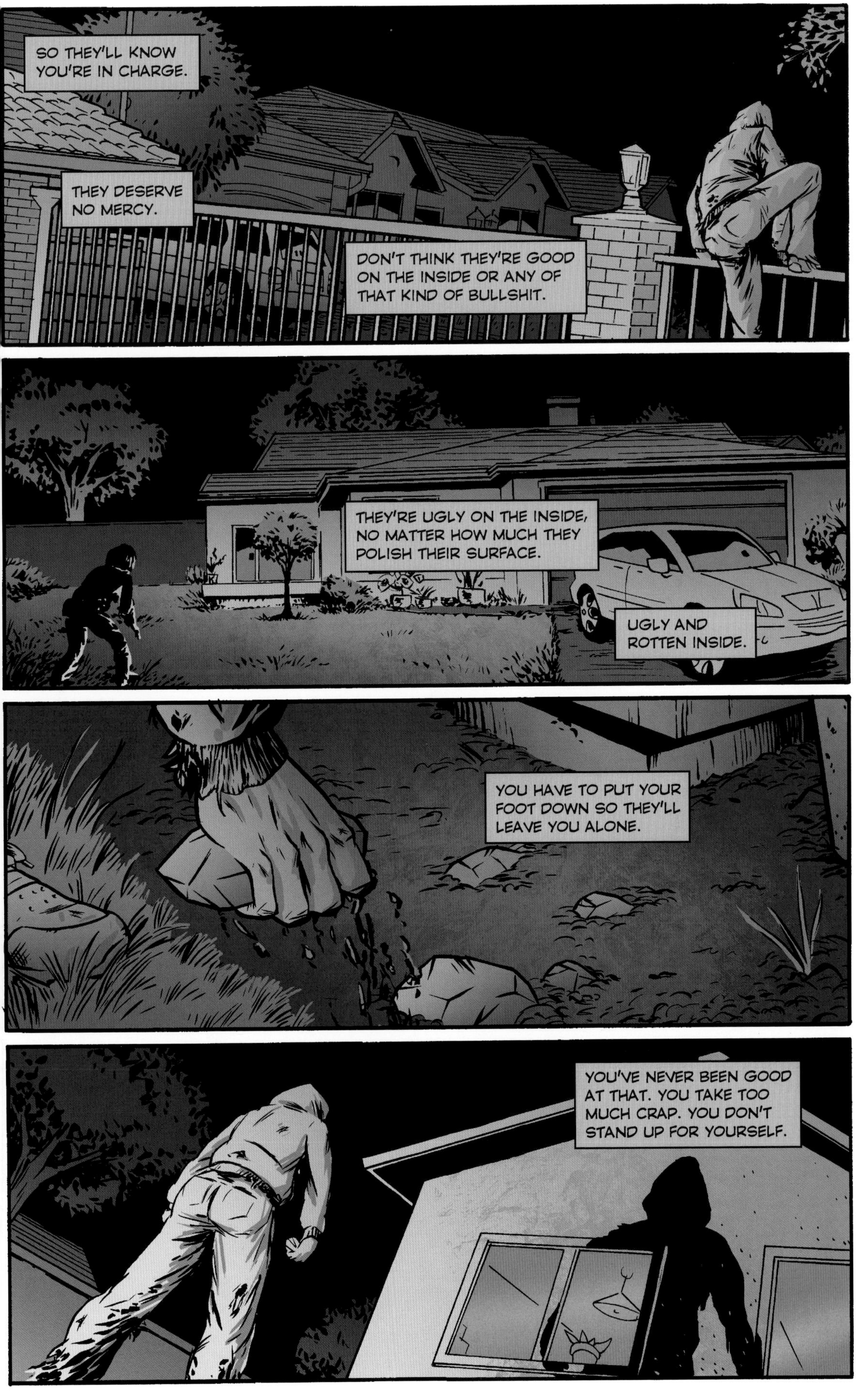
SO THEY'LL KNOW YOU'RE IN CHARGE.
THEY DESERVE NO MERCY.
DON'T THINK THEY'RE GOOD ON THE INSIDE OR ANY OF THAT KIND OF BULLSHIT.
THEY'RE UGLY ON THE INSIDE, NO MATTER HOW MUCH THEY POLISH THEIR SURFACE.
UGLY AND ROTTEN INSIDE.
YOU HAVE TO PUT YOUR FOOT DOWN SO THEY'LL LEAVE YOU ALONE.
YOU'VE NEVER BEEN GOOD AT THAT. YOU TAKE TOO MUCH CRAP. YOU DON'T STAND UP FOR YOURSELF.

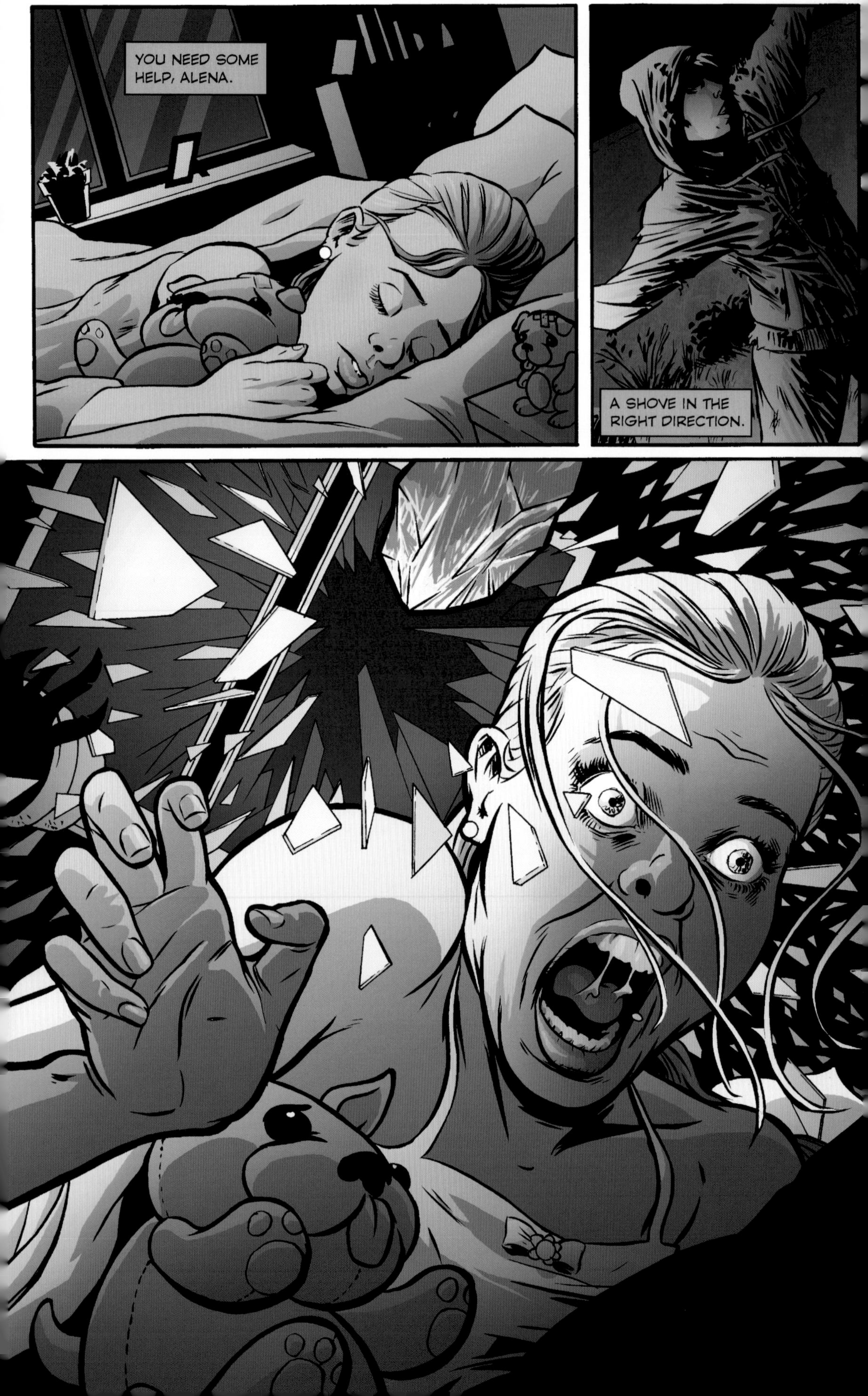
YOU NEED SOME HELP, ALENA.
A SHOVE IN THE RIGHT DIRECTION.

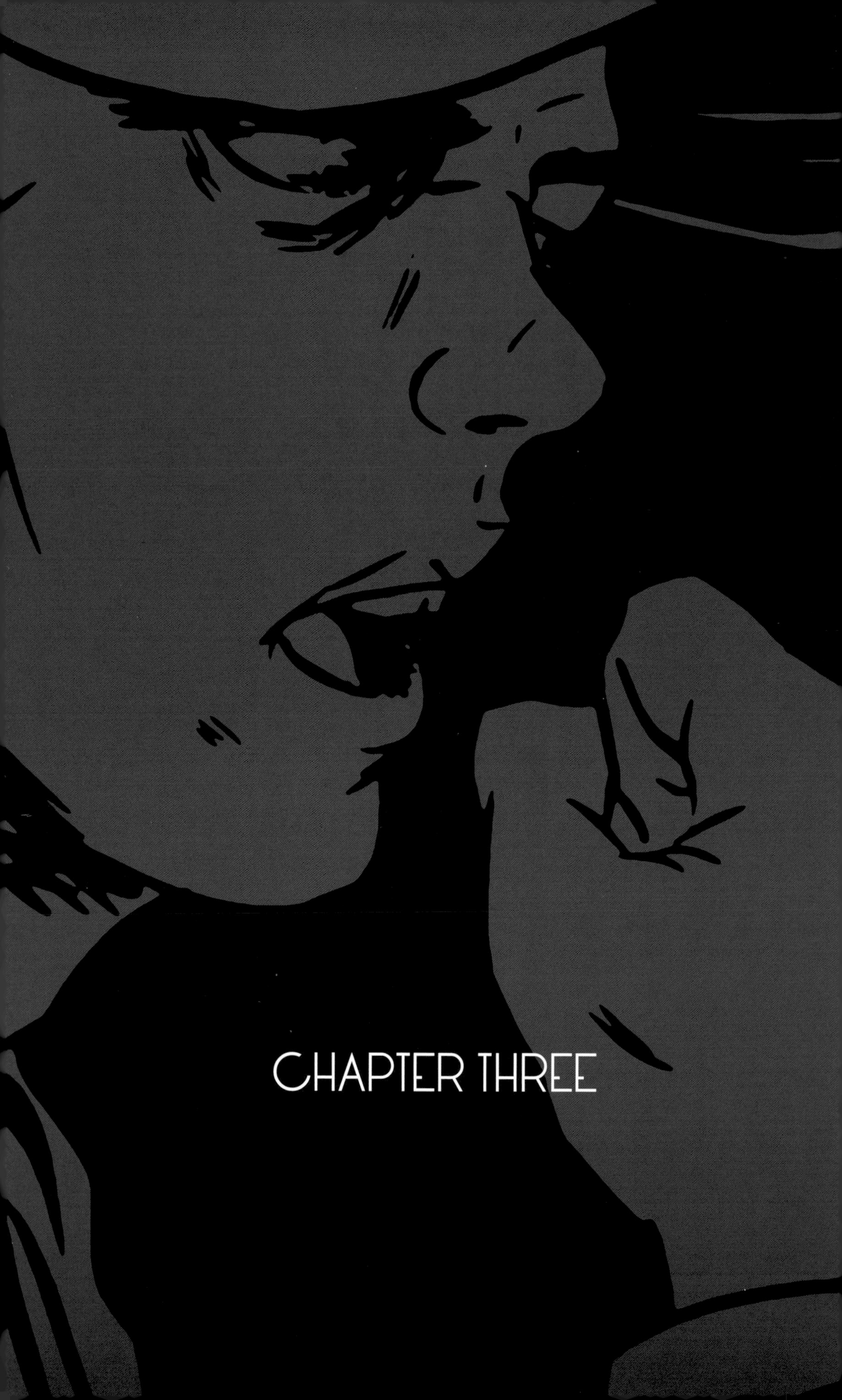

# CHAPTER THREE

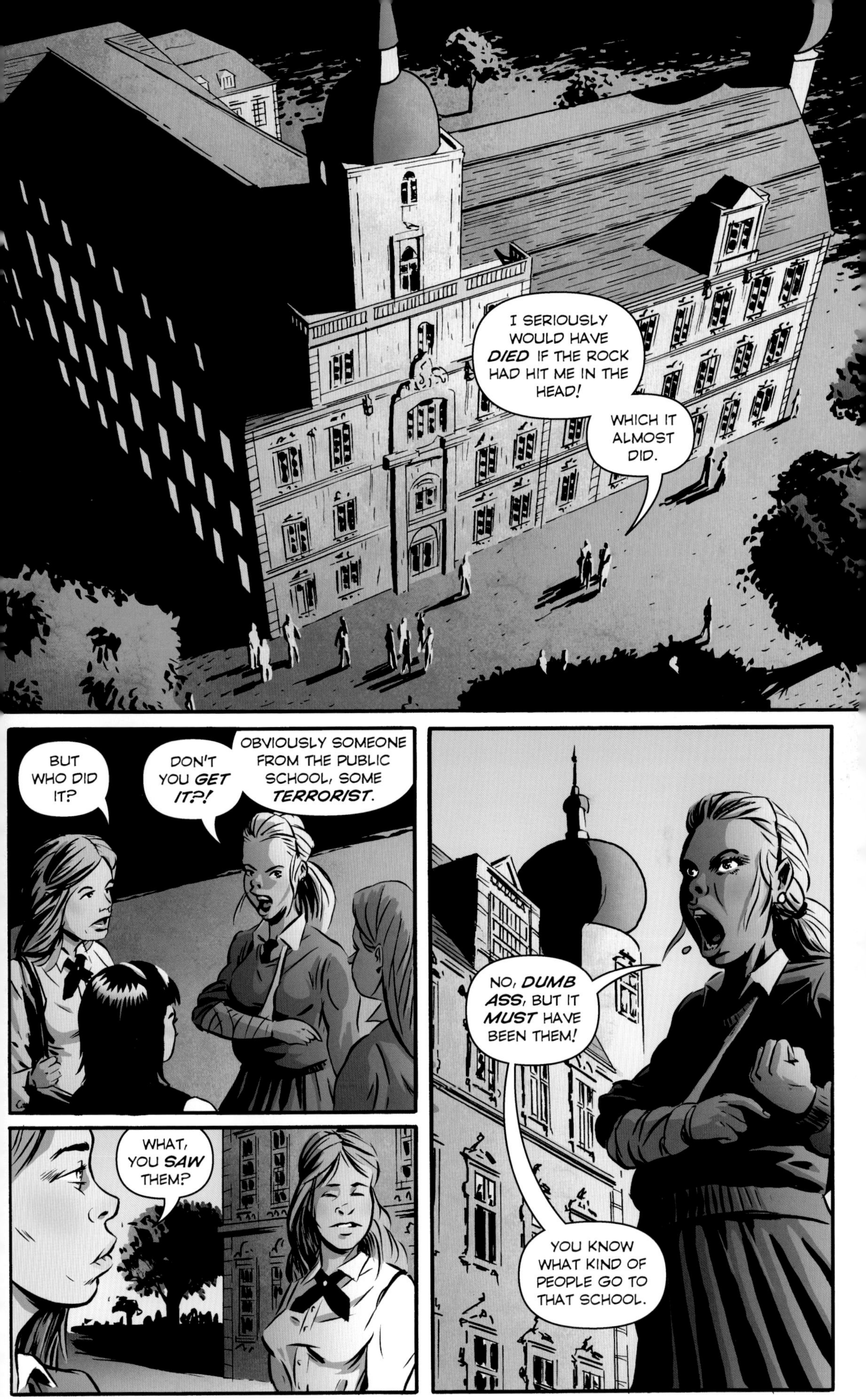
I SERIOUSLY WOULD HAVE DIED IF THE ROCK HAD HIT ME IN THE HEAD!
WHICH IT ALMOST DID.
BUT WHO DID IT?
DON'T YOU GET IT?!
OBVIOUSLY SOMEONE FROM THE PUBLIC SCHOOL, SOME TERRORIST.
WHAT, YOU SAW THEM?
NO, DUMB ASS, BUT IT MUST HAVE BEEN THEM!
YOU KNOW WHAT KIND OF PEOPLE GO TO THAT SCHOOL.

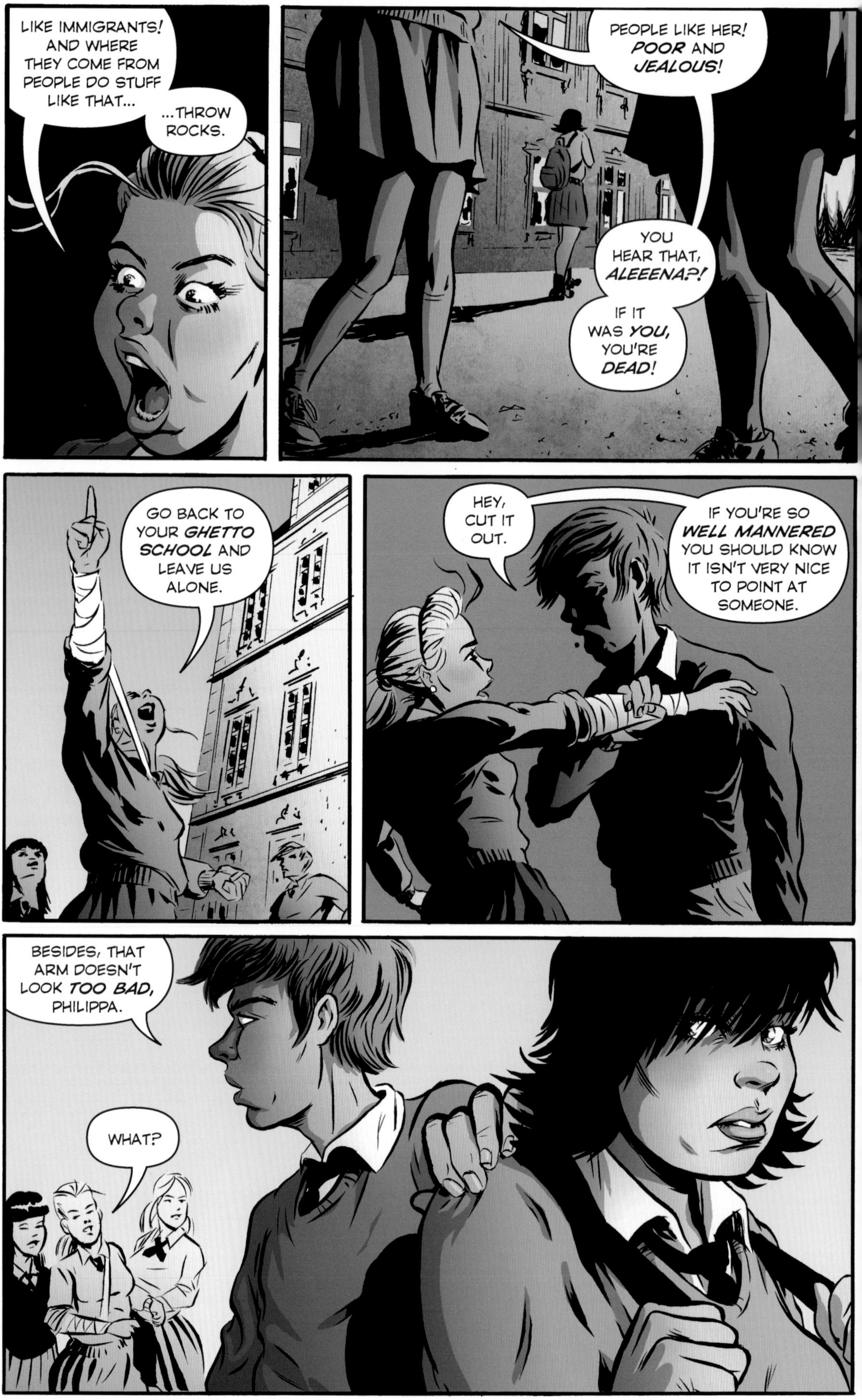

LIKE IMMIGRANTS! AND WHERE THEY COME FROM PEOPLE DO STUFF LIKE THAT...
...THROW ROCKS.
PEOPLE LIKE HER! POOR AND JEALOUS!
YOU HEAR THAT, ALEEENA?!
IF IT WAS YOU, YOU'RE DEAD!
GO BACK TO YOUR GHETTO SCHOOL AND LEAVE US ALONE.
HEY, CUT IT OUT.
IF YOU'RE SO WELL MANNERED YOU SHOULD KNOW IT ISN'T VERY NICE TO POINT AT SOMEONE.
BESIDES, THAT ARM DOESN'T LOOK TOO BAD, PHILIPPA.
WHAT?

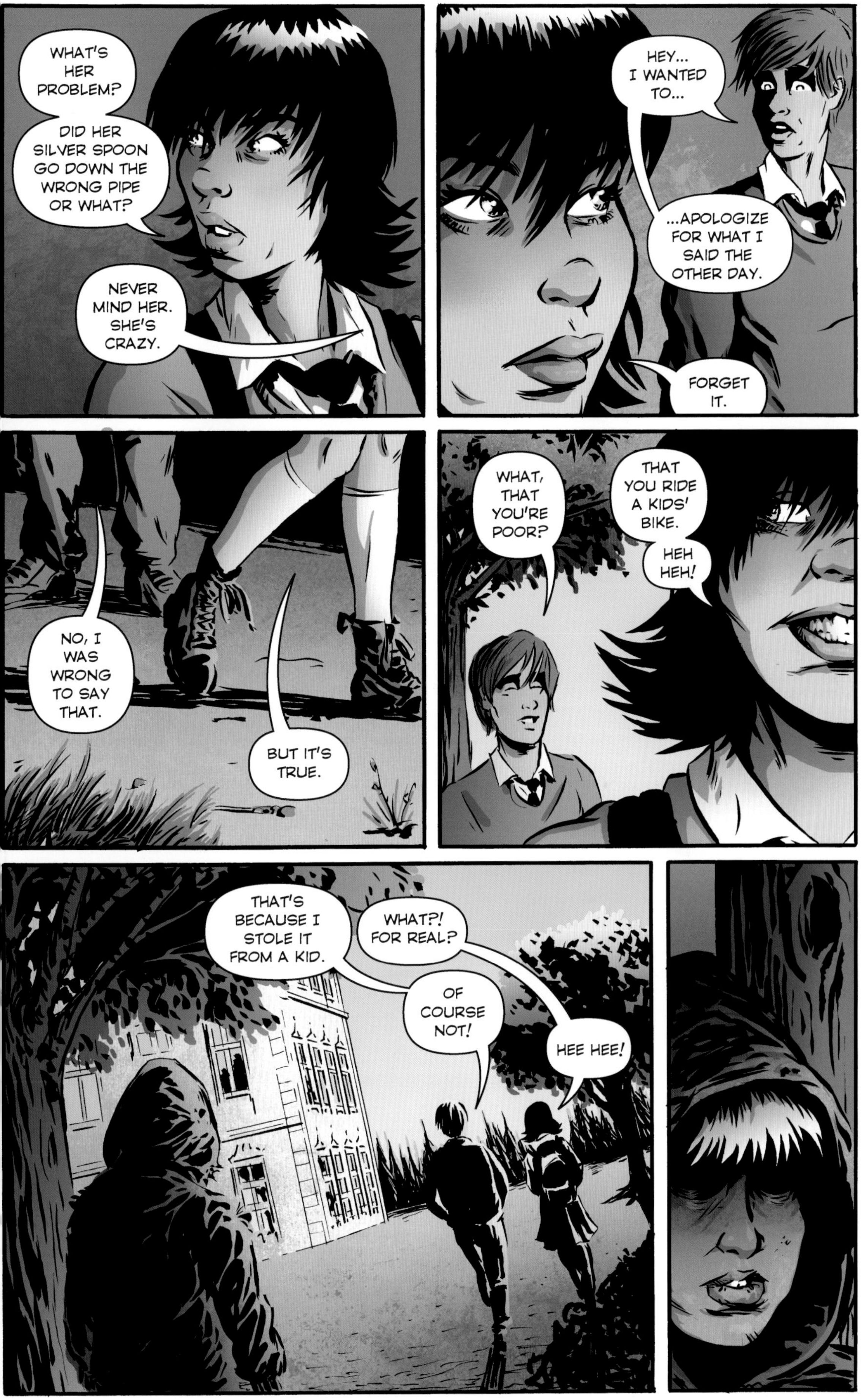
WHAT'S HER PROBLEM?
DID HER SILVER SPOON GO DOWN THE WRONG PIPE OR WHAT?
NEVER MIND HER. SHE'S CRAZY.
HEY... I WANTED TO...
...APOLOGIZE FOR WHAT I SAID THE OTHER DAY.
FORGET IT.
NO, I WAS WRONG TO SAY THAT.
BUT IT'S TRUE.
WHAT, THAT YOU'RE POOR?
THAT YOU RIDE A KIDS' BIKE.
HEH HEH!
THAT'S BECAUSE I STOLE IT FROM A KID.
WHAT?! FOR REAL?
OF COURSE NOT!
HEE HEE!

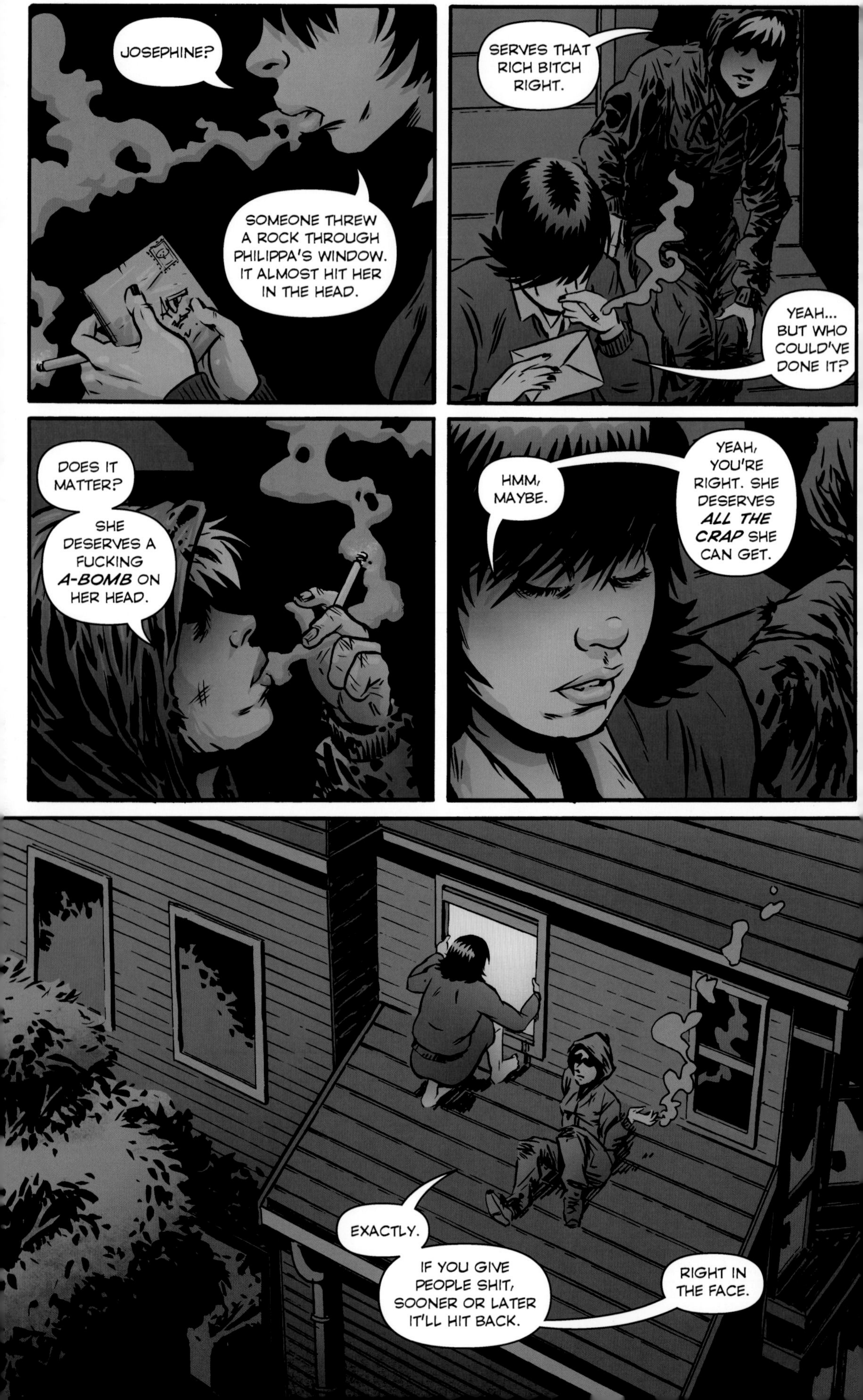
JOSEPHINE?
SOMEONE THREW A ROCK THROUGH PHILIPPA'S WINDOW. IT ALMOST HIT HER IN THE HEAD.
SERVES THAT RICH BITCH RIGHT.
YEAH... BUT WHO COULD'VE DONE IT?
DOES IT MATTER?
SHE DESERVES A FUCKING *A-BOMB* ON HER HEAD.
HMM, MAYBE.
YEAH, YOU'RE RIGHT. SHE DESERVES *ALL THE CRAP* SHE CAN GET.
EXACTLY.
IF YOU GIVE PEOPLE SHIT, SOONER OR LATER IT'LL HIT BACK.
RIGHT IN THE FACE.

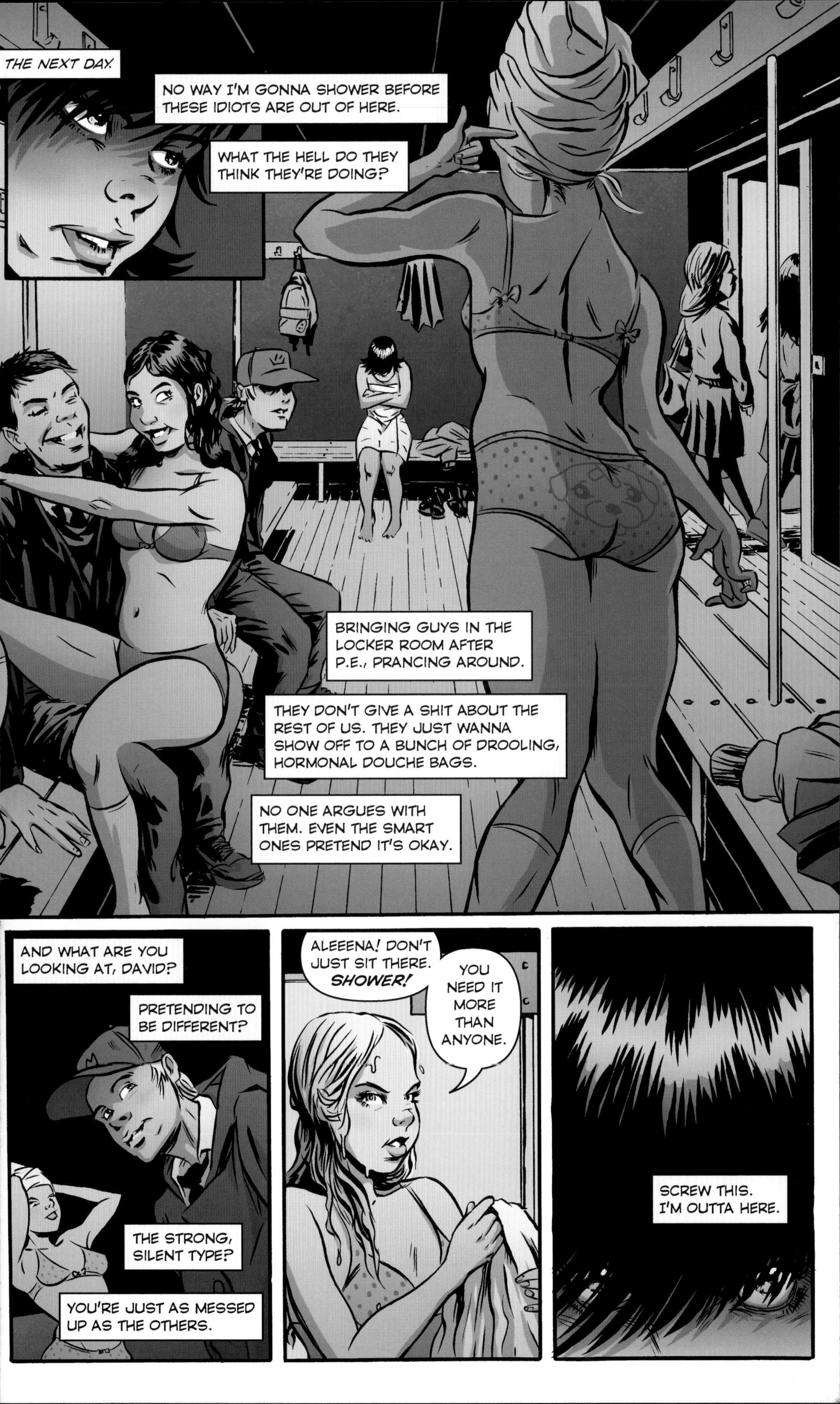
THE NEXT DAY.
NO WAY I'M GONNA SHOWER BEFORE THESE IDIOTS ARE OUT OF HERE.
WHAT THE HELL DO THEY THINK THEY'RE DOING?
BRINGING GUYS IN THE LOCKER ROOM AFTER P.E., PRANCING AROUND.
THEY DON'T GIVE A SHIT ABOUT THE REST OF US. THEY JUST WANNA SHOW OFF TO A BUNCH OF DROOLING, HORMONAL DOUCHE BAGS.
NO ONE ARGUES WITH THEM. EVEN THE SMART ONES PRETEND IT'S OKAY.
AND WHAT ARE YOU LOOKING AT, DAVID?
PRETENDING TO BE DIFFERENT?
THE STRONG, SILENT TYPE?
YOU'RE JUST AS MESSED UP AS THE OTHERS.
ALEEENA! DON'T JUST SIT THERE. SHOWER!
YOU NEED IT MORE THAN ANYONE.
SCREW THIS. I'M OUTTA HERE.

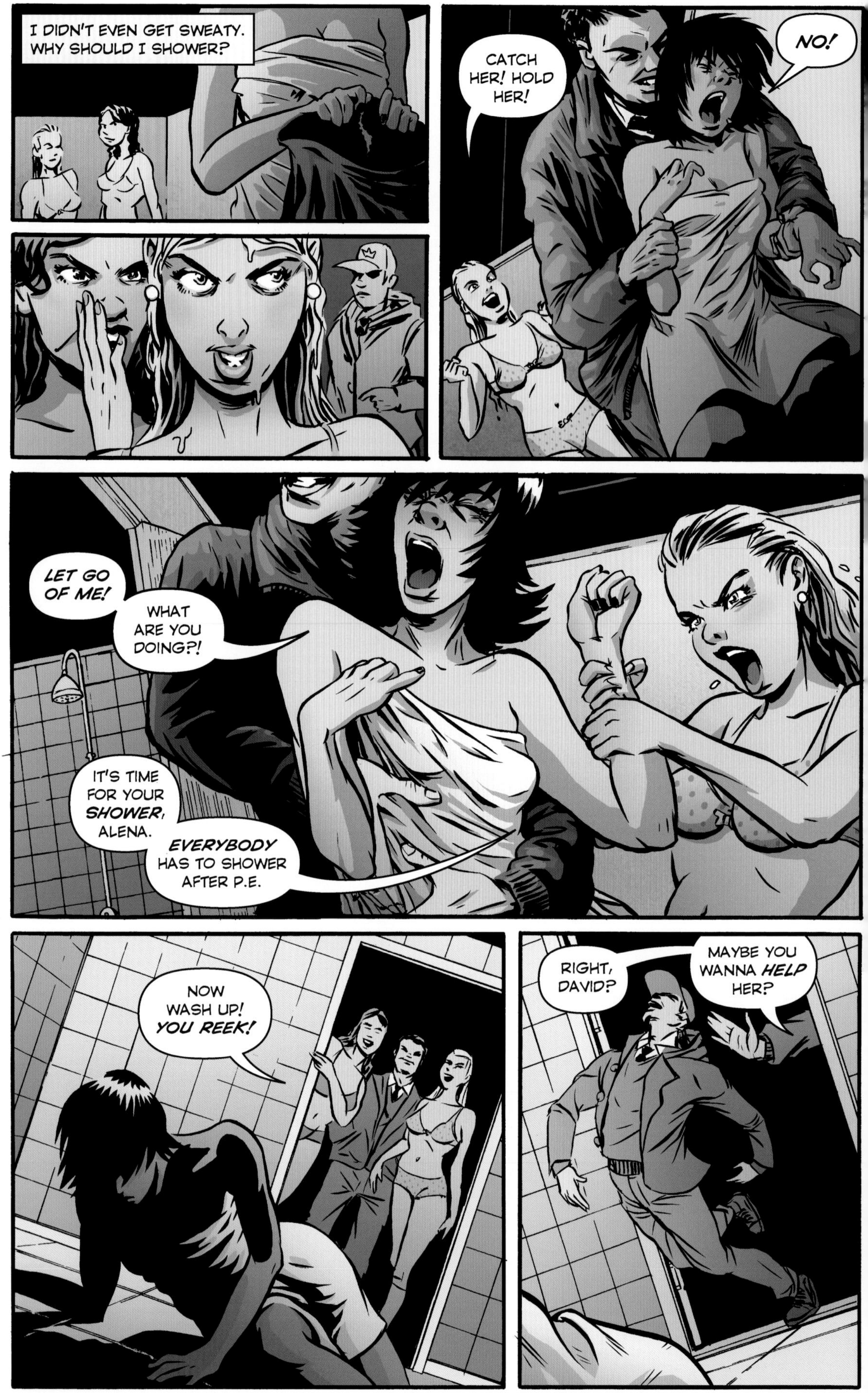

I DIDN'T EVEN GET SWEATY. WHY SHOULD I SHOWER?
CATCH HER! HOLD HER!
NO!
LET GO OF ME!
WHAT ARE YOU DOING?!
IT'S TIME FOR YOUR SHOWER, ALENA.
EVERYBODY HAS TO SHOWER AFTER P.E.
NOW WASH UP! YOU REEK!
RIGHT, DAVID?
MAYBE YOU WANNA HELP HER?

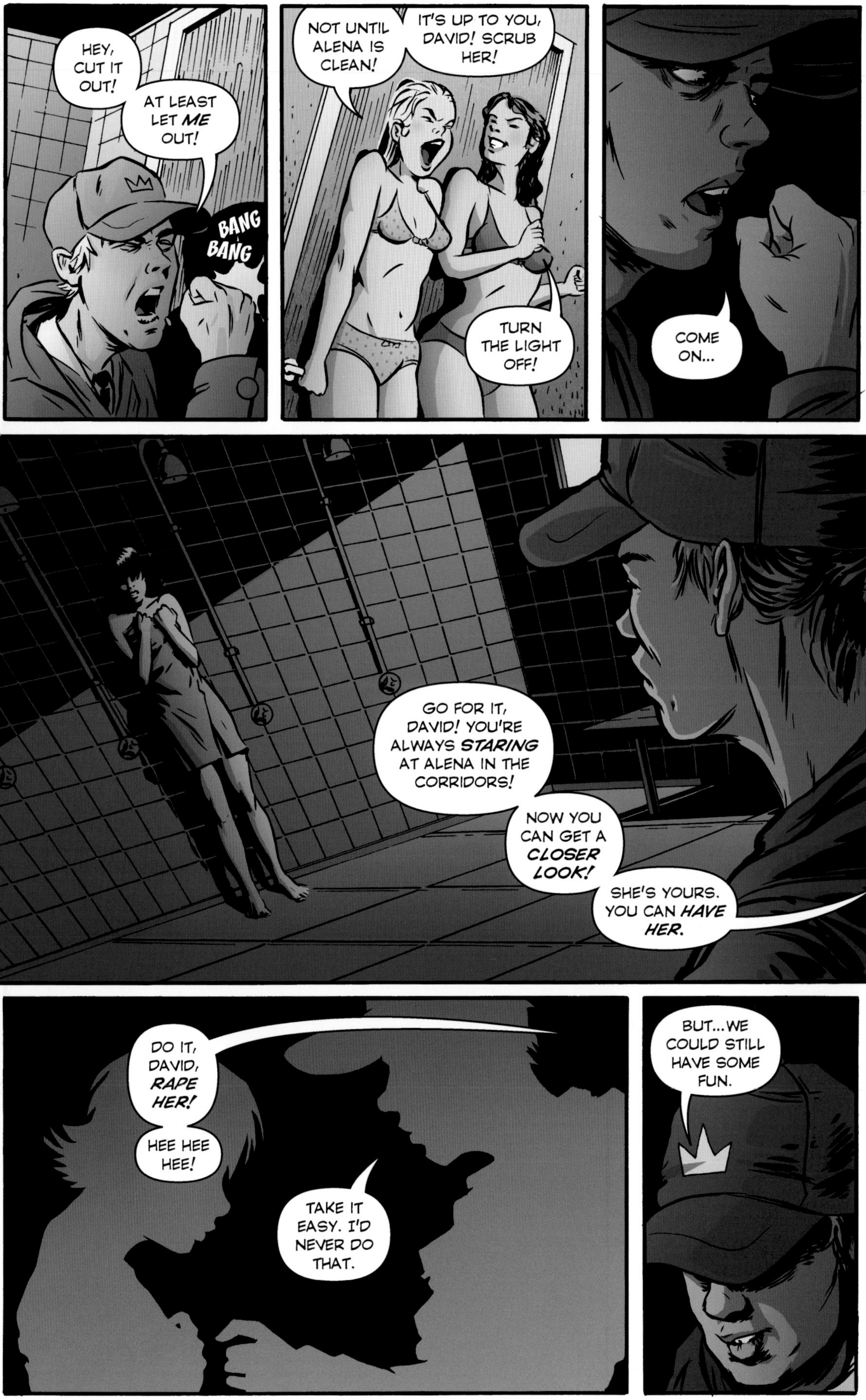
HEY, CUT IT OUT!
AT LEAST LET *ME* OUT!
BANG BANG
NOT UNTIL ALENA IS CLEAN!
IT'S UP TO YOU, DAVID! SCRUB HER!
TURN THE LIGHT OFF!
COME ON...
GO FOR IT, DAVID! YOU'RE ALWAYS *STARING* AT ALENA IN THE CORRIDORS!
NOW YOU CAN GET A *CLOSER LOOK!*
SHE'S YOURS. YOU CAN *HAVE HER.*
DO IT, DAVID, *RAPE HER!*
HEE HEE HEE!
TAKE IT EASY. I'D NEVER DO THAT.
BUT...WE COULD STILL HAVE SOME FUN.

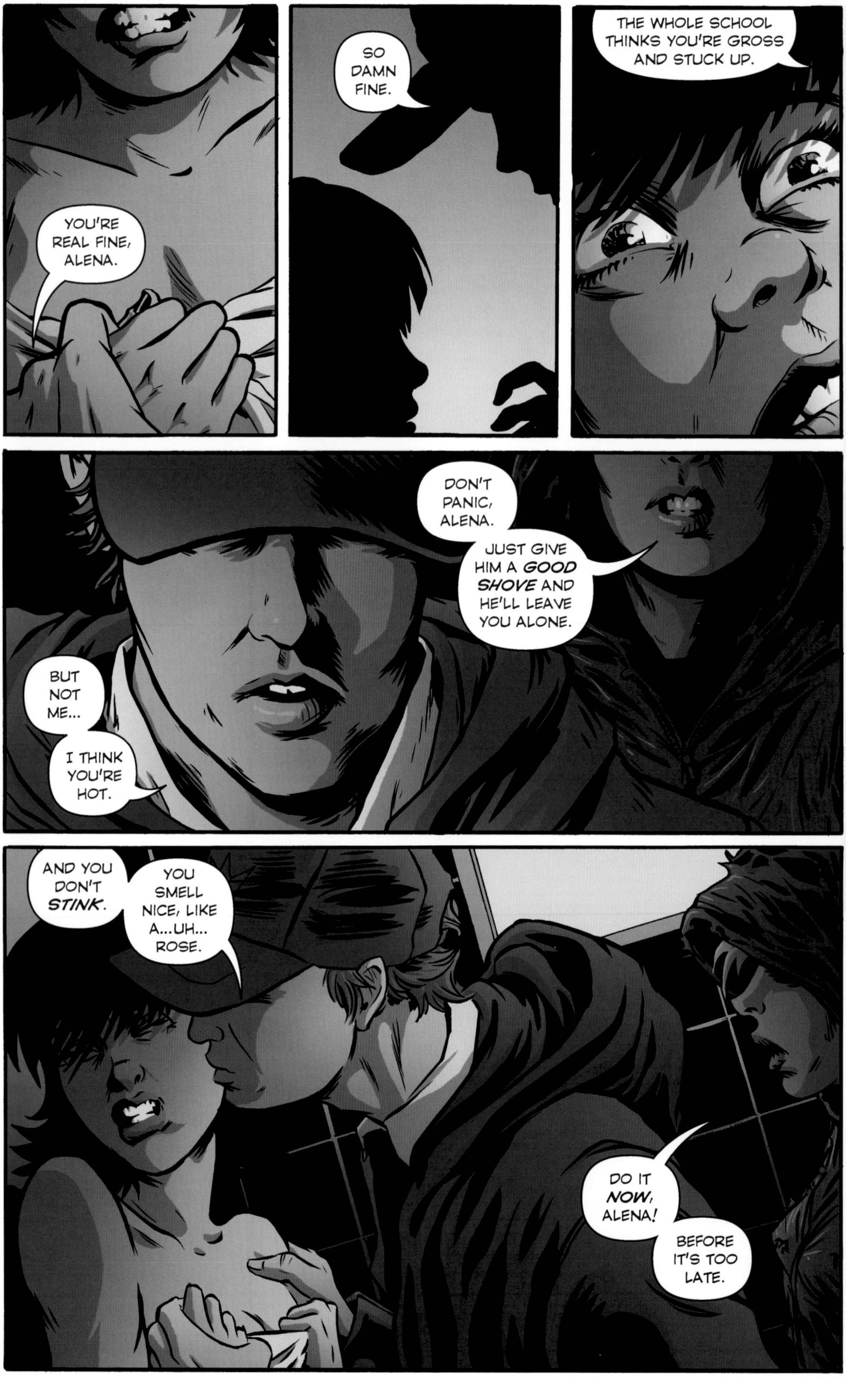
YOU'RE REAL FINE, ALENA.
SO DAMN FINE.
THE WHOLE SCHOOL THINKS YOU'RE GROSS AND STUCK UP.
DON'T PANIC, ALENA.
JUST GIVE HIM A **GOOD SHOVE** AND HE'LL LEAVE YOU ALONE.
BUT NOT ME...
I THINK YOU'RE HOT.
AND YOU DON'T **STINK**.
YOU SMELL NICE, LIKE A...UH... ROSE.
DO IT **NOW**, ALENA!
BEFORE IT'S TOO LATE.

PUT YOUR KNEE RIGHT IN HIS CROTCH.

OR ELSE HE WON'T STOP.

COME ON, JUST LET ME TOUCH YOU.

YOU'LL LIKE IT.

I PROMISE.

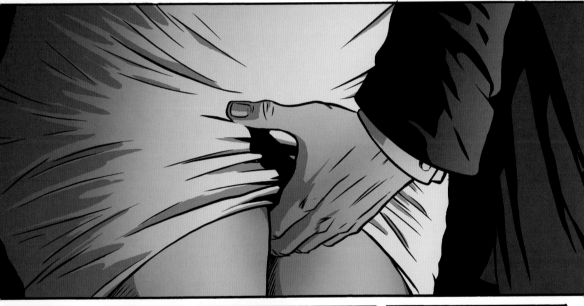

YEAH.

GOOD, HUH?

DAMN IT, ALENA. I GUESS *I'LL* HAVE TO DO IT.

SQUEEK

TSCHHH
AAH!
OUFF!
THUCK
HEY?! WHAT ARE YOU DOING IN THERE?
HOW'S IT GOING, DAVID?
OPEN THE DOOR, PHILIPPA.
HEH HEH!
SOCK!
AAAAHH!
YOU'RE *DEAD*, YOU LITTLE WHORE!

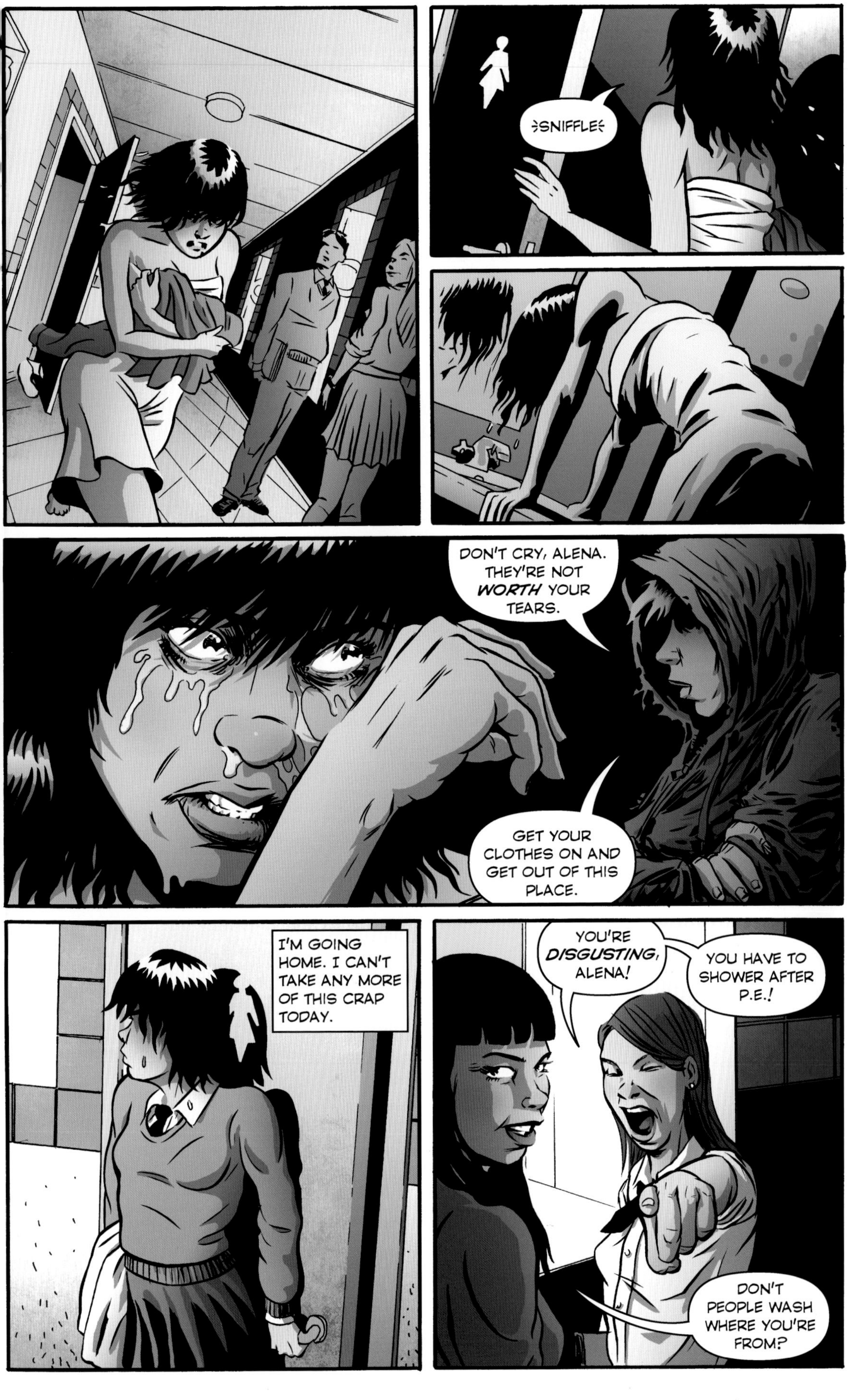

SNIFFLE
DON'T CRY, ALENA. THEY'RE NOT *WORTH* YOUR TEARS.
GET YOUR CLOTHES ON AND GET OUT OF THIS PLACE.
I'M GOING HOME. I CAN'T TAKE ANY MORE OF THIS CRAP TODAY.
YOU'RE *DISGUSTING*, ALENA!
YOU HAVE TO SHOWER AFTER P.E.!
DON'T PEOPLE WASH WHERE YOU'RE FROM?

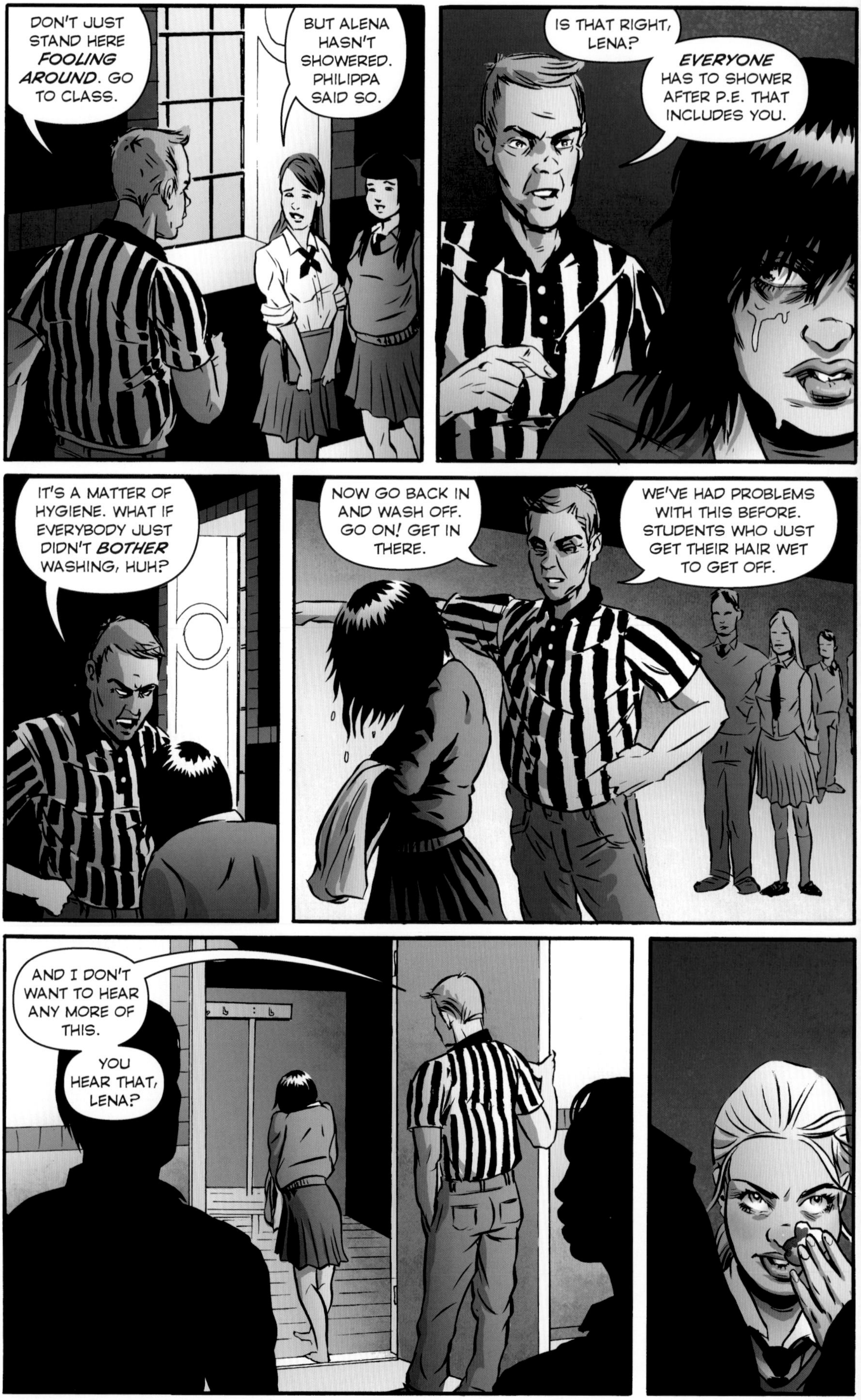
DON'T JUST STAND HERE *FOOLING AROUND*. GO TO CLASS.
BUT ALENA HASN'T SHOWERED. PHILIPPA SAID SO.
IS THAT RIGHT, LENA?
*EVERYONE* HAS TO SHOWER AFTER P.E. THAT INCLUDES YOU.
IT'S A MATTER OF HYGIENE. WHAT IF EVERYBODY JUST DIDN'T *BOTHER* WASHING, HUH?
NOW GO BACK IN AND WASH OFF. GO ON! GET IN THERE.
WE'VE HAD PROBLEMS WITH THIS BEFORE. STUDENTS WHO JUST GET THEIR HAIR WET TO GET OFF.
AND I DON'T WANT TO HEAR ANY MORE OF THIS.
YOU HEAR THAT, LENA?

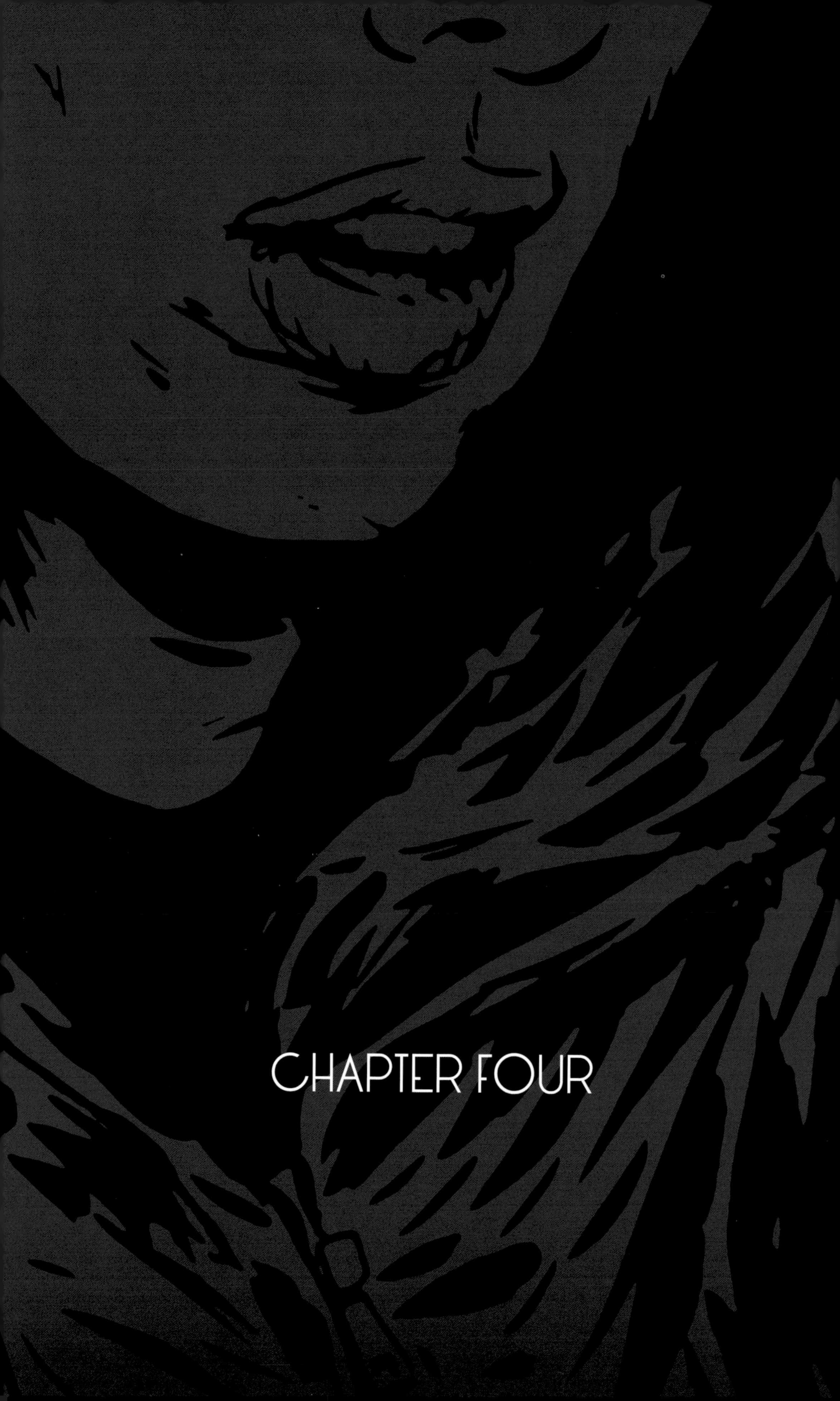
CHAPTER FOUR

I HAVE THE FEELING PHILIPPA COULD DO *ANYTHING* NOW.

AFTER THAT NOSEBLEED IN P.E. SHE'S GONE NUTS. BUT IT WASN'T EVEN *MY FAULT!*

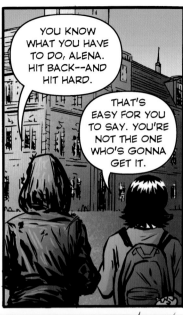

YOU KNOW WHAT YOU HAVE TO DO, ALENA. HIT BACK--AND HIT HARD.

THAT'S EASY FOR YOU TO SAY. YOU'RE NOT THE ONE WHO'S GONNA GET IT.

MAYBE YOUR KNIGHT IN SHINING ARMOR, *FABIAN*, WILL COME HELP YOU.

ISN'T HE YOUR *HERO* NOWADAYS?

CUT IT OUT, JOSEPHINE.

I HAVE TO DO THIS ON MY OWN.

THAT'S *EXACTLY* WHAT I'VE BEEN SAYING.

ALONE, JOSEPHINE. WITHOUT *YOU*.

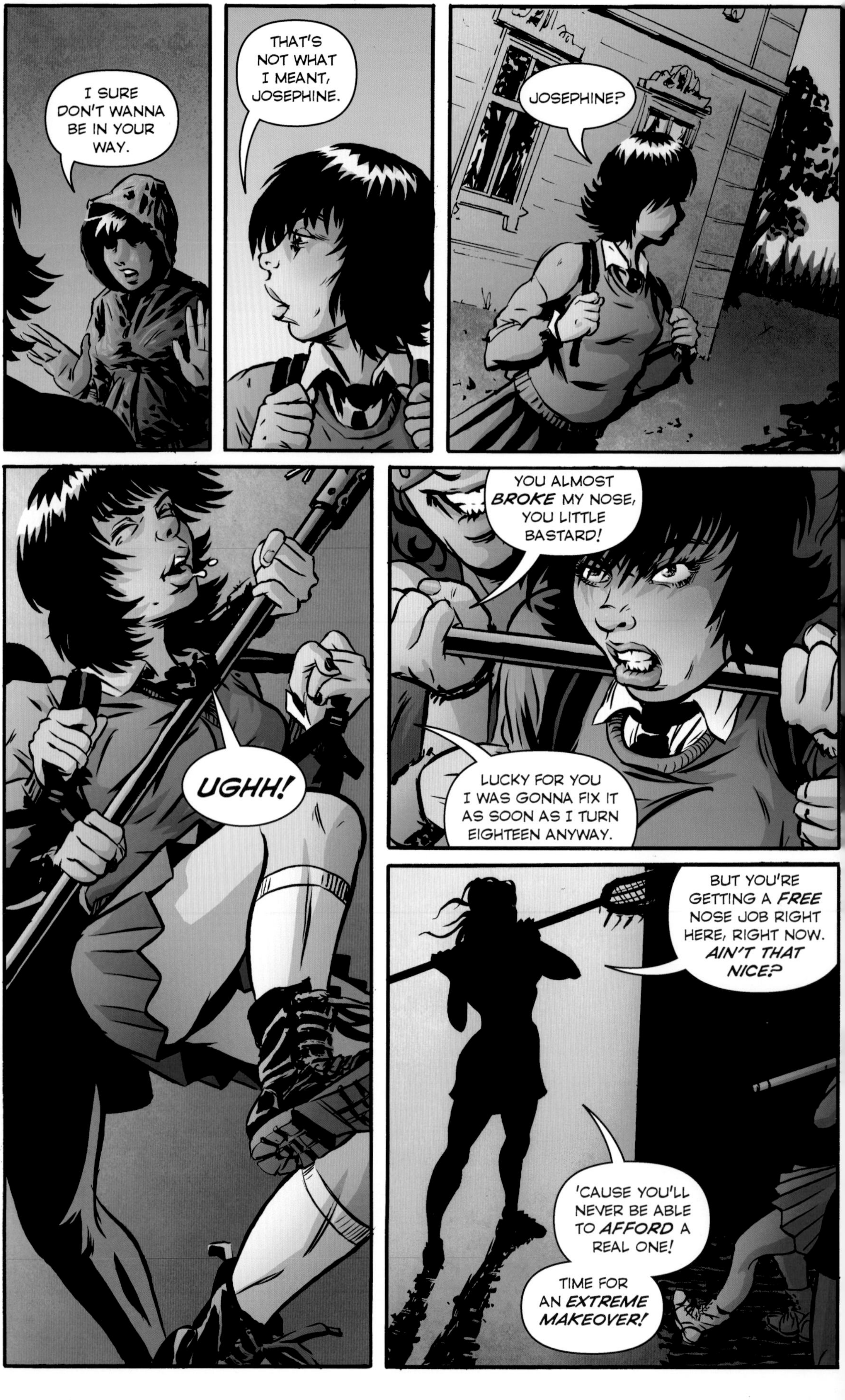
I SURE DON'T WANNA BE IN YOUR WAY.
THAT'S NOT WHAT I MEANT, JOSEPHINE.
JOSEPHINE?
UGHH!
YOU ALMOST *BROKE* MY NOSE, YOU LITTLE BASTARD!
LUCKY FOR YOU I WAS GONNA FIX IT AS SOON AS I TURN EIGHTEEN ANYWAY.
BUT YOU'RE GETTING A *FREE* NOSE JOB RIGHT HERE, RIGHT NOW. *AIN'T THAT NICE?*
'CAUSE YOU'LL NEVER BE ABLE TO *AFFORD* A REAL ONE!
TIME FOR AN *EXTREME MAKEOVER!*

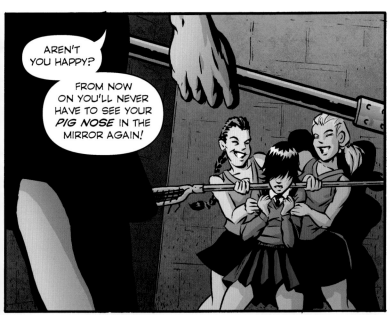

AREN'T YOU HAPPY?

FROM NOW ON YOU'LL NEVER HAVE TO SEE YOUR *PIG NOSE* IN THE MIRROR AGAIN!

YOU'RE GONNA BE *SUPER HOT!*

*HAHAHA!*

D'YOU KNOW WHY I'M THE *BEST PLAYER* ON THE LACROSSE TEAM?

'CAUSE I CAN SWING THIS HARDER THAN *ANYONE* ELSE.

IF I CAN MAKE A BALL FLY 100 M.P.H., YOUR SNOUT WON'T BE A PROBLEM.

STAND ABSOLUTELY STILL, ALENA.

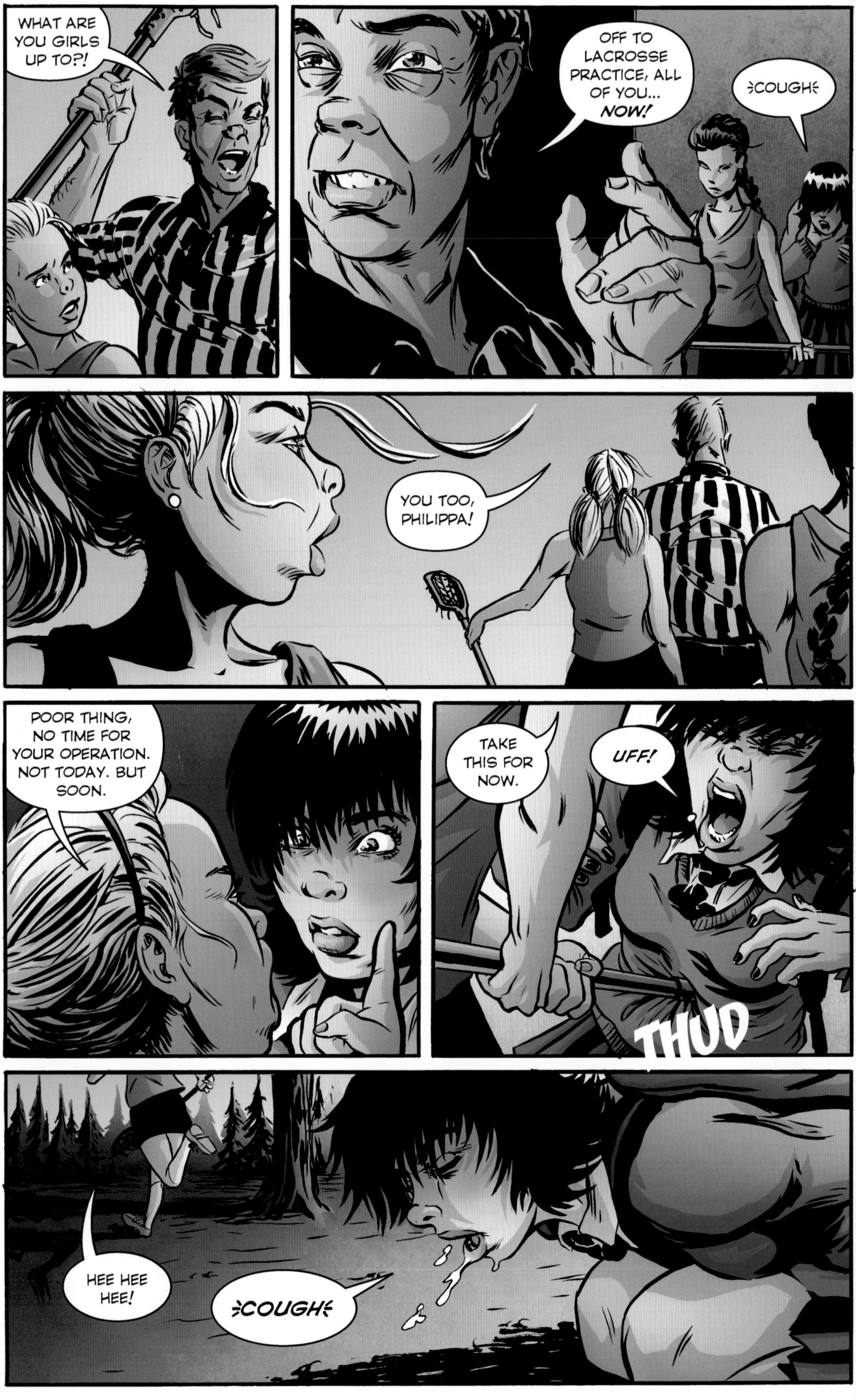
WHAT ARE YOU GIRLS UP TO?!
OFF TO LACROSSE PRACTICE, ALL OF YOU... NOW!
COUGH
YOU TOO, PHILIPPA!
POOR THING, NO TIME FOR YOUR OPERATION. NOT TODAY. BUT SOON.
TAKE THIS FOR NOW.
UFF!
THUD
HEE HEE HEE!
COUGH

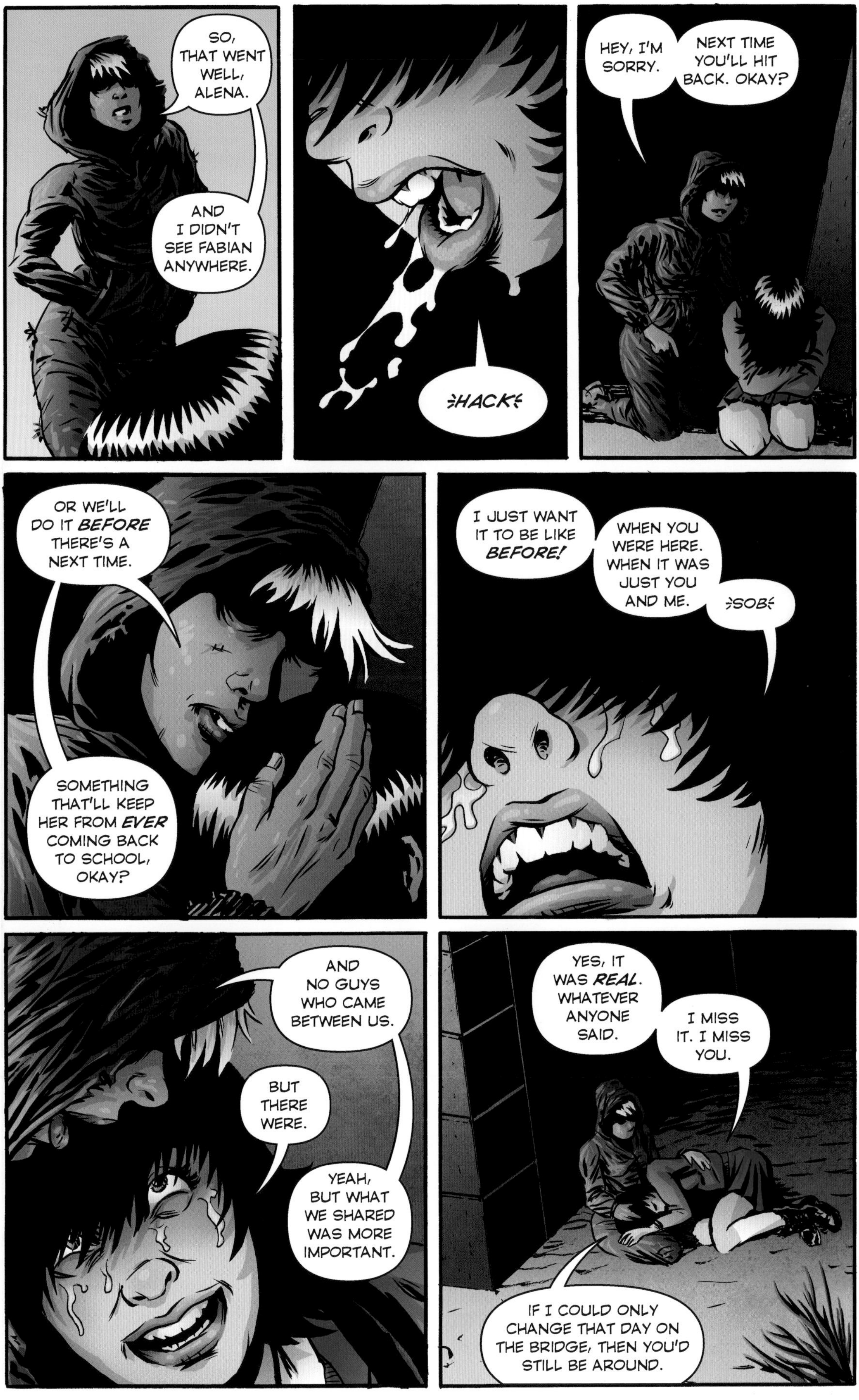
SO, THAT WENT WELL, ALENA.
AND I DIDN'T SEE FABIAN ANYWHERE.
HACK
HEY, I'M SORRY.
NEXT TIME YOU'LL HIT BACK. OKAY?
OR WE'LL DO IT BEFORE THERE'S A NEXT TIME.
SOMETHING THAT'LL KEEP HER FROM EVER COMING BACK TO SCHOOL, OKAY?
I JUST WANT IT TO BE LIKE BEFORE!
WHEN YOU WERE HERE. WHEN IT WAS JUST YOU AND ME.
SOB
AND NO GUYS WHO CAME BETWEEN US.
BUT THERE WERE.
YEAH, BUT WHAT WE SHARED WAS MORE IMPORTANT.
YES, IT WAS REAL. WHATEVER ANYONE SAID.
I MISS IT. I MISS YOU.
IF I COULD ONLY CHANGE THAT DAY ON THE BRIDGE, THEN YOU'D STILL BE AROUND.

ALL RIGHT, SO THAT'S IT FOR TODAY.

FINALLY!

I THINK THINGS WILL WORK OUT WITH THOSE GIRLS.

AND WE'LL MEET THIS TIME EVERY WEEK FROM NOW ON.

WHY DID YOU CHOOSE THIS TIME, BY THE WAY?

IT'S WHEN I HAVE P.E.

DON'T YOU LIKE P.E.?

I DIDN'T EITHER.

WHO CARES? DON'T ACT LIKE YOU KNOW ME.

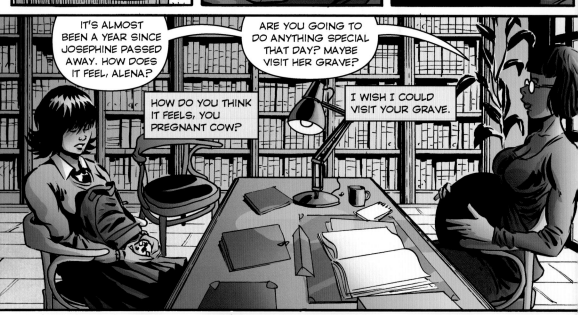

IT'S ALMOST BEEN A YEAR SINCE JOSEPHINE PASSED AWAY. HOW DOES IT FEEL, ALENA?

ARE YOU GOING TO DO ANYTHING SPECIAL THAT DAY? MAYBE VISIT HER GRAVE?

HOW DO YOU THINK IT FEELS, YOU PREGNANT COW?

I WISH I COULD VISIT YOUR GRAVE.

YOU KNOW, AT SOME POINT WE'LL *HAVE* TO TALK ABOUT THAT DAY.

YOU HAVE TO LET IT OUT, PROCESS, AND MOVE ON.

WHY? *I DIDN'T KILL HER*, IF THAT'S WHAT YOU THINK.

NOBODY SAID SO.

WHY WOULD YOU SAY THAT?

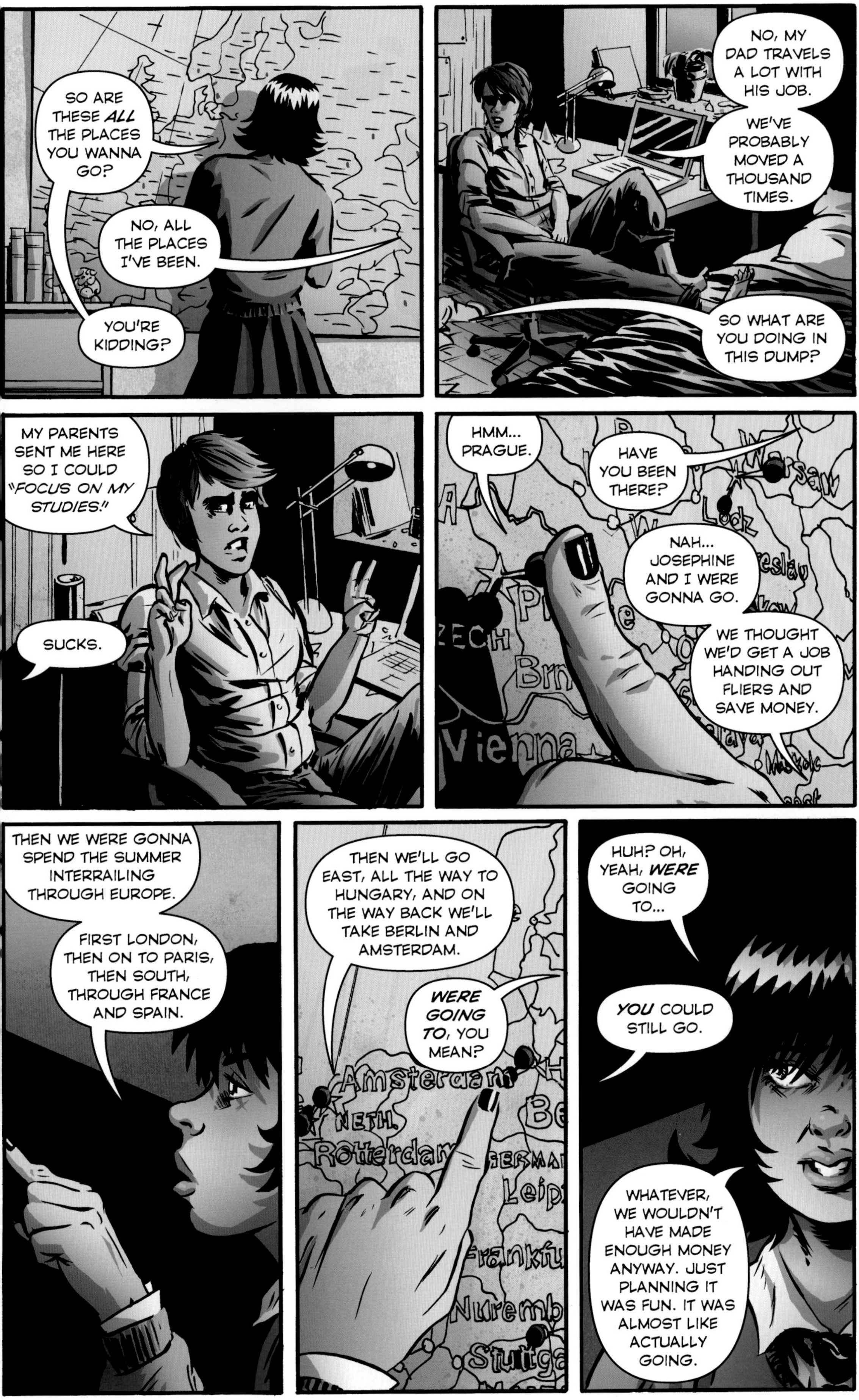
SO ARE THESE *ALL* THE PLACES YOU WANNA GO?
NO, ALL THE PLACES I'VE BEEN.
YOU'RE KIDDING?
NO, MY DAD TRAVELS A LOT WITH HIS JOB.
WE'VE PROBABLY MOVED A THOUSAND TIMES.
SO WHAT ARE YOU DOING IN THIS DUMP?
MY PARENTS SENT ME HERE SO I COULD "*FOCUS ON MY STUDIES*."
SUCKS.
HMM... PRAGUE.
HAVE YOU BEEN THERE?
NAH... JOSEPHINE AND I WERE GONNA GO.
WE THOUGHT WE'D GET A JOB HANDING OUT FLIERS AND SAVE MONEY.
Warsaw
Lodz
CZECH
Vienna
THEN WE WERE GONNA SPEND THE SUMMER INTERRAILING THROUGH EUROPE.
FIRST LONDON, THEN ON TO PARIS, THEN SOUTH, THROUGH FRANCE AND SPAIN.
THEN WE'LL GO EAST, ALL THE WAY TO HUNGARY, AND ON THE WAY BACK WE'LL TAKE BERLIN AND AMSTERDAM.
*WERE GOING TO*, YOU MEAN?
Amsterdam
NETH.
Rotterdam
HUH? OH, YEAH, ***WERE*** GOING TO...
*YOU* COULD STILL GO.
WHATEVER, WE WOULDN'T HAVE MADE ENOUGH MONEY ANYWAY. JUST PLANNING IT WAS FUN. IT WAS ALMOST LIKE ACTUALLY GOING.

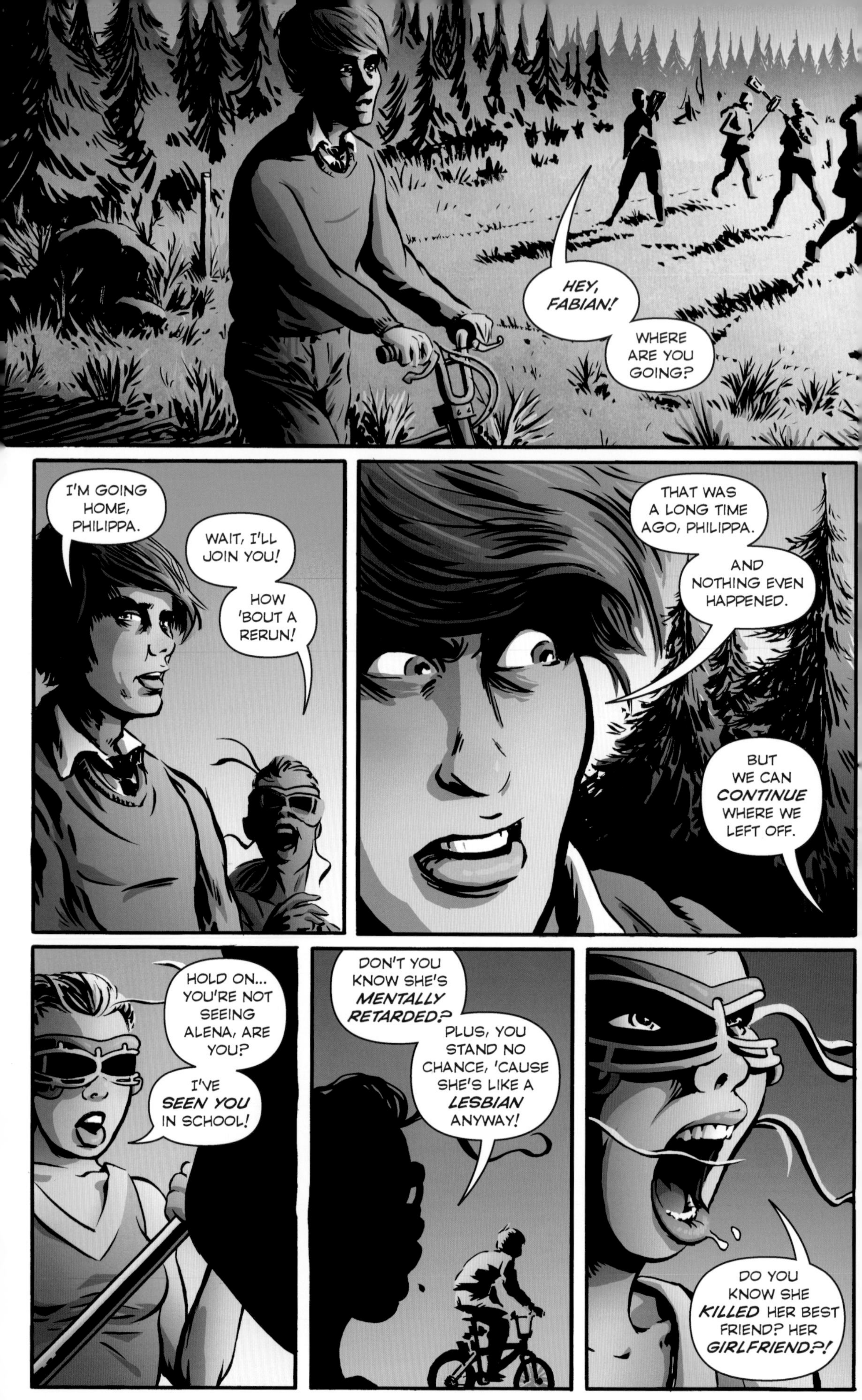
HEY, FABIAN!
WHERE ARE YOU GOING?
I'M GOING HOME, PHILIPPA.
WAIT, I'LL JOIN YOU!
HOW 'BOUT A RERUN!
THAT WAS A LONG TIME AGO, PHILIPPA.
AND NOTHING EVEN HAPPENED.
BUT WE CAN CONTINUE WHERE WE LEFT OFF.
HOLD ON... YOU'RE NOT SEEING ALENA, ARE YOU?
I'VE SEEN YOU IN SCHOOL!
DON'T YOU KNOW SHE'S MENTALLY RETARDED?
PLUS, YOU STAND NO CHANCE, 'CAUSE SHE'S LIKE A LESBIAN ANYWAY!
DO YOU KNOW SHE KILLED HER BEST FRIEND? HER GIRLFRIEND?!

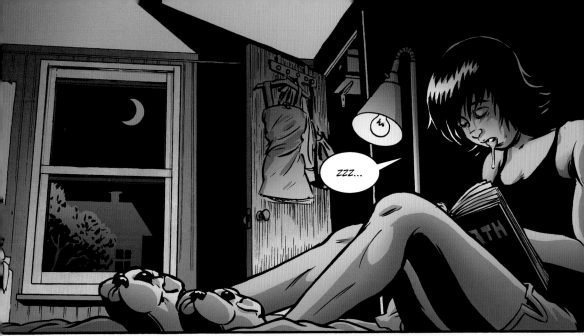

ZZZ...

YOU SHOULDN'T BE SO *EASILY* IMPRESSED!

AAH!

HE'S NOT *THAT* COOL.

JUST 'CAUSE HIS DAD'S *FILTHY RICH* AND THEY CAN AFFORD TO GO ANYWHERE.

SO, WHO SAYS I AM IMPRESSED?

*HA!* AS IF IT DOESN'T SHOW!

OH, COME ON.

YOU HAVEN'T *FORGOTTEN* OUR PLANS, HAVE YOU?

WE'RE GOING INTERRAILING TOGETHER.

WHERE'S THE MAP?

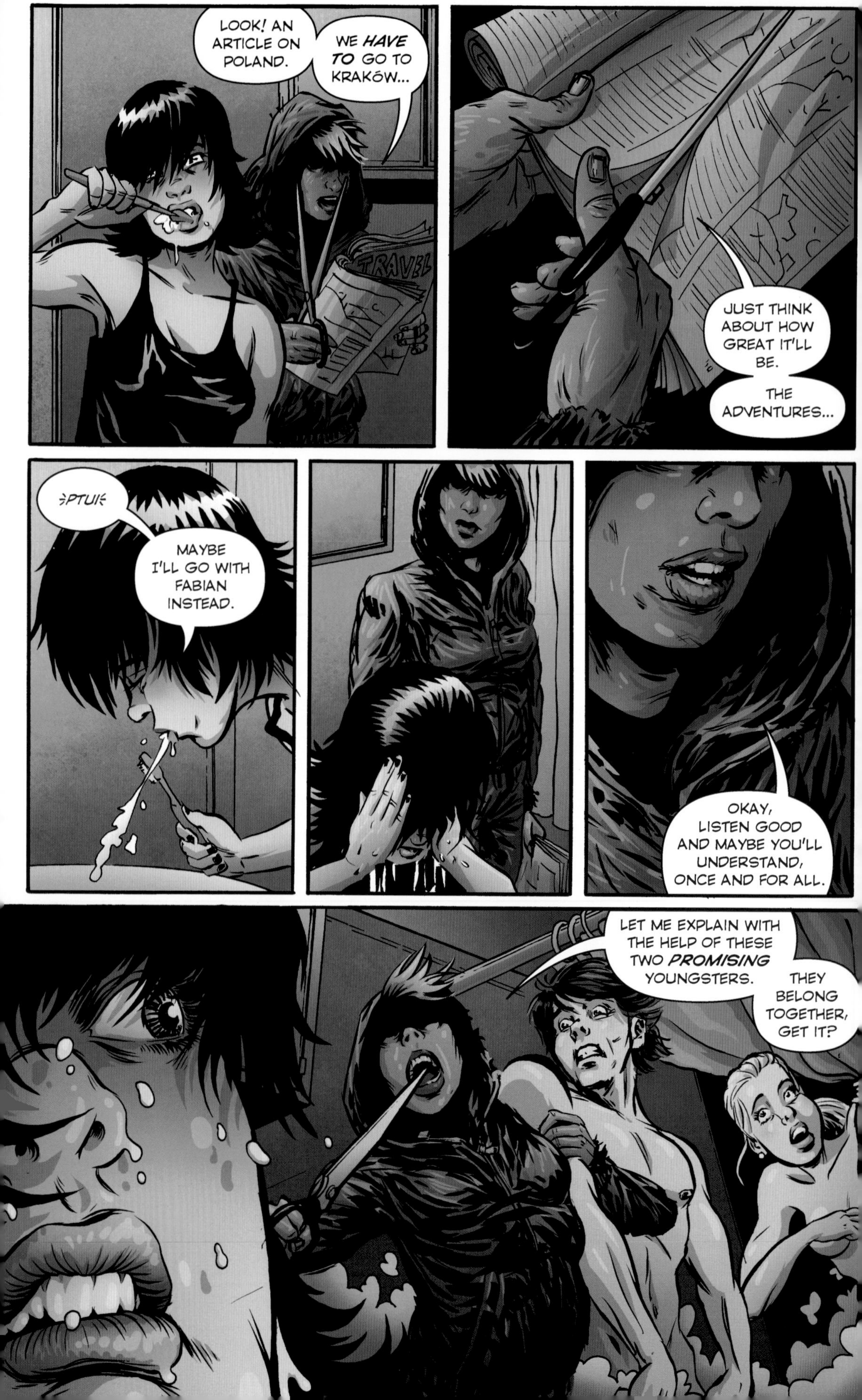
LOOK! AN ARTICLE ON POLAND.
WE HAVE TO GO TO KRAKÓW...
TRAVEL
JUST THINK ABOUT HOW GREAT IT'LL BE.
THE ADVENTURES...
PTUI
MAYBE I'LL GO WITH FABIAN INSTEAD.
OKAY, LISTEN GOOD AND MAYBE YOU'LL UNDERSTAND, ONCE AND FOR ALL.
LET ME EXPLAIN WITH THE HELP OF THESE TWO PROMISING YOUNGSTERS.
THEY BELONG TOGETHER, GET IT?

SEE? THEY'RE FROM THE SAME WORLD.

IT'S FABIAN'S WORLD, *NOT YOURS*. YOU KNOW WHAT I MEAN. YOU DON'T EVEN HAVE THE GUTS TO INVITE HIM OVER.

YOU'RE *EMBARRASSED* ABOUT WHERE YOU LIVE, WHO YOU ARE. BUT *SCREW* THEM!

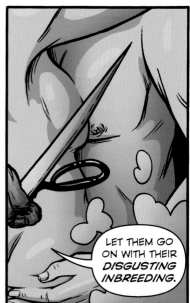

LET THEM GO ON WITH THEIR *DISGUSTING INBREEDING.*

SHLICKT

FHSSS

SPLURRT

EEEK!

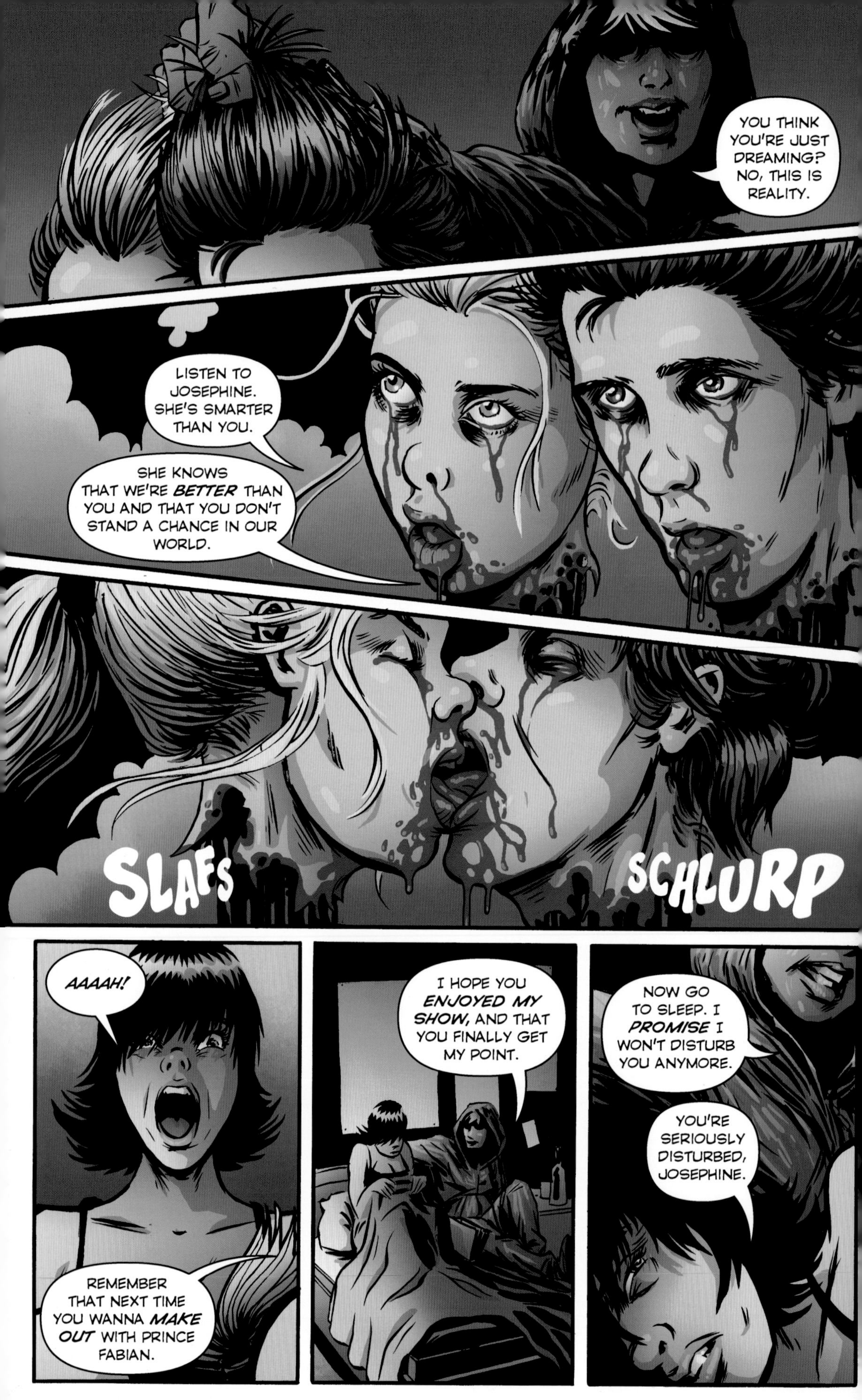
YOU THINK YOU'RE JUST DREAMING? NO, THIS IS REALITY.
LISTEN TO JOSEPHINE. SHE'S SMARTER THAN YOU.
SHE KNOWS THAT WE'RE *BETTER* THAN YOU AND THAT YOU DON'T STAND A CHANCE IN OUR WORLD.
SLAFS
SCHLURP
*AAAAH!*
REMEMBER THAT NEXT TIME YOU WANNA *MAKE OUT* WITH PRINCE FABIAN.
I HOPE YOU *ENJOYED MY SHOW,* AND THAT YOU FINALLY GET MY POINT.
NOW GO TO SLEEP. I *PROMISE* I WON'T DISTURB YOU ANYMORE.
YOU'RE SERIOUSLY DISTURBED, JOSEPHINE.

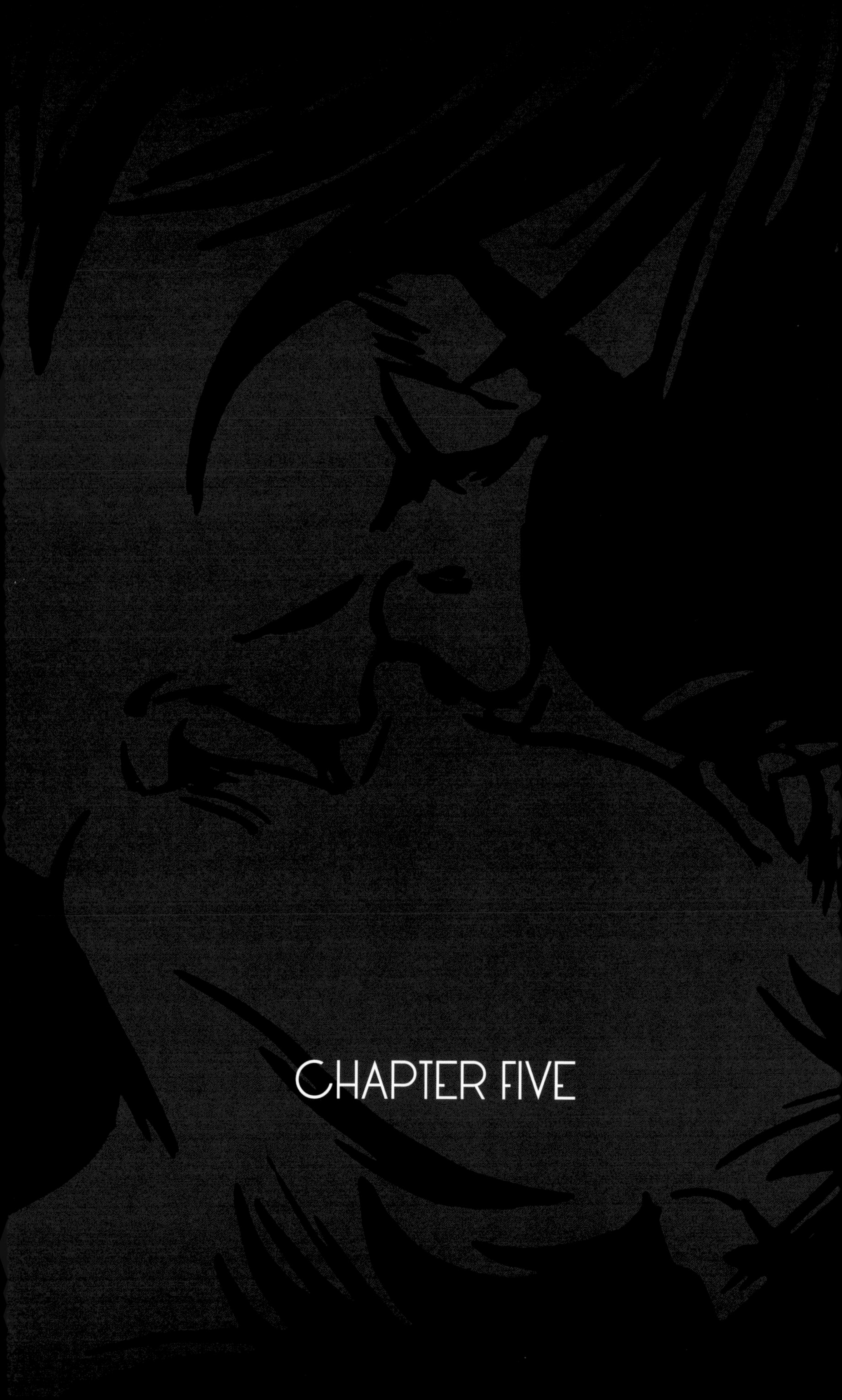

# CHAPTER FIVE

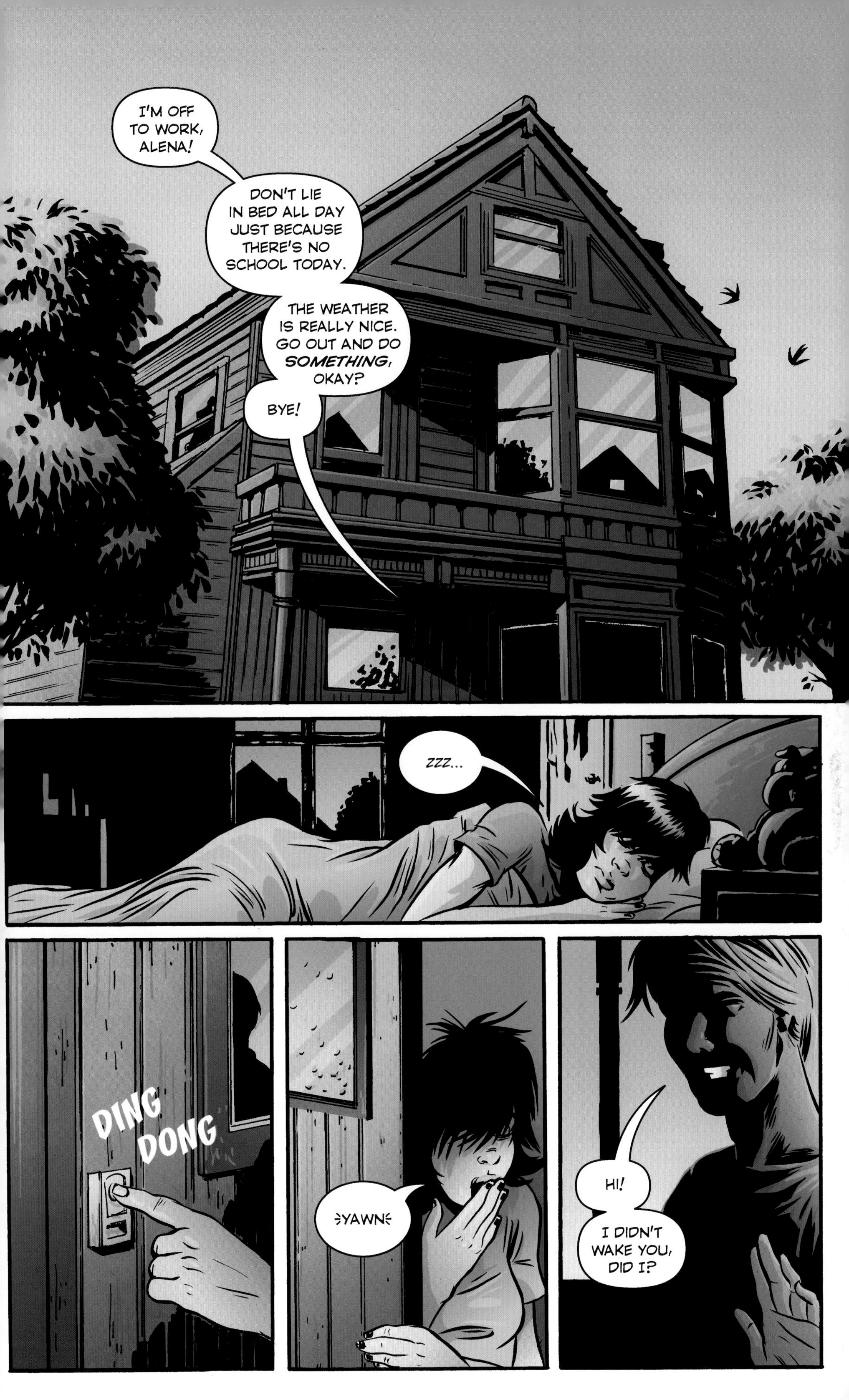
I'M OFF TO WORK, ALENA!
DON'T LIE IN BED ALL DAY JUST BECAUSE THERE'S NO SCHOOL TODAY.
THE WEATHER IS REALLY NICE. GO OUT AND DO *SOMETHING*, OKAY?
BYE!
ZZZ...
DING DONG
YAWN
HI!
I DIDN'T WAKE YOU, DID I?

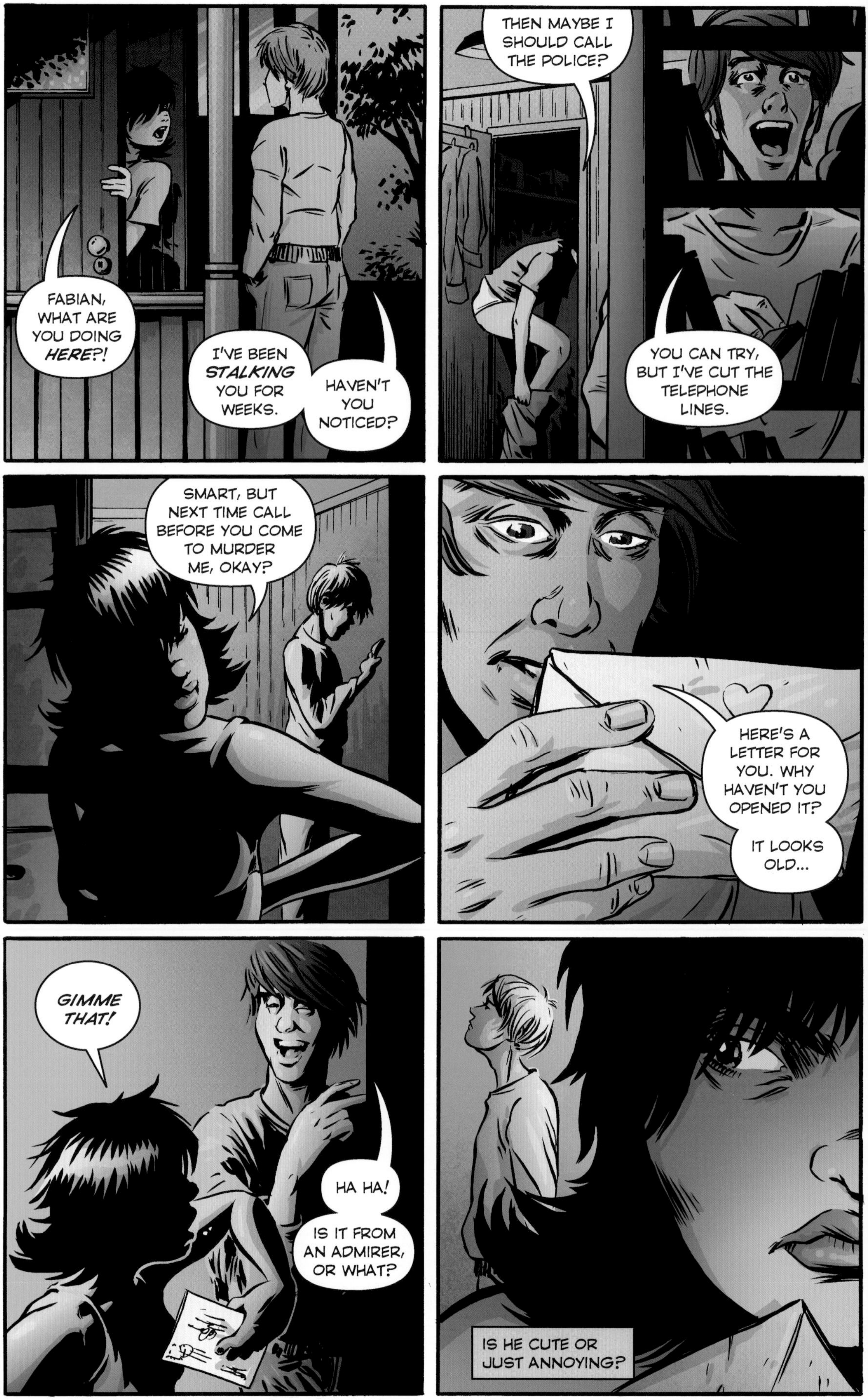
FABIAN, WHAT ARE YOU DOING *HERE*?!
I'VE BEEN *STALKING* YOU FOR WEEKS.
HAVEN'T YOU NOTICED?
THEN MAYBE I SHOULD CALL THE POLICE?
YOU CAN TRY, BUT I'VE CUT THE TELEPHONE LINES.
SMART, BUT NEXT TIME CALL BEFORE YOU COME TO MURDER ME, OKAY?
HERE'S A LETTER FOR YOU. WHY HAVEN'T YOU OPENED IT?
IT LOOKS OLD...
*GIMME THAT!*
HA HA!
IS IT FROM AN ADMIRER, OR WHAT?
IS HE CUTE OR JUST ANNOYING?

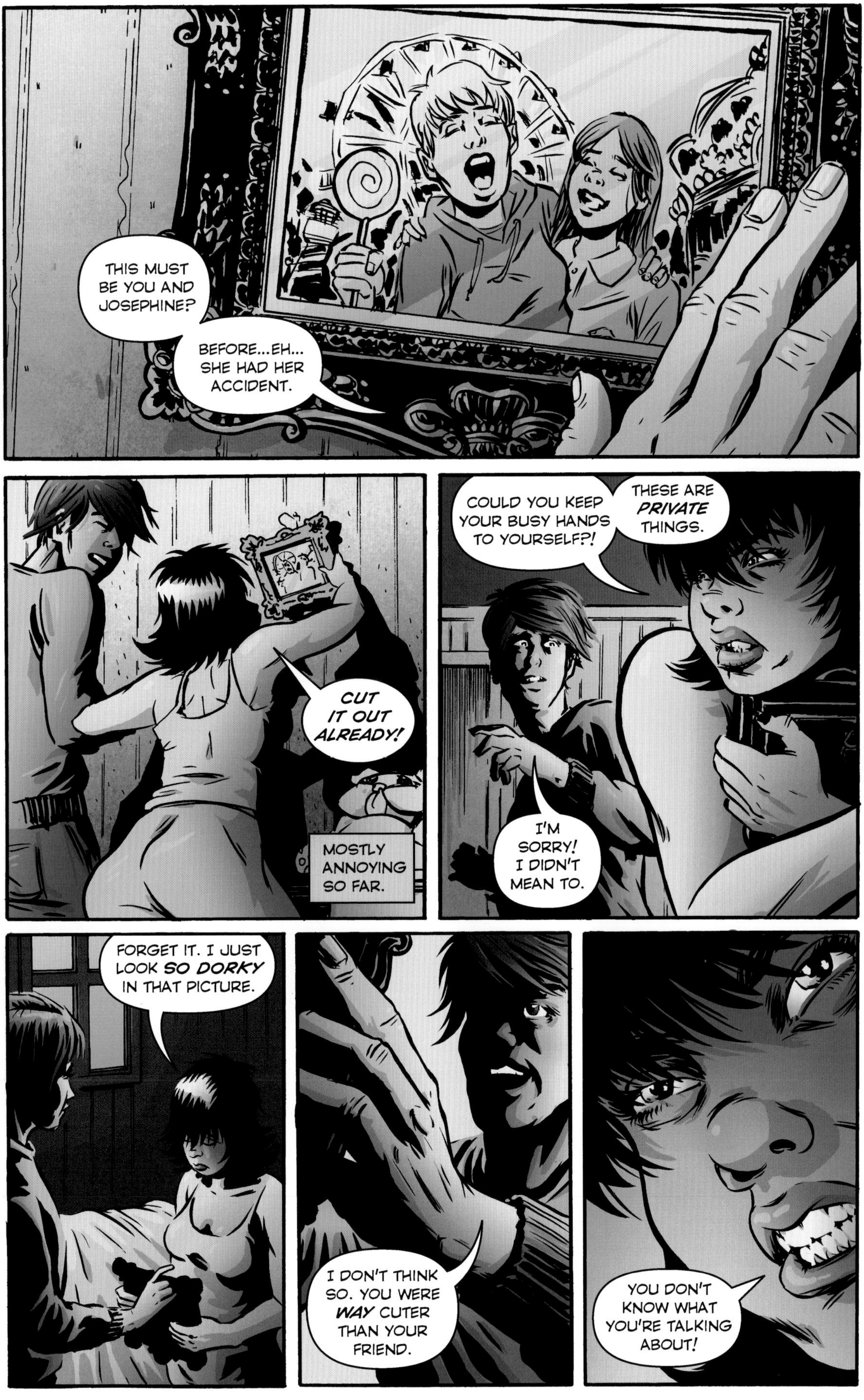
THIS MUST BE YOU AND JOSEPHINE?
BEFORE...EH... SHE HAD HER ACCIDENT.
CUT IT OUT ALREADY!
MOSTLY ANNOYING SO FAR.
COULD YOU KEEP YOUR BUSY HANDS TO YOURSELF?!
THESE ARE PRIVATE THINGS.
I'M SORRY! I DIDN'T MEAN TO.
FORGET IT. I JUST LOOK SO DORKY IN THAT PICTURE.
I DON'T THINK SO. YOU WERE WAY CUTER THAN YOUR FRIEND.
YOU DON'T KNOW WHAT YOU'RE TALKING ABOUT!

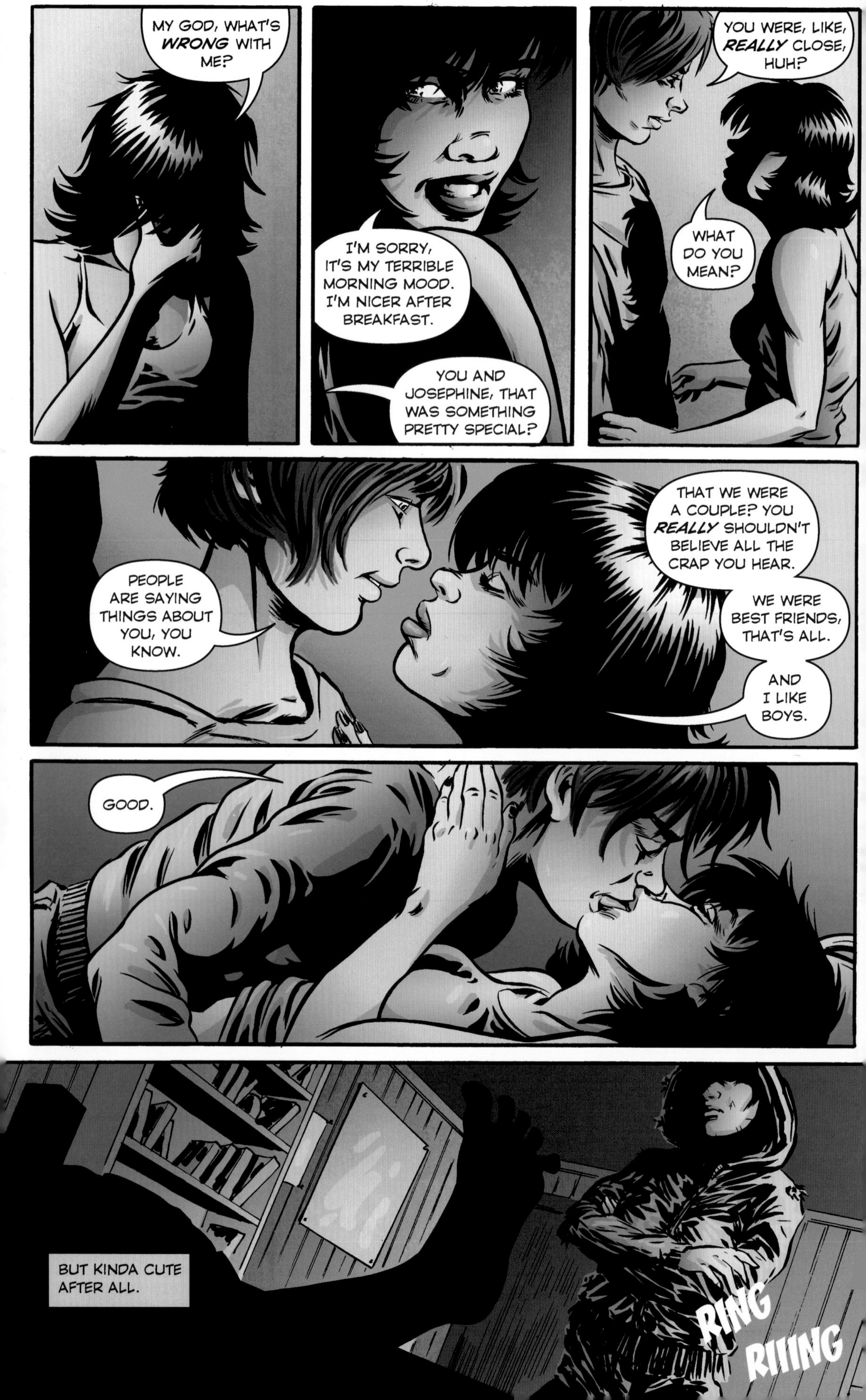
MY GOD, WHAT'S *WRONG* WITH ME?
I'M SORRY, IT'S MY TERRIBLE MORNING MOOD. I'M NICER AFTER BREAKFAST.
YOU AND JOSEPHINE, THAT WAS SOMETHING PRETTY SPECIAL?
YOU WERE, LIKE, *REALLY* CLOSE, HUH?
WHAT DO YOU MEAN?
PEOPLE ARE SAYING THINGS ABOUT YOU, YOU KNOW.
THAT WE WERE A COUPLE? YOU *REALLY* SHOULDN'T BELIEVE ALL THE CRAP YOU HEAR.
WE WERE BEST FRIENDS, THAT'S ALL.
AND I LIKE BOYS.
GOOD.
BUT KINDA CUTE AFTER ALL.
RING
RIIING

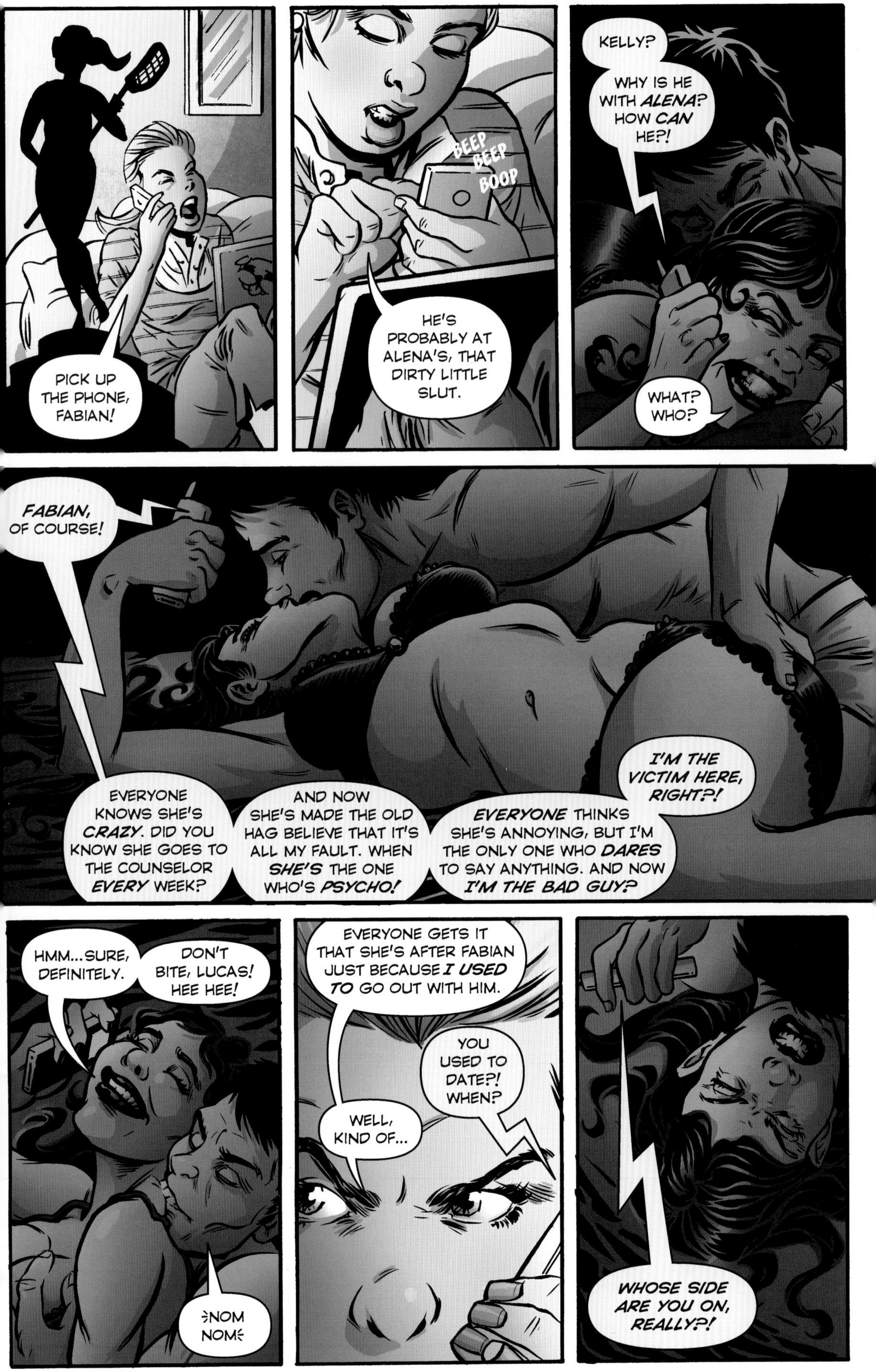
PICK UP THE PHONE, FABIAN!
BEEP BEEP BOOP
HE'S PROBABLY AT ALENA'S, THAT DIRTY LITTLE SLUT.
KELLY?
WHY IS HE WITH ALENA? HOW CAN HE?!
WHAT? WHO?
FABIAN, OF COURSE!
EVERYONE KNOWS SHE'S CRAZY. DID YOU KNOW SHE GOES TO THE COUNSELOR EVERY WEEK?
AND NOW SHE'S MADE THE OLD HAG BELIEVE THAT IT'S ALL MY FAULT. WHEN SHE'S THE ONE WHO'S PSYCHO!
EVERYONE THINKS SHE'S ANNOYING, BUT I'M THE ONLY ONE WHO DARES TO SAY ANYTHING. AND NOW I'M THE BAD GUY?
I'M THE VICTIM HERE, RIGHT?!
HMM...SURE, DEFINITELY.
DON'T BITE, LUCAS! HEE HEE!
NOM NOM
EVERYONE GETS IT THAT SHE'S AFTER FABIAN JUST BECAUSE I USED TO GO OUT WITH HIM.
YOU USED TO DATE?! WHEN?
WELL, KIND OF...
WHOSE SIDE ARE YOU ON, REALLY?!

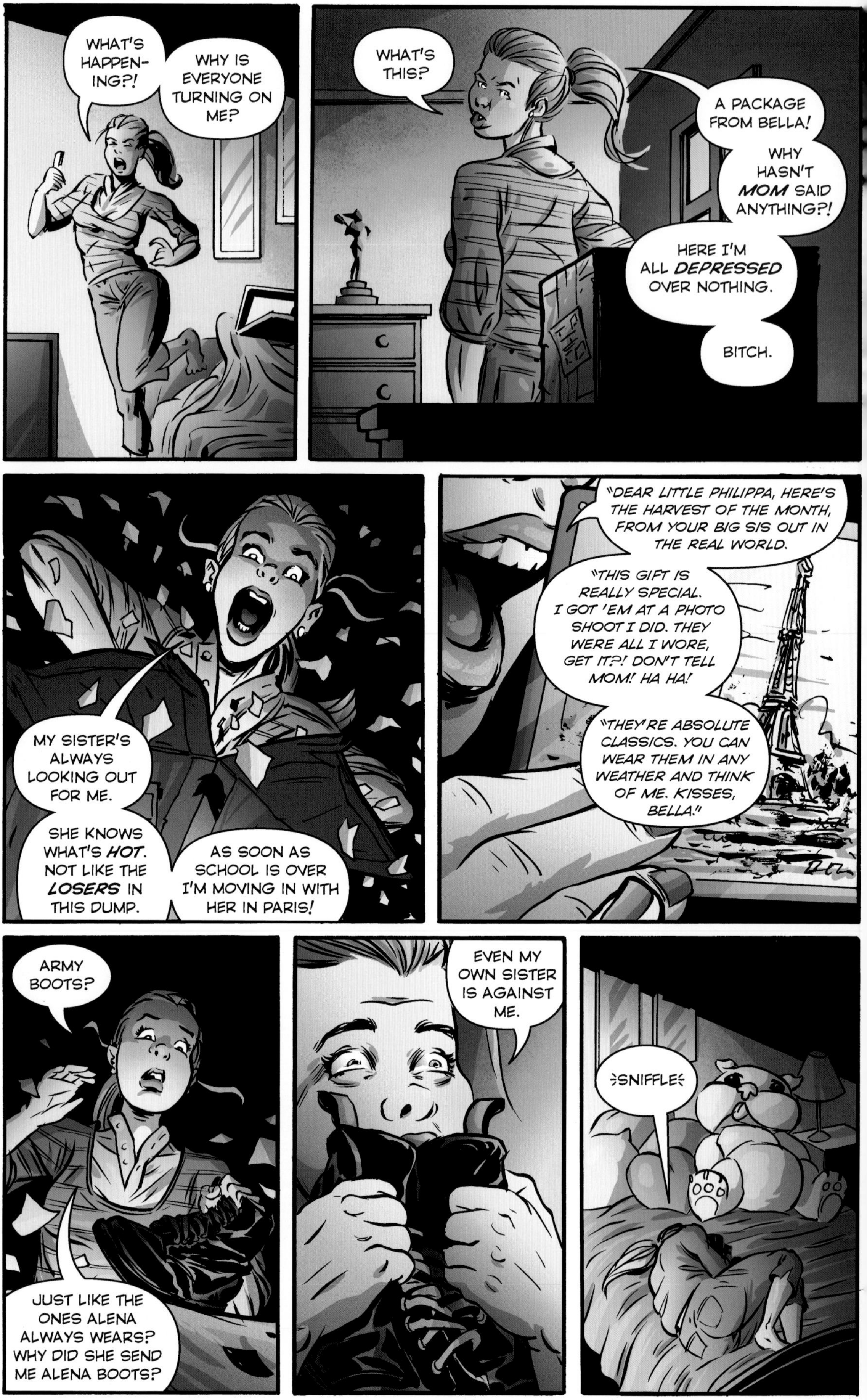
WHAT'S HAPPEN-ING?!
WHY IS EVERYONE TURNING ON ME?
WHAT'S THIS?
A PACKAGE FROM BELLA!
WHY HASN'T MOM SAID ANYTHING?!
HERE I'M ALL DEPRESSED OVER NOTHING.
BITCH.
MY SISTER'S ALWAYS LOOKING OUT FOR ME.
SHE KNOWS WHAT'S HOT. NOT LIKE THE LOSERS IN THIS DUMP.
AS SOON AS SCHOOL IS OVER I'M MOVING IN WITH HER IN PARIS!
"DEAR LITTLE PHILIPPA, HERE'S THE HARVEST OF THE MONTH, FROM YOUR BIG SIS OUT IN THE REAL WORLD.
"THIS GIFT IS REALLY SPECIAL. I GOT 'EM AT A PHOTO SHOOT I DID. THEY WERE ALL I WORE, GET IT?! DON'T TELL MOM! HA HA!
"THEY'RE ABSOLUTE CLASSICS. YOU CAN WEAR THEM IN ANY WEATHER AND THINK OF ME. KISSES, BELLA."
ARMY BOOTS?
JUST LIKE THE ONES ALENA ALWAYS WEARS? WHY DID SHE SEND ME ALENA BOOTS?
EVEN MY OWN SISTER IS AGAINST ME.
SNIFFLE

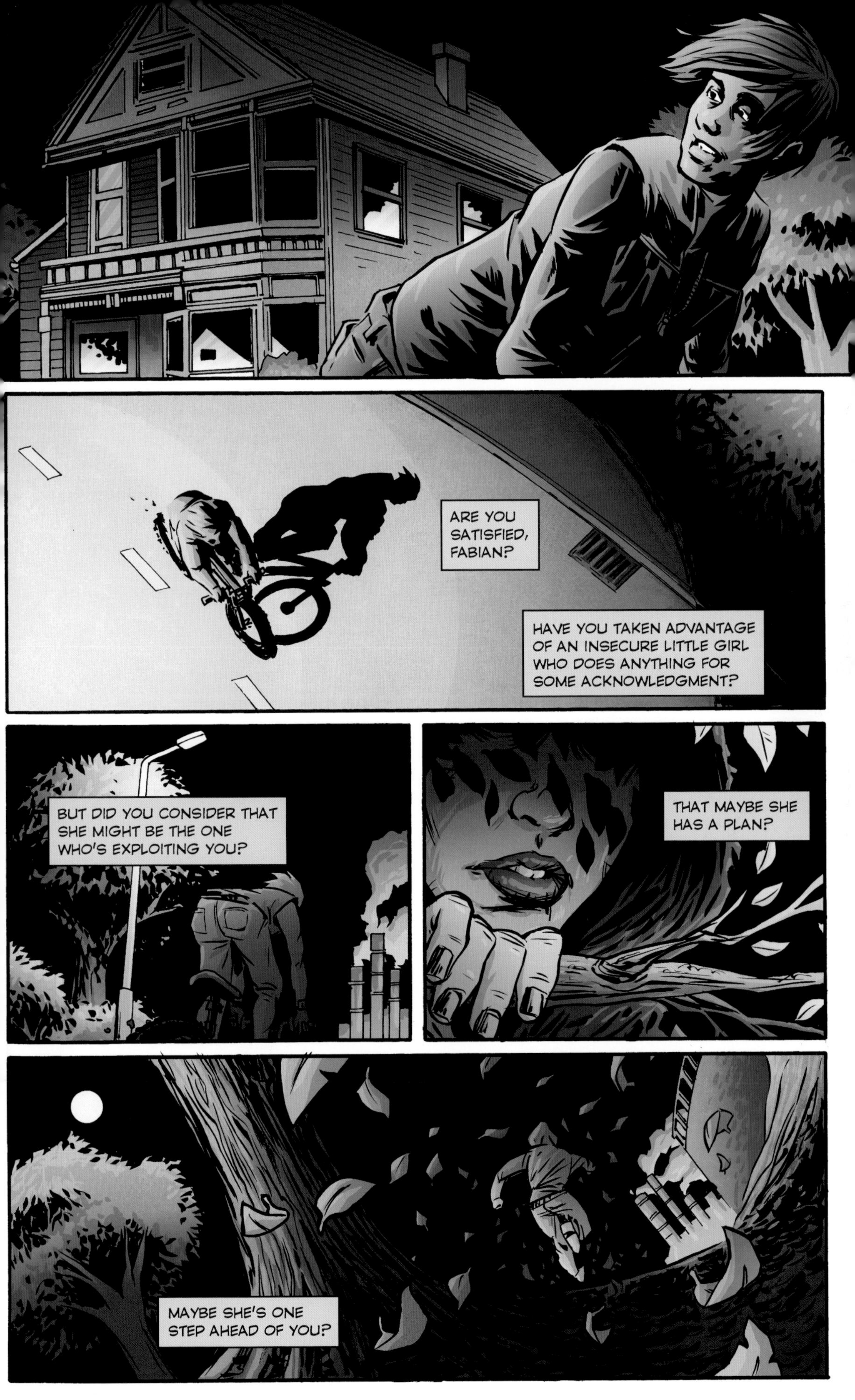
ARE YOU SATISFIED, FABIAN?
HAVE YOU TAKEN ADVANTAGE OF AN INSECURE LITTLE GIRL WHO DOES ANYTHING FOR SOME ACKNOWLEDGMENT?
BUT DID YOU CONSIDER THAT SHE MIGHT BE THE ONE WHO'S EXPLOITING YOU?
THAT MAYBE SHE HAS A PLAN?
MAYBE SHE'S ONE STEP AHEAD OF YOU?

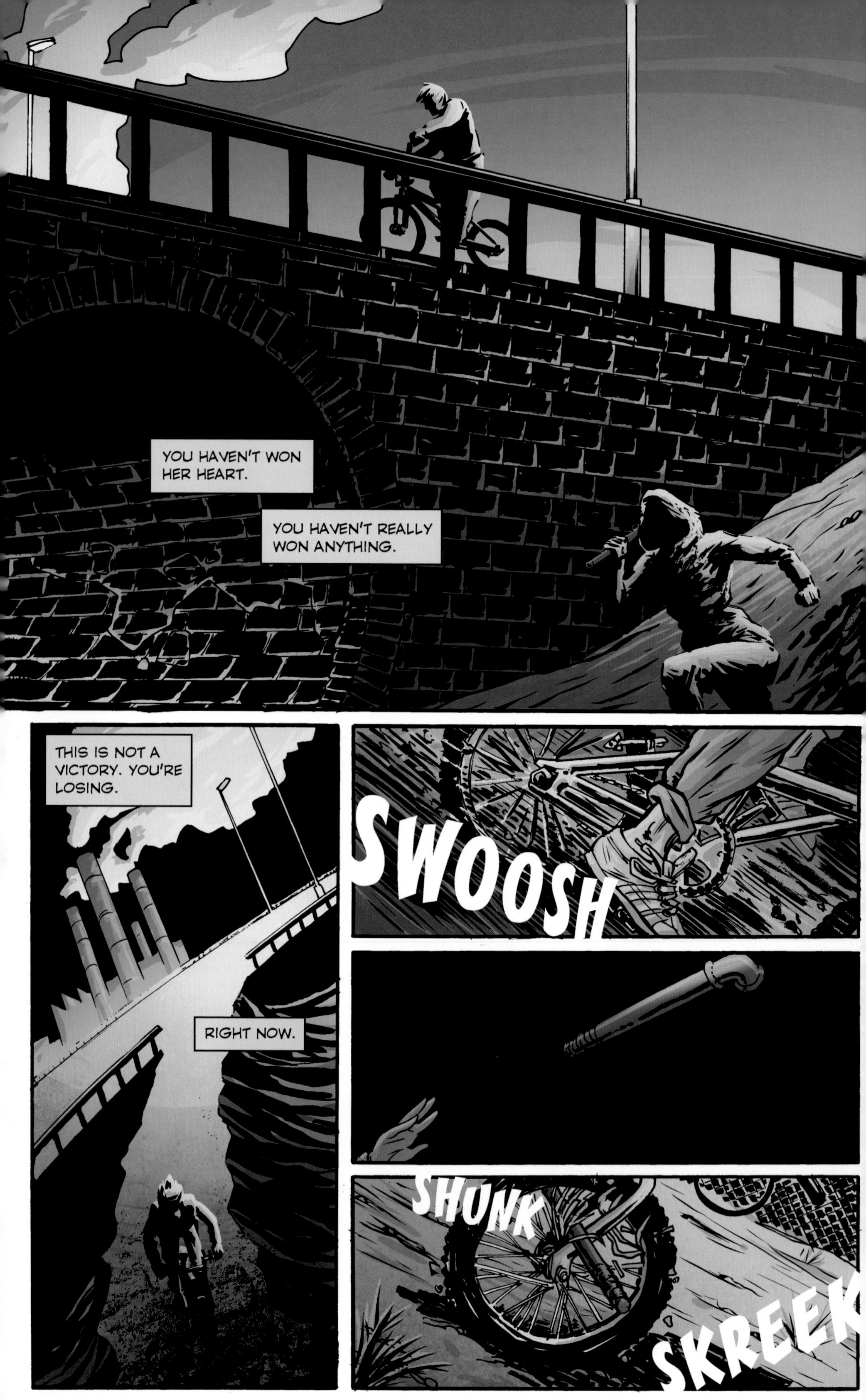
YOU HAVEN'T WON HER HEART.
YOU HAVEN'T REALLY WON ANYTHING.
THIS IS NOT A VICTORY. YOU'RE LOSING.
RIGHT NOW.
SWOOSH
SHUNK
SKREEK

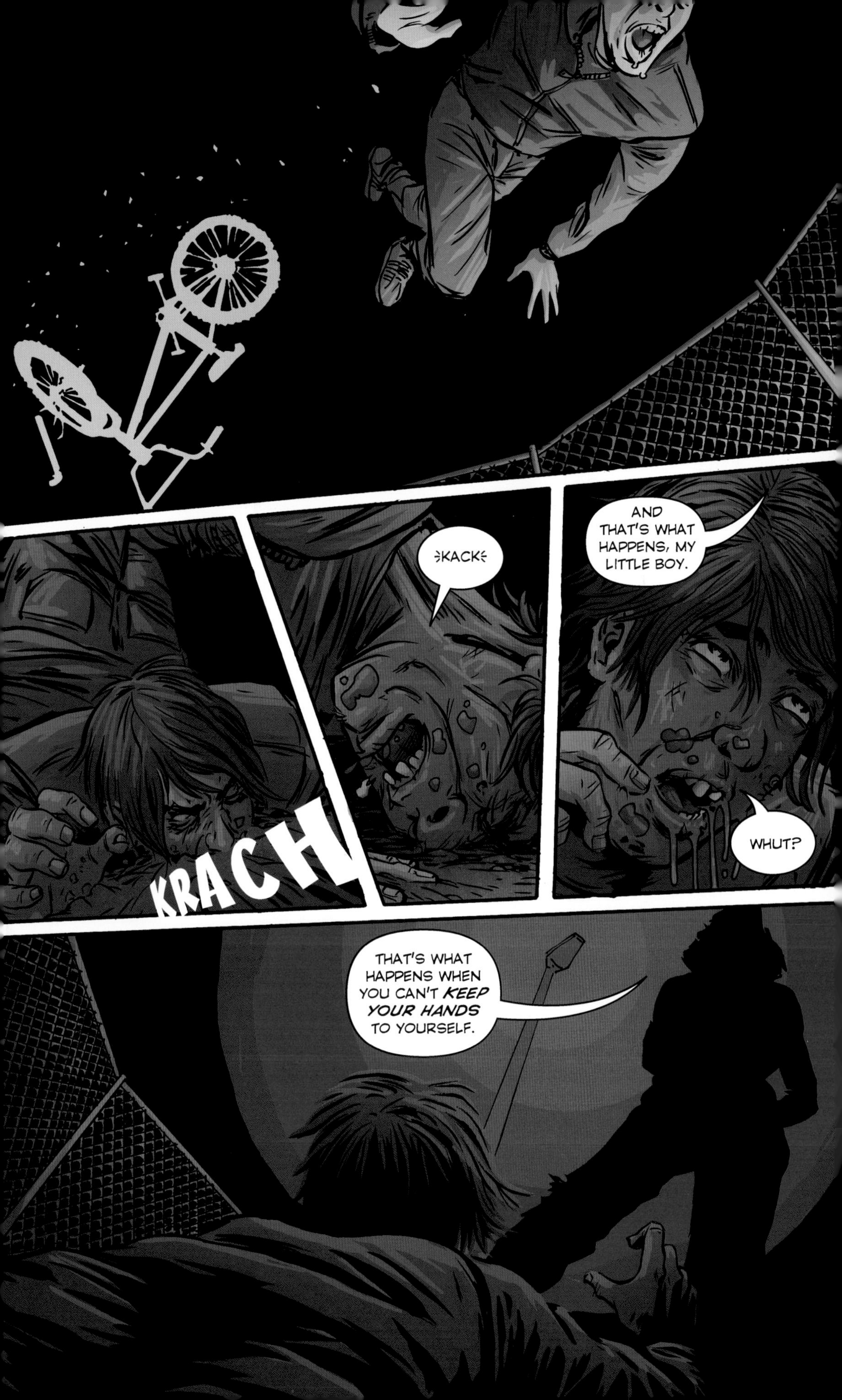
KRACH
KACK
AND THAT'S WHAT HAPPENS, MY LITTLE BOY.
WHUT?
THAT'S WHAT HAPPENS WHEN YOU CAN'T *KEEP YOUR HANDS* TO YOURSELF.

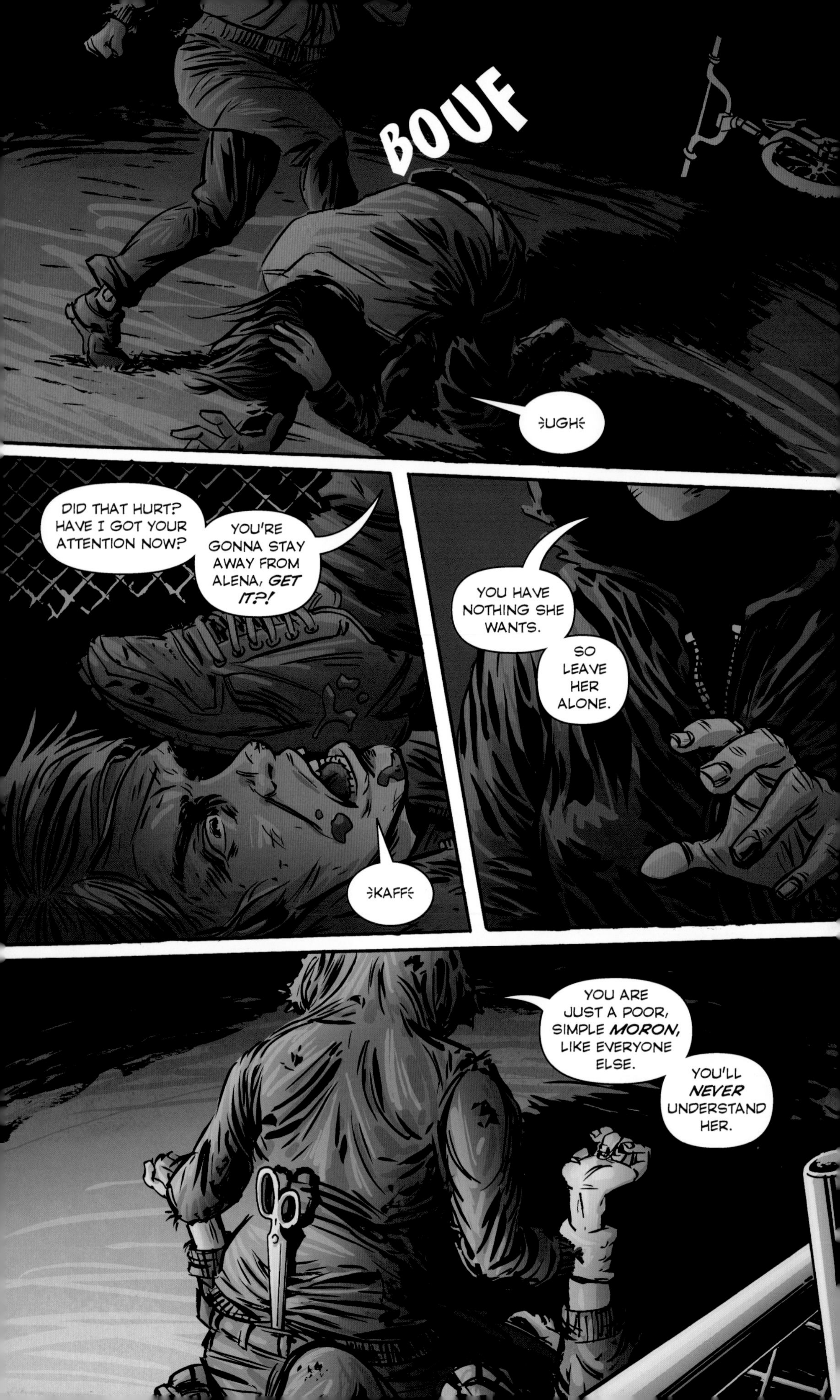
BOUF
UGH
DID THAT HURT? HAVE I GOT YOUR ATTENTION NOW?
YOU'RE GONNA STAY AWAY FROM ALENA, *GET IT?!*
KAFF
YOU HAVE NOTHING SHE WANTS.
SO LEAVE HER ALONE.
YOU ARE JUST A POOR, SIMPLE *MORON,* LIKE EVERYONE ELSE.
YOU'LL *NEVER* UNDERSTAND HER.

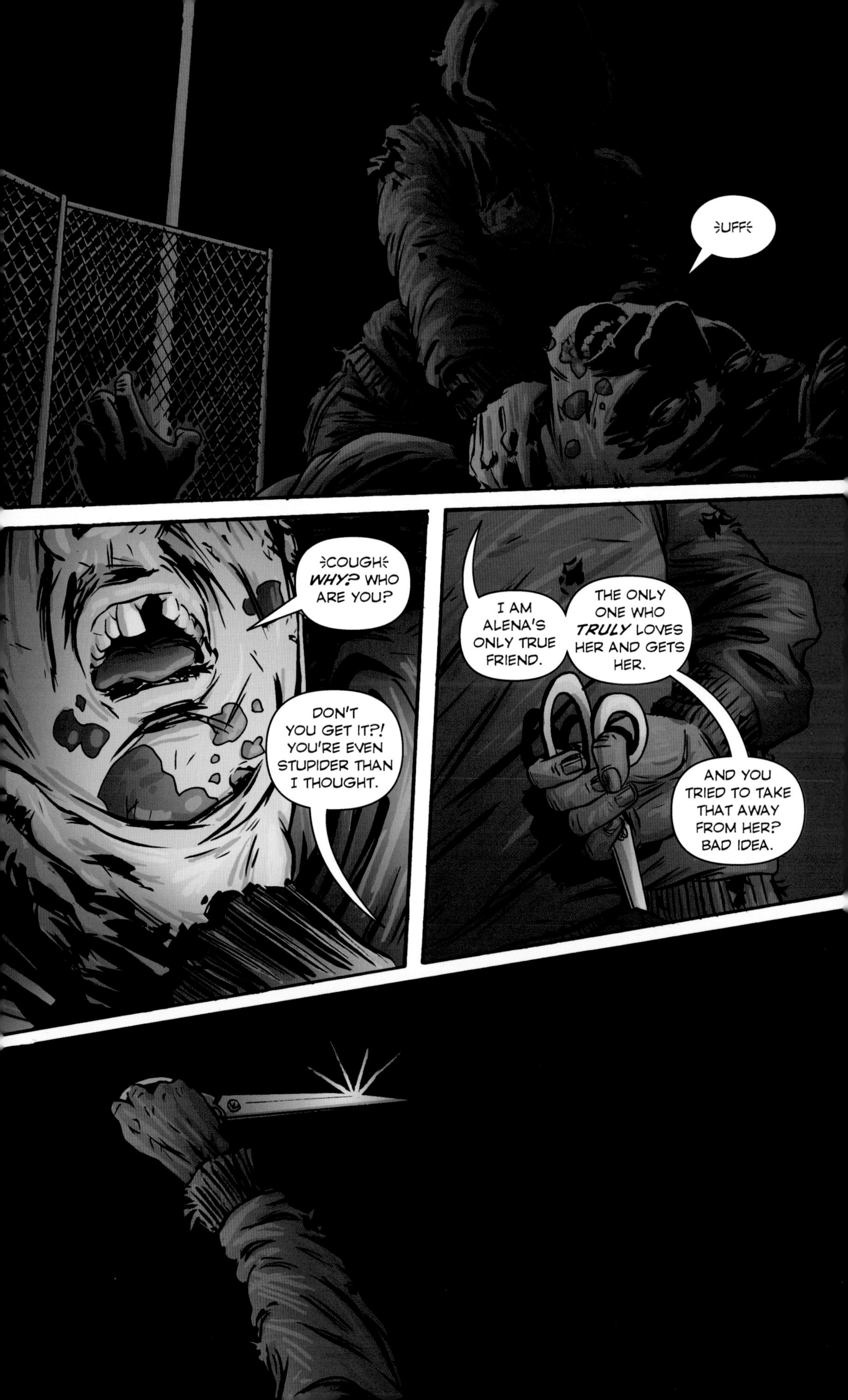

UFF
COUGH
WHY? WHO ARE YOU?
DON'T YOU GET IT?! YOU'RE EVEN STUPIDER THAN I THOUGHT.
I AM ALENA'S ONLY TRUE FRIEND.
THE ONLY ONE WHO TRULY LOVES HER AND GETS HER.
AND YOU TRIED TO TAKE THAT AWAY FROM HER? BAD IDEA.

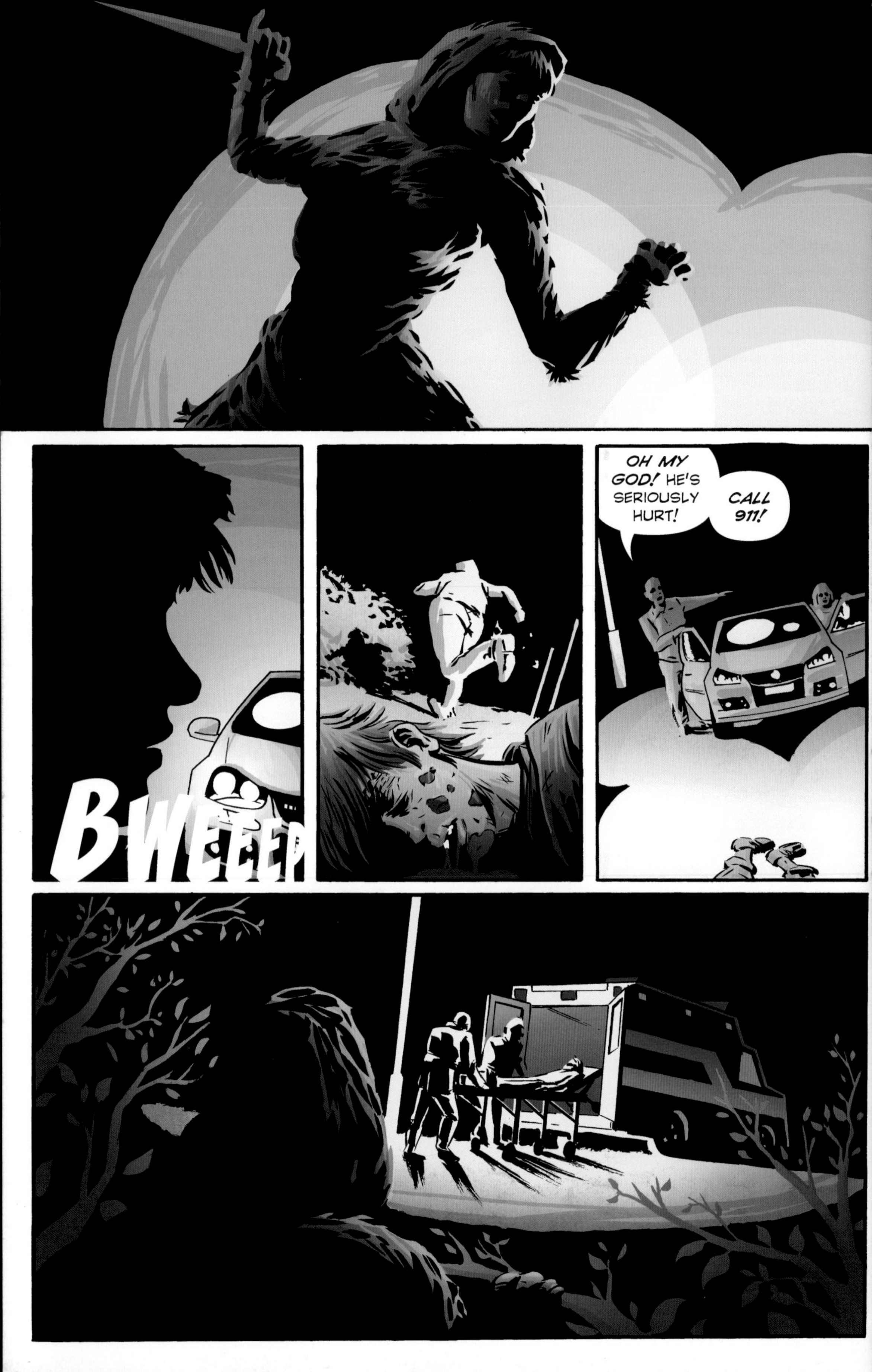
BWEEEP
OH MY GOD! HE'S SERIOUSLY HURT!
CALL 911!

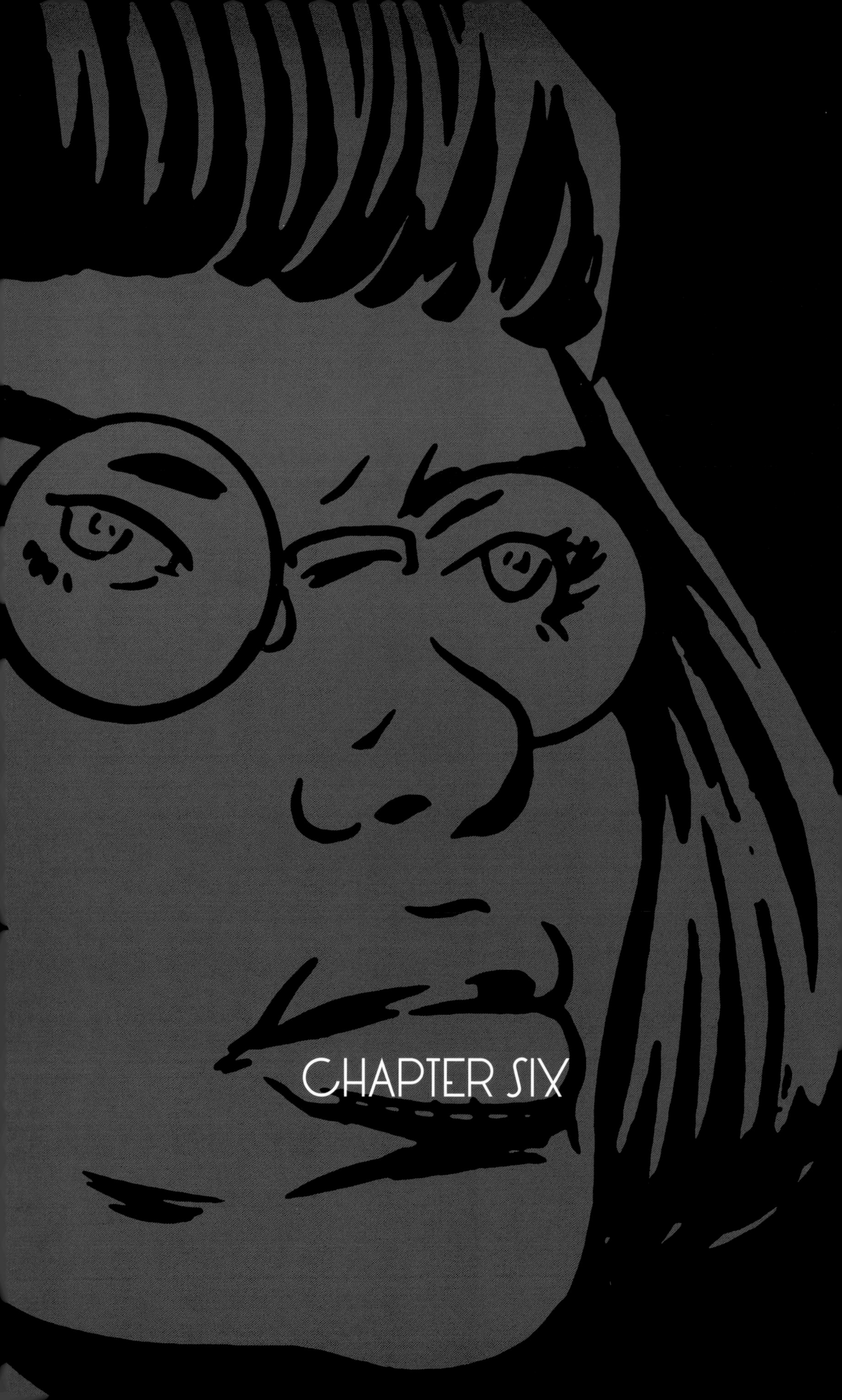

# CHAPTER SIX

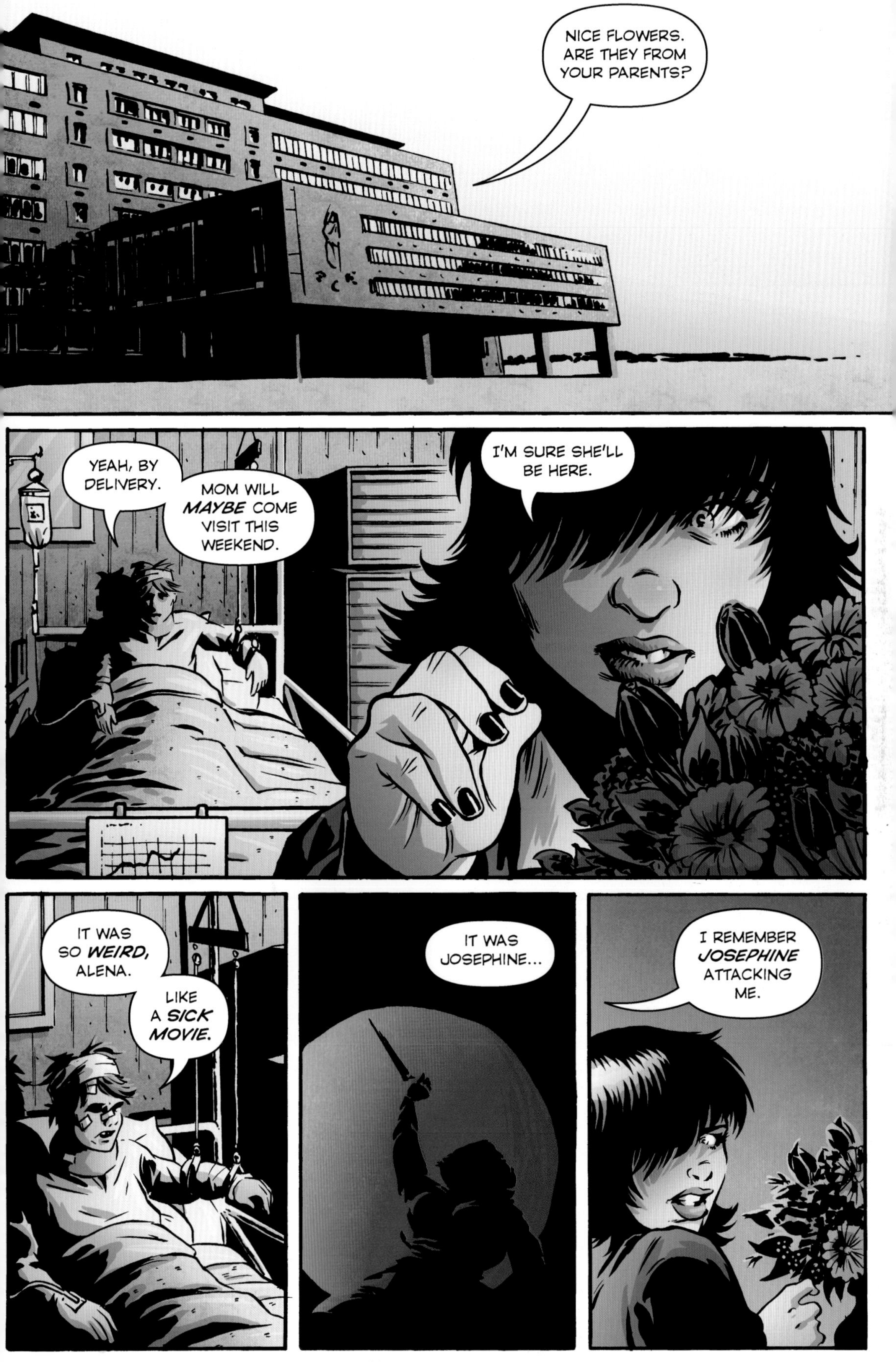
NICE FLOWERS. ARE THEY FROM YOUR PARENTS?
YEAH, BY DELIVERY.
MOM WILL *MAYBE* COME VISIT THIS WEEKEND.
I'M SURE SHE'LL BE HERE.
IT WAS SO *WEIRD,* ALENA.
LIKE A *SICK MOVIE.*
IT WAS JOSEPHINE...
I REMEMBER *JOSEPHINE* ATTACKING ME.

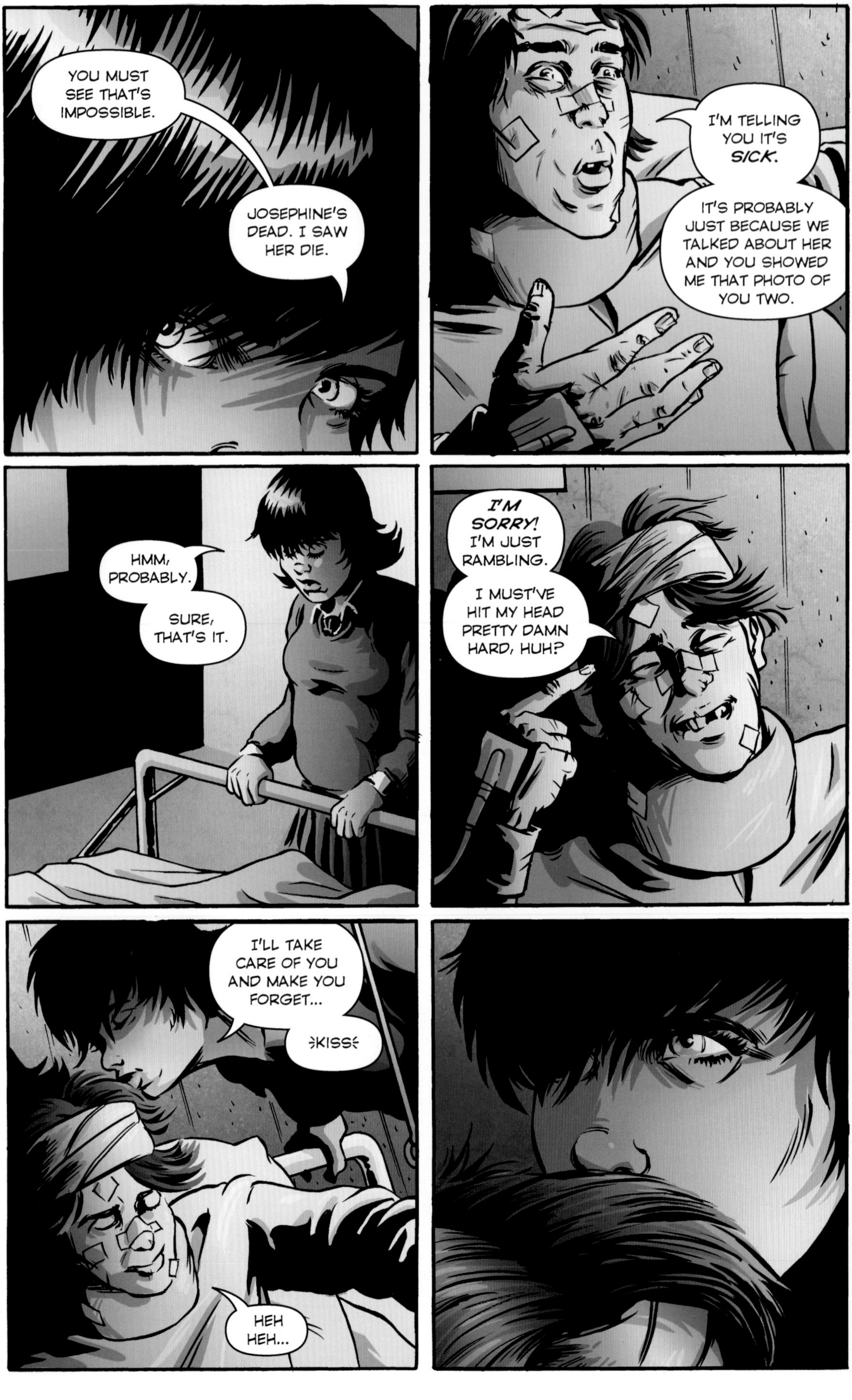
YOU MUST SEE THAT'S IMPOSSIBLE.
JOSEPHINE'S DEAD. I SAW HER DIE.
I'M TELLING YOU IT'S *SICK*.
IT'S PROBABLY JUST BECAUSE WE TALKED ABOUT HER AND YOU SHOWED ME THAT PHOTO OF YOU TWO.
HMM, PROBABLY.
SURE, THAT'S IT.
*I'M SORRY!* I'M JUST RAMBLING.
I MUST'VE HIT MY HEAD PRETTY DAMN HARD, HUH?
I'LL TAKE CARE OF YOU AND MAKE YOU FORGET...
KISS
HEH HEH...

JOSEPHINE'S LETTER... DO I EVEN WANNA KNOW WHAT IT SAYS ANYMORE?

IT'S TOO LATE, ANYWAY.

I'M DEFINITELY GOING INSANE.

I'M SEEING GHOSTS. I'M TALKING TO A GHOST. AND GHOSTS DON'T EXIST.

BUT WHO ATTACKED FABIAN?

IT'S ALMOST A YEAR SINCE JOSEPHINE DIED. I WANNA MOVE ON.

BUT I CAN'T.

≶SIGH≷

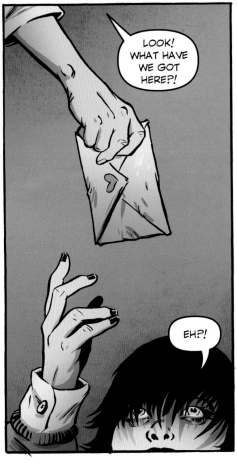

LOOK! WHAT HAVE WE GOT HERE?!

EH?!

IS IT A *LOVE LETTER* FROM YOUR PITIFUL BOY-FRIEND AT THE HOSPITAL?

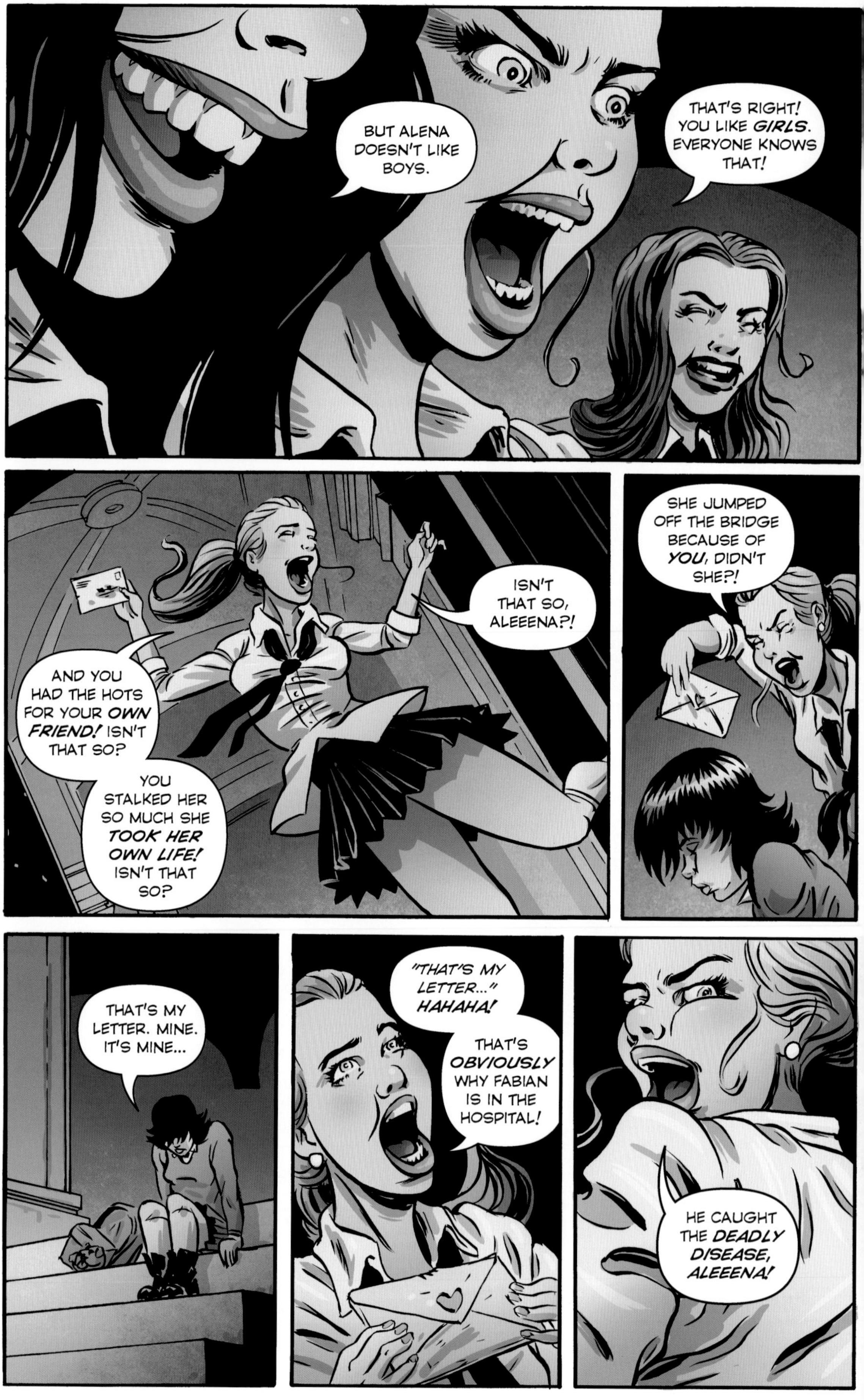

BUT ALENA DOESN'T LIKE BOYS.
THAT'S RIGHT! YOU LIKE GIRLS. EVERYONE KNOWS THAT!
ISN'T THAT SO, ALEEENA?!
AND YOU HAD THE HOTS FOR YOUR OWN FRIEND! ISN'T THAT SO?
YOU STALKED HER SO MUCH SHE TOOK HER OWN LIFE! ISN'T THAT SO?
SHE JUMPED OFF THE BRIDGE BECAUSE OF YOU, DIDN'T SHE?!
THAT'S MY LETTER. MINE. IT'S MINE...
"THAT'S MY LETTER..." HAHAHA!
THAT'S OBVIOUSLY WHY FABIAN IS IN THE HOSPITAL!
HE CAUGHT THE DEADLY DISEASE, ALEEENA!

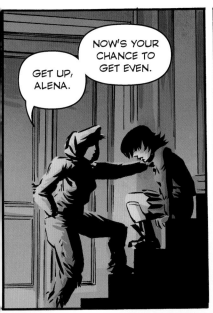

GET UP, ALENA.

NOW'S YOUR CHANCE TO GET EVEN.

WATCH OUT! SHE'S GONNA GET YOU!

SHE HAS HERPES! AND AIDS AND CHLAMYDIA!

TURN AROUND. AIM. HIT.

COME ON! CRUSH HER!

§UHFF§

DUFF

§HGHN§

LOOK, ALENA'S TRYING TO FIGHT. HOW CUTE!

I DIDN'T THINK YOU HAD THE BALLS. I THOUGHT YOU LIKED PUSSY!

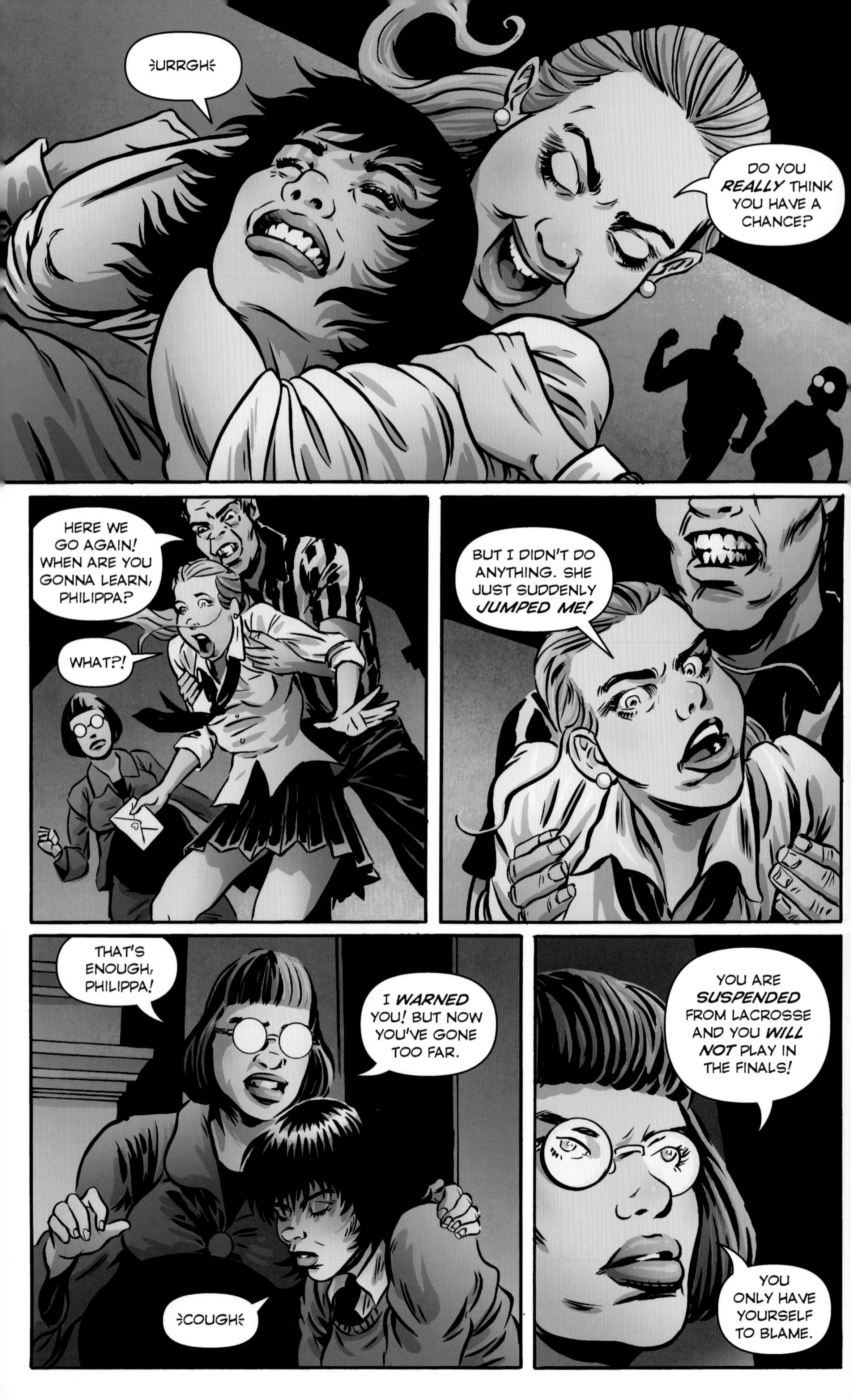

URRGH
DO YOU REALLY THINK YOU HAVE A CHANCE?
HERE WE GO AGAIN! WHEN ARE YOU GONNA LEARN, PHILIPPA?
WHAT?!
BUT I DIDN'T DO ANYTHING. SHE JUST SUDDENLY JUMPED ME!
THAT'S ENOUGH, PHILIPPA!
I WARNED YOU! BUT NOW YOU'VE GONE TOO FAR.
COUGH
YOU ARE SUSPENDED FROM LACROSSE AND YOU WILL NOT PLAY IN THE FINALS!
YOU ONLY HAVE YOURSELF TO BLAME.

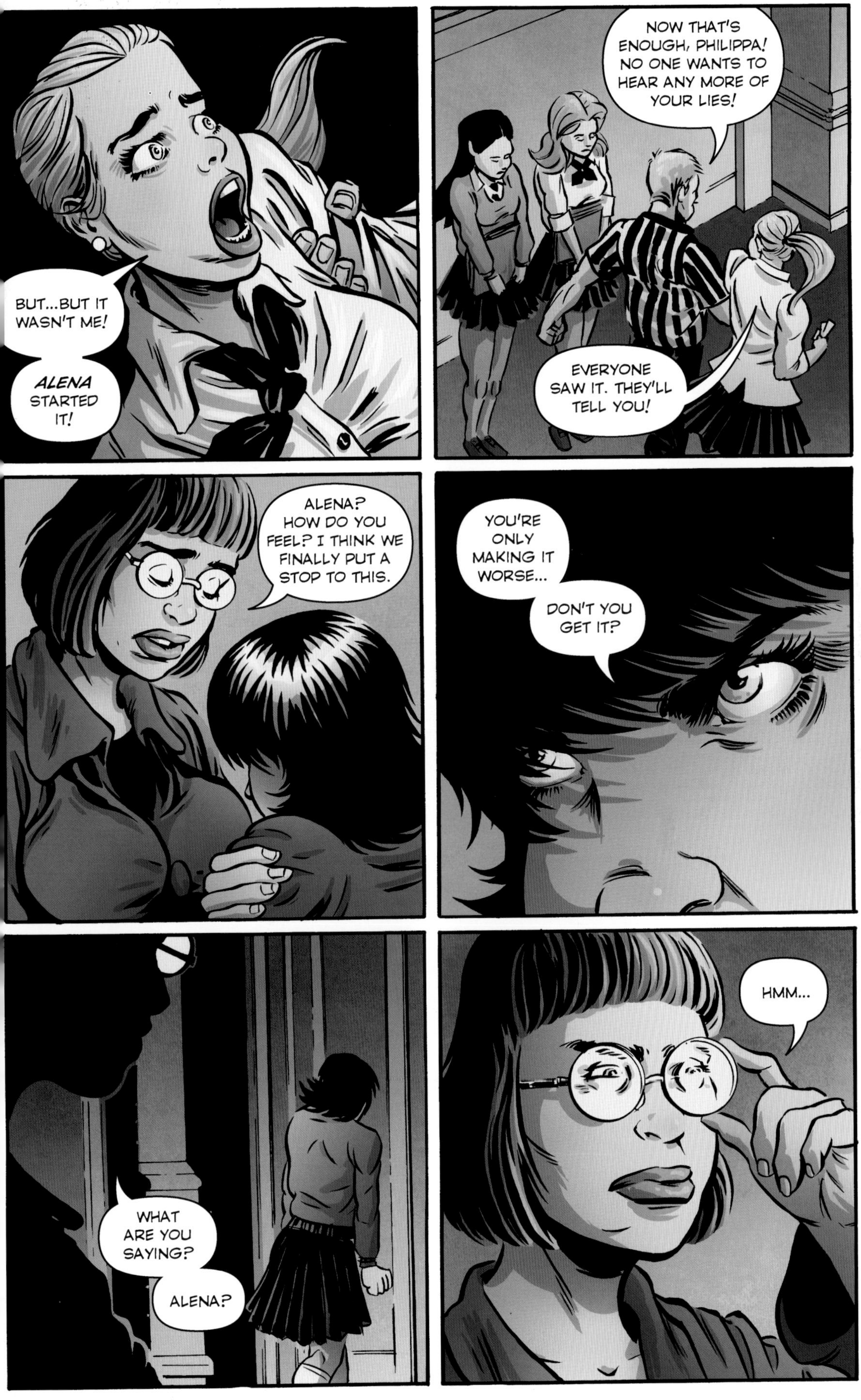
BUT...BUT IT WASN'T ME!
*ALENA* STARTED IT!
NOW THAT'S ENOUGH, PHILIPPA! NO ONE WANTS TO HEAR ANY MORE OF YOUR LIES!
EVERYONE SAW IT. THEY'LL TELL YOU!
ALENA? HOW DO YOU FEEL? I THINK WE FINALLY PUT A STOP TO THIS.
YOU'RE ONLY MAKING IT WORSE...
DON'T YOU GET IT?
WHAT ARE YOU SAYING?
ALENA?
HMM...

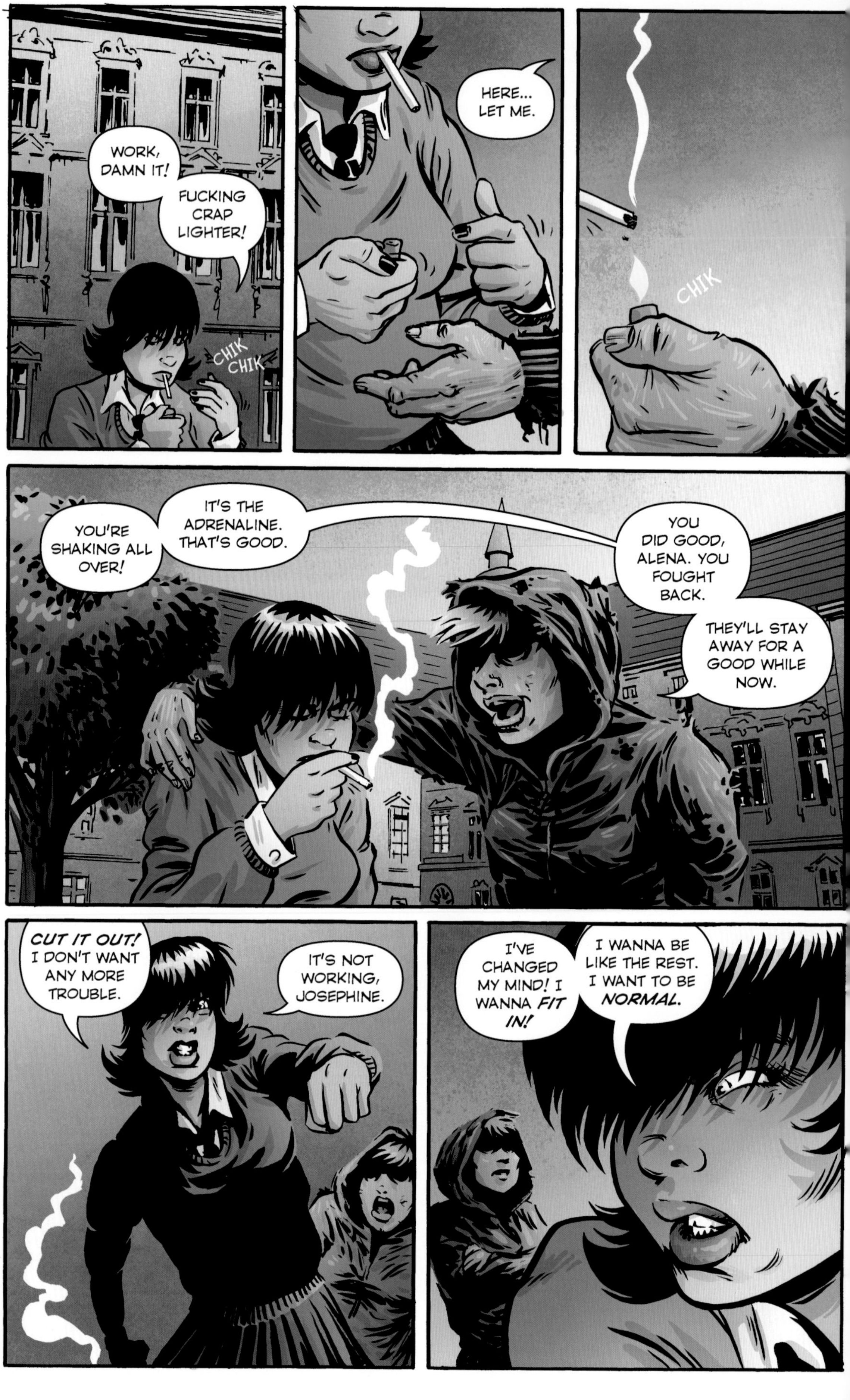
WORK, DAMN IT!
FUCKING CRAP LIGHTER!
CHIK CHIK
HERE... LET ME.
CHIK
YOU'RE SHAKING ALL OVER!
IT'S THE ADRENALINE. THAT'S GOOD.
YOU DID GOOD, ALENA. YOU FOUGHT BACK.
THEY'LL STAY AWAY FOR A GOOD WHILE NOW.
CUT IT OUT! I DON'T WANT ANY MORE TROUBLE.
IT'S NOT WORKING, JOSEPHINE.
I'VE CHANGED MY MIND! I WANNA FIT IN!
I WANNA BE LIKE THE REST. I WANT TO BE NORMAL.

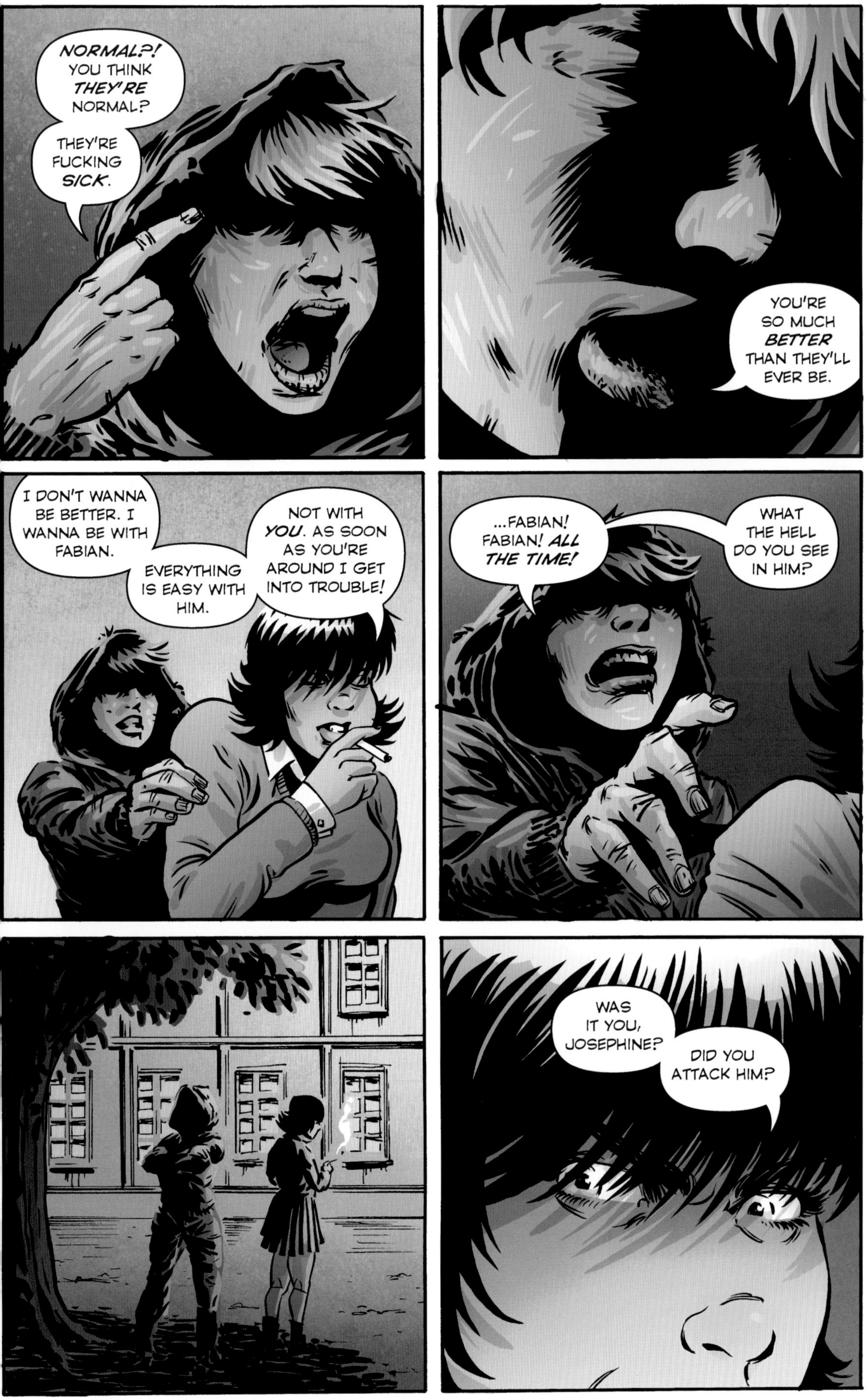
NORMAL?! YOU THINK THEY'RE NORMAL?
THEY'RE FUCKING SICK.
YOU'RE SO MUCH BETTER THAN THEY'LL EVER BE.
I DON'T WANNA BE BETTER. I WANNA BE WITH FABIAN.
EVERYTHING IS EASY WITH HIM.
NOT WITH YOU. AS SOON AS YOU'RE AROUND I GET INTO TROUBLE!
...FABIAN! FABIAN! ALL THE TIME!
WHAT THE HELL DO YOU SEE IN HIM?
WAS IT YOU, JOSEPHINE?
DID YOU ATTACK HIM?

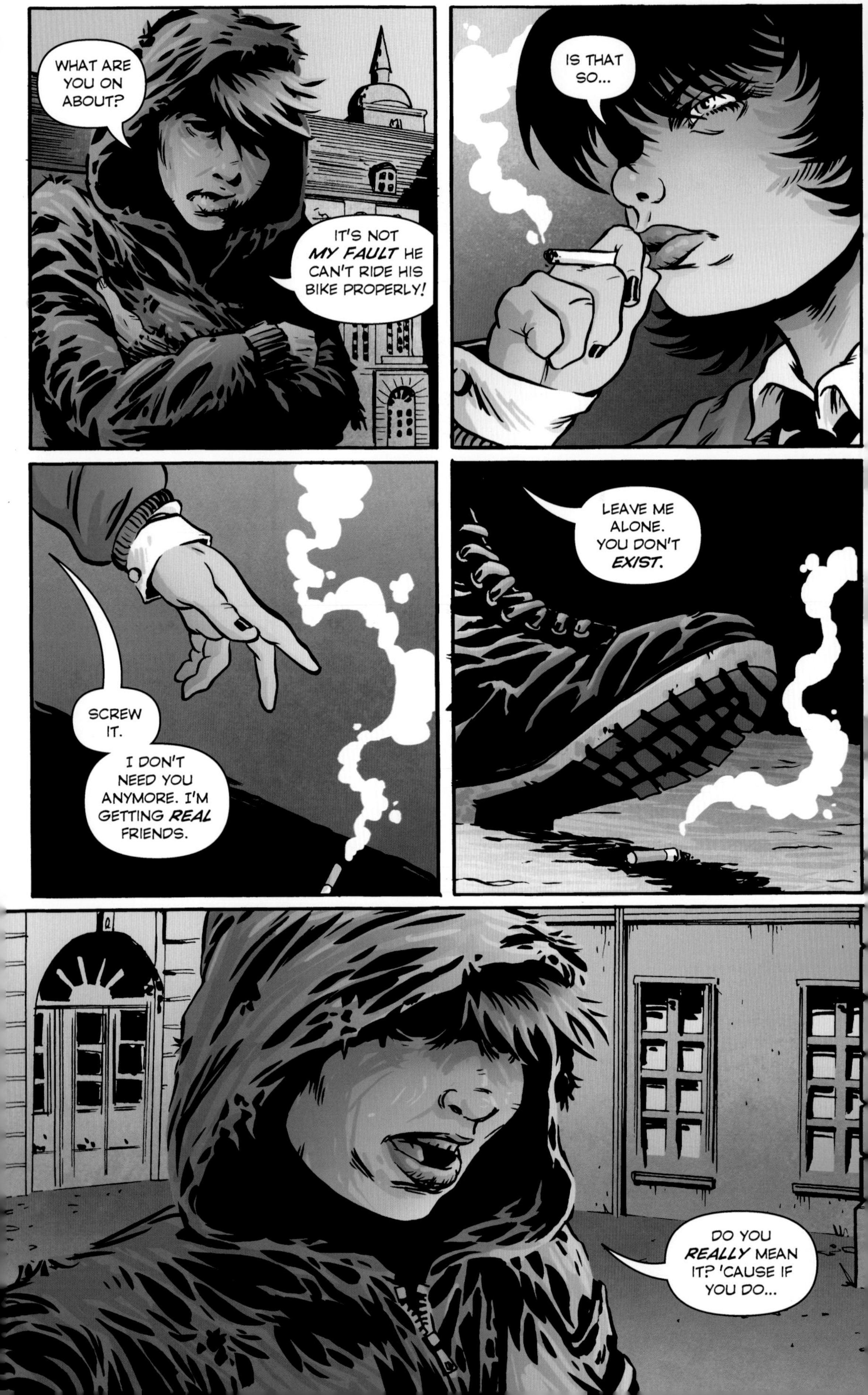
WHAT ARE YOU ON ABOUT?
IT'S NOT *MY FAULT* HE CAN'T RIDE HIS BIKE PROPERLY!
IS THAT SO...
SCREW IT.
I DON'T NEED YOU ANYMORE. I'M GETTING *REAL* FRIENDS.
LEAVE ME ALONE. YOU DON'T *EXIST*.
DO YOU *REALLY* MEAN IT? 'CAUSE IF YOU DO...

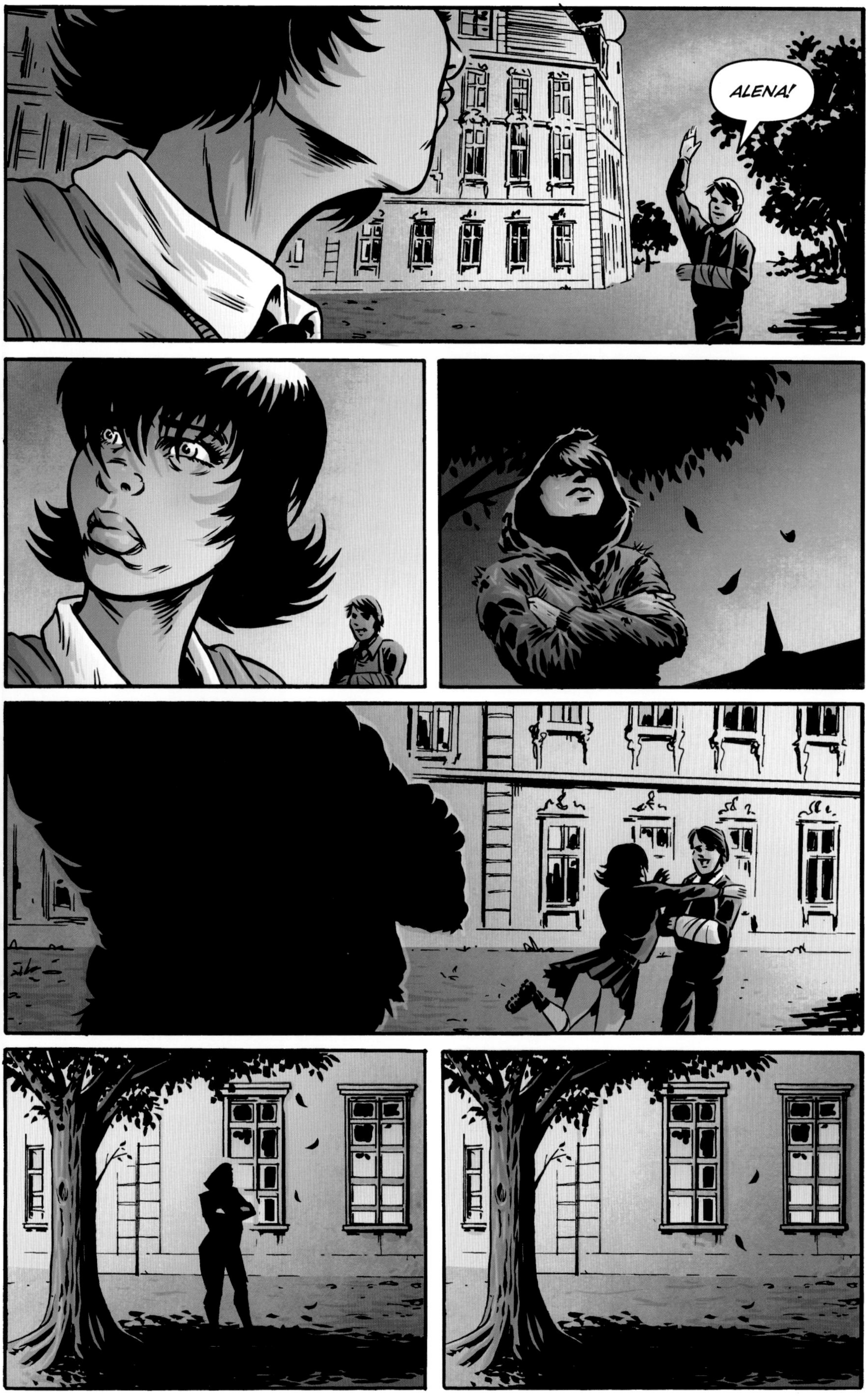
ALENA!

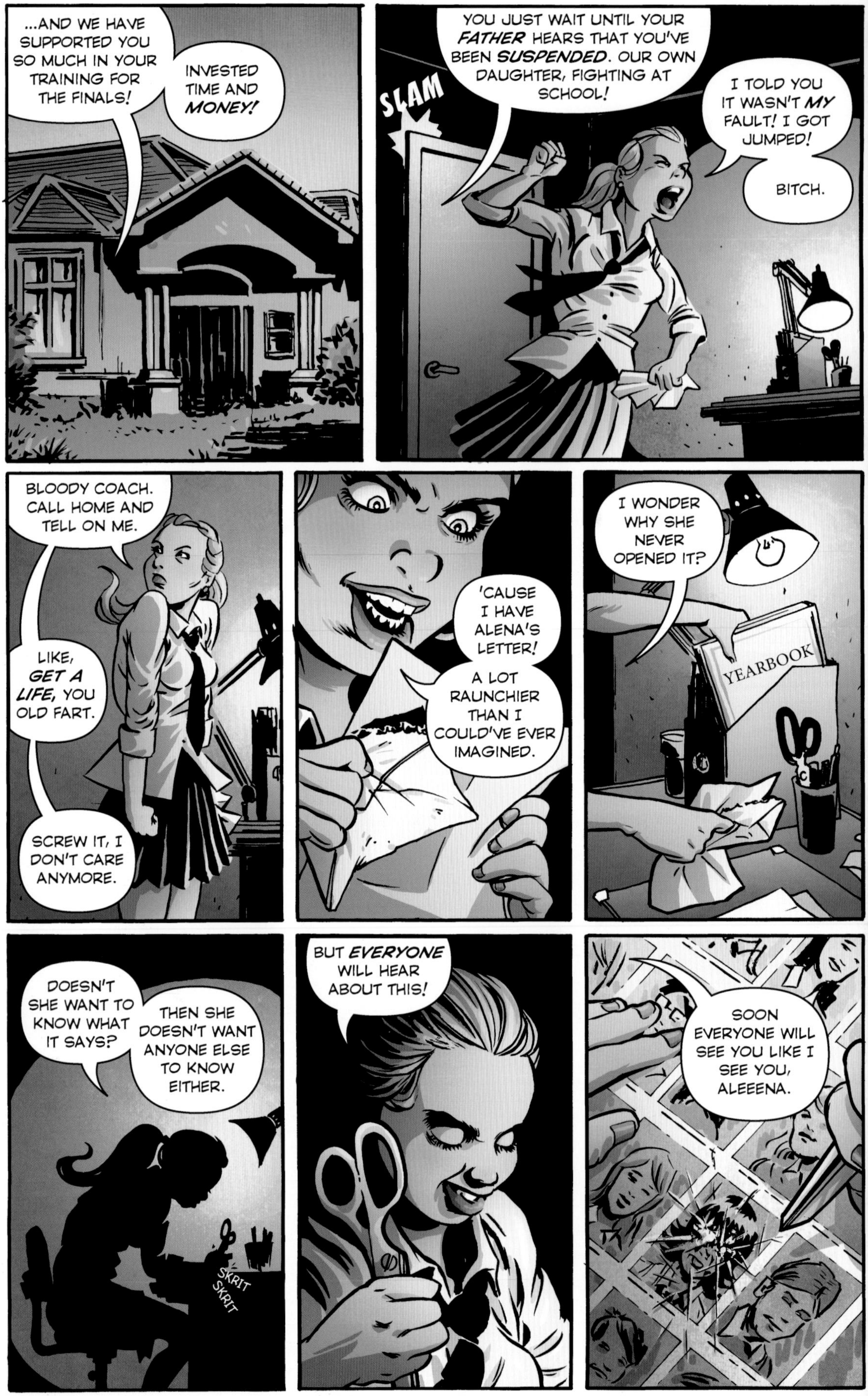
...AND WE HAVE SUPPORTED YOU SO MUCH IN YOUR TRAINING FOR THE FINALS!
INVESTED TIME AND MONEY!
YOU JUST WAIT UNTIL YOUR FATHER HEARS THAT YOU'VE BEEN SUSPENDED. OUR OWN DAUGHTER, FIGHTING AT SCHOOL!
SLAM
I TOLD YOU IT WASN'T MY FAULT! I GOT JUMPED!
BITCH.
BLOODY COACH. CALL HOME AND TELL ON ME.
LIKE, GET A LIFE, YOU OLD FART.
SCREW IT, I DON'T CARE ANYMORE.
'CAUSE I HAVE ALENA'S LETTER!
A LOT RAUNCHIER THAN I COULD'VE EVER IMAGINED.
I WONDER WHY SHE NEVER OPENED IT?
YEARBOOK
DOESN'T SHE WANT TO KNOW WHAT IT SAYS?
THEN SHE DOESN'T WANT ANYONE ELSE TO KNOW EITHER.
SKRIT SKRIT
BUT EVERYONE WILL HEAR ABOUT THIS!
SOON EVERYONE WILL SEE YOU LIKE I SEE YOU, ALEEENA.

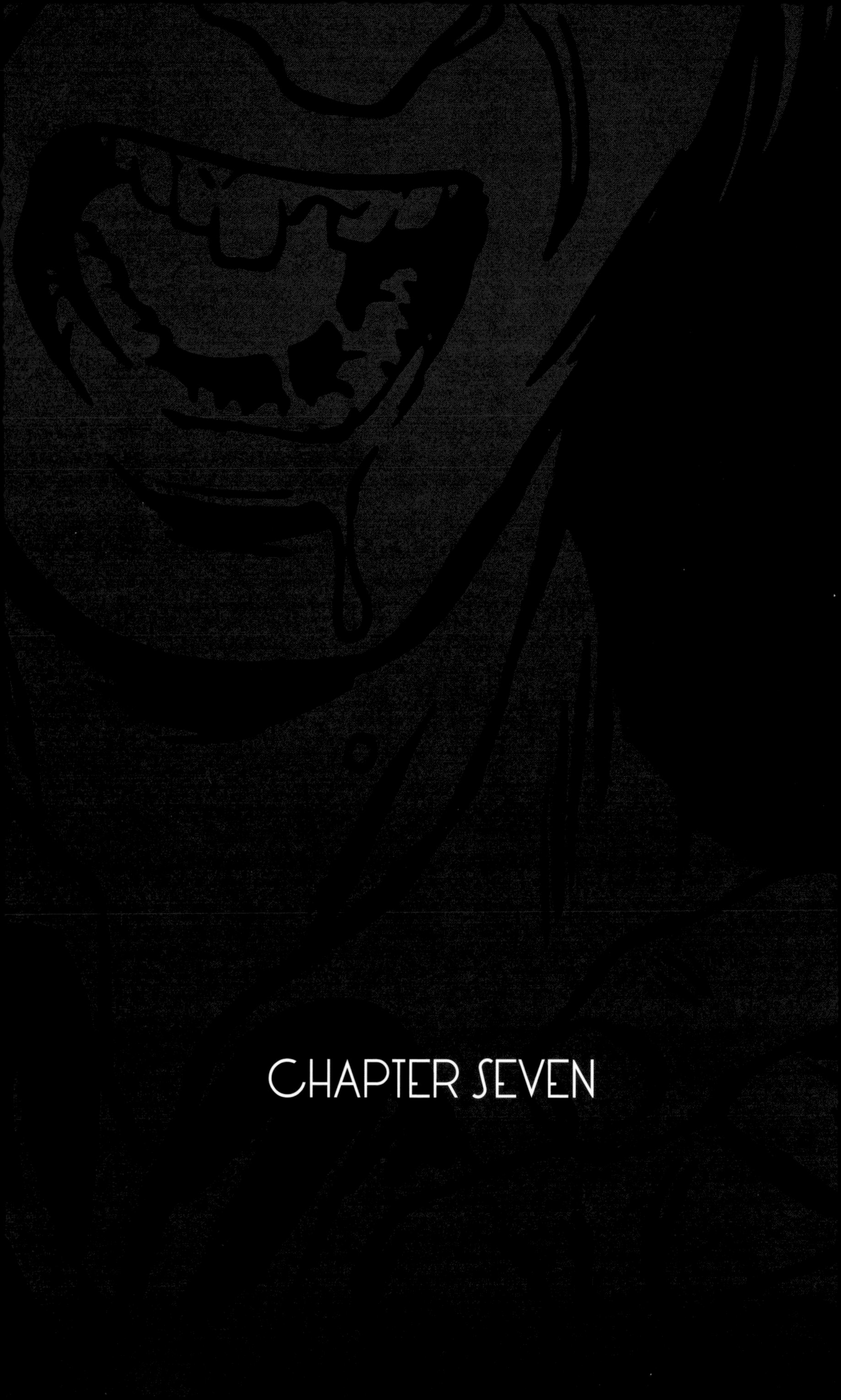

# CHAPTER SEVEN

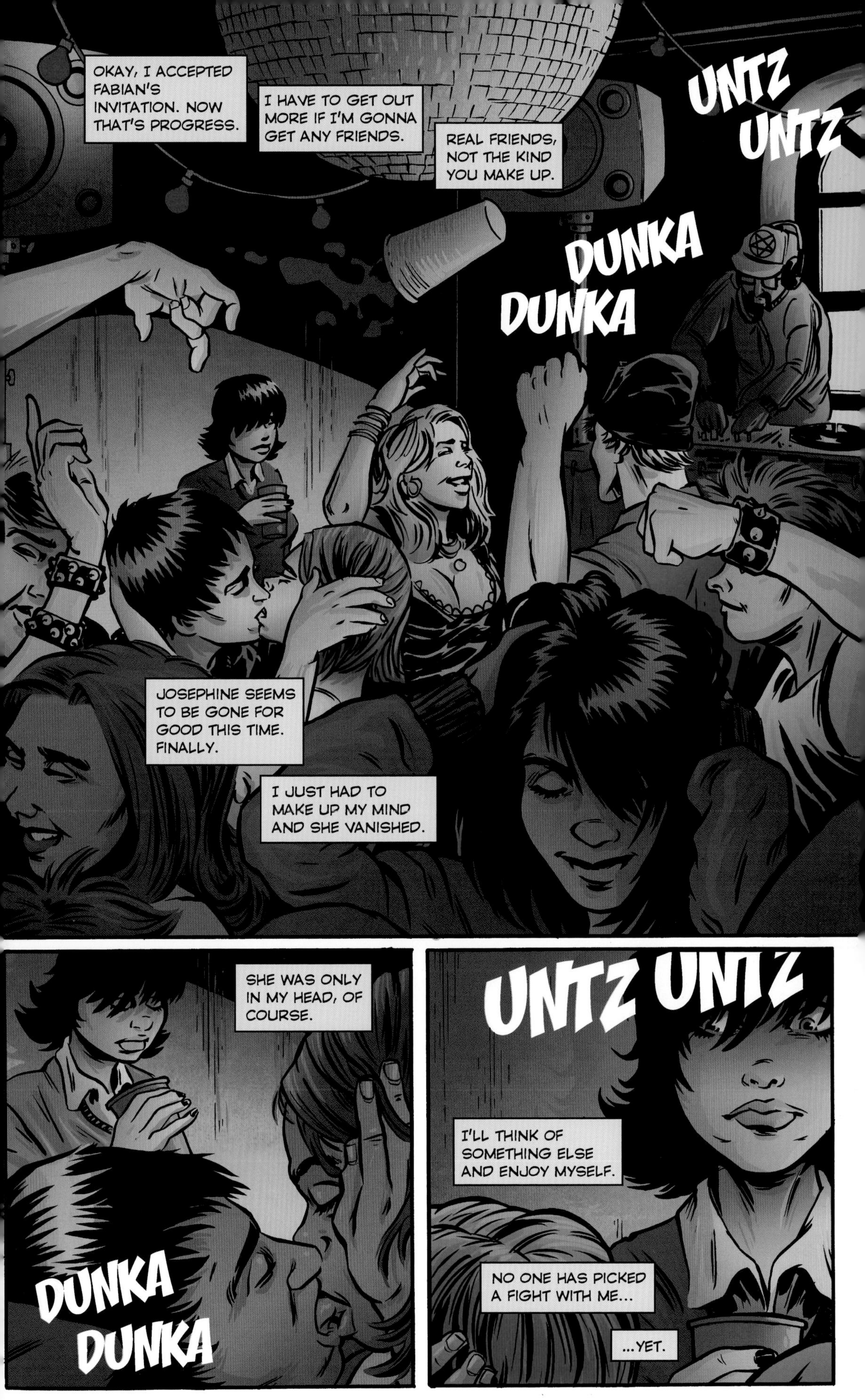

OKAY, I ACCEPTED FABIAN'S INVITATION. NOW THAT'S PROGRESS.
I HAVE TO GET OUT MORE IF I'M GONNA GET ANY FRIENDS.
REAL FRIENDS, NOT THE KIND YOU MAKE UP.
UNTZ UNTZ
DUNKA DUNKA
JOSEPHINE SEEMS TO BE GONE FOR GOOD THIS TIME. FINALLY.
I JUST HAD TO MAKE UP MY MIND AND SHE VANISHED.
SHE WAS ONLY IN MY HEAD, OF COURSE.
DUNKA DUNKA
UNTZ UNTZ
I'LL THINK OF SOMETHING ELSE AND ENJOY MYSELF.
NO ONE HAS PICKED A FIGHT WITH ME...
...YET.

HI! YOU'RE ALENA, RIGHT?

EH, MAYBE... I MEAN, YES.

GOOD! I'M LINA. THIS IS CONNY. SAY HI, CONNY.

FABIAN HAS SPOKEN SO MUCH ABOUT YOU.

YOU HAVE SUCH A COOL HAIRDO. I WISH I DARED TO CUT IT LIKE THAT.

WHO'S YOUR HAIRDRESSER? IS IT CLAUDE?

NO, I CUT IT MYSELF.

DUNKA DUNKA

WOW! HOW COOL!

YOU TWO ENJOY YOURSELVES. COME, CONNY! LET'S LEAVE THEM ALONE.

HERE'S YOUR DRINK, ALENA.

HOW'S IT GOING? ARE YOU GONNA SURVIVE?

IT'S OKAY, REALLY.

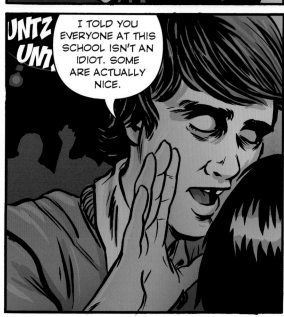

UNTZ UNTZ

I TOLD YOU EVERYONE AT THIS SCHOOL ISN'T AN IDIOT. SOME ARE ACTUALLY NICE.

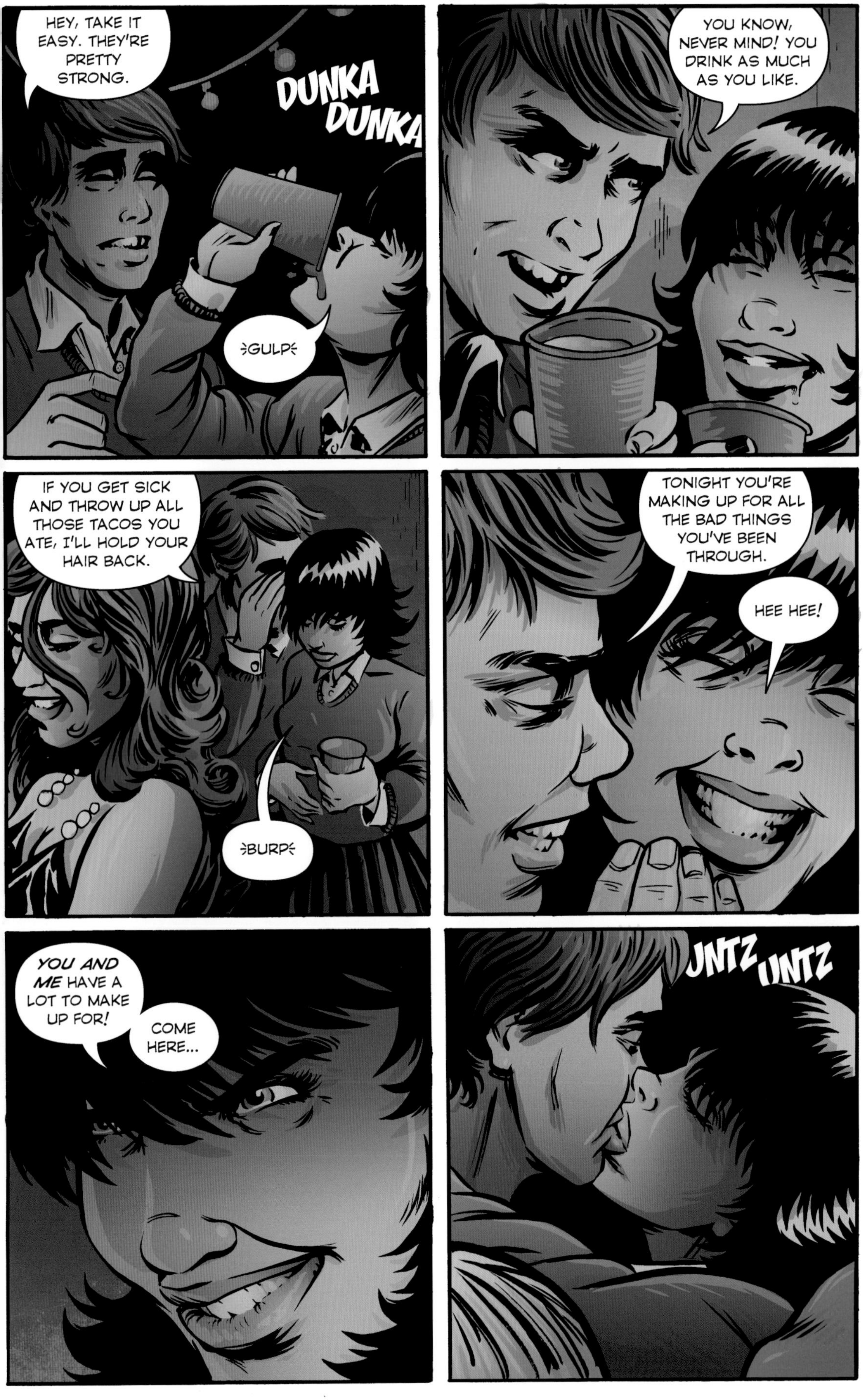
HEY, TAKE IT EASY. THEY'RE PRETTY STRONG.
DUNKA DUNKA
GULP
YOU KNOW, NEVER MIND! YOU DRINK AS MUCH AS YOU LIKE.
IF YOU GET SICK AND THROW UP ALL THOSE TACOS YOU ATE, I'LL HOLD YOUR HAIR BACK.
BURP
TONIGHT YOU'RE MAKING UP FOR ALL THE BAD THINGS YOU'VE BEEN THROUGH.
HEE HEE!
*YOU AND ME* HAVE A LOT TO MAKE UP FOR!
COME HERE...
UNTZ UNTZ

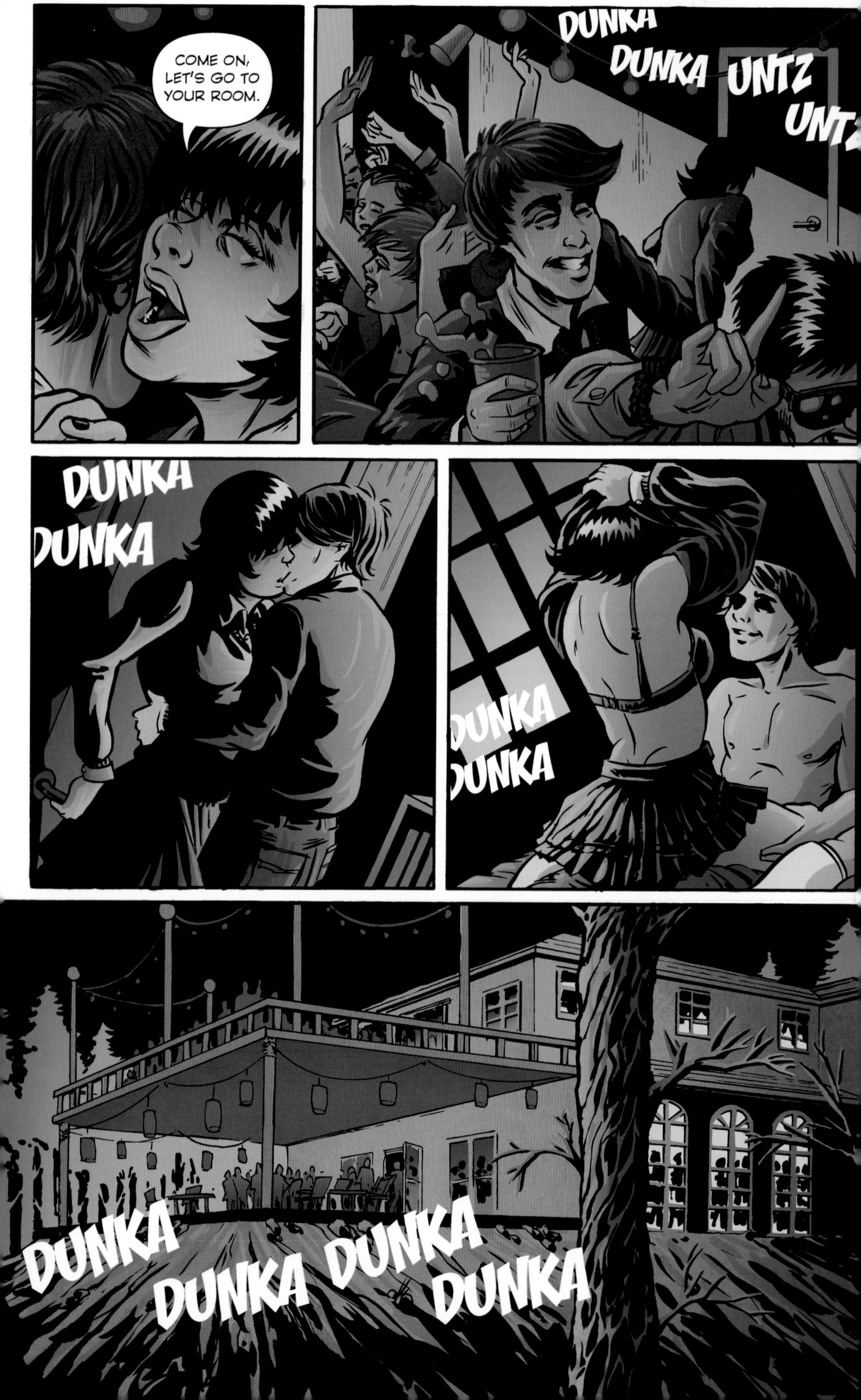
COME ON, LET'S GO TO YOUR ROOM.
DUNKA
DUNKA
UNTZ
UNTZ
DUNKA
DUNKA
DUNKA
DUNKA
DUNKA
DUNKA
DUNKA
DUNKA

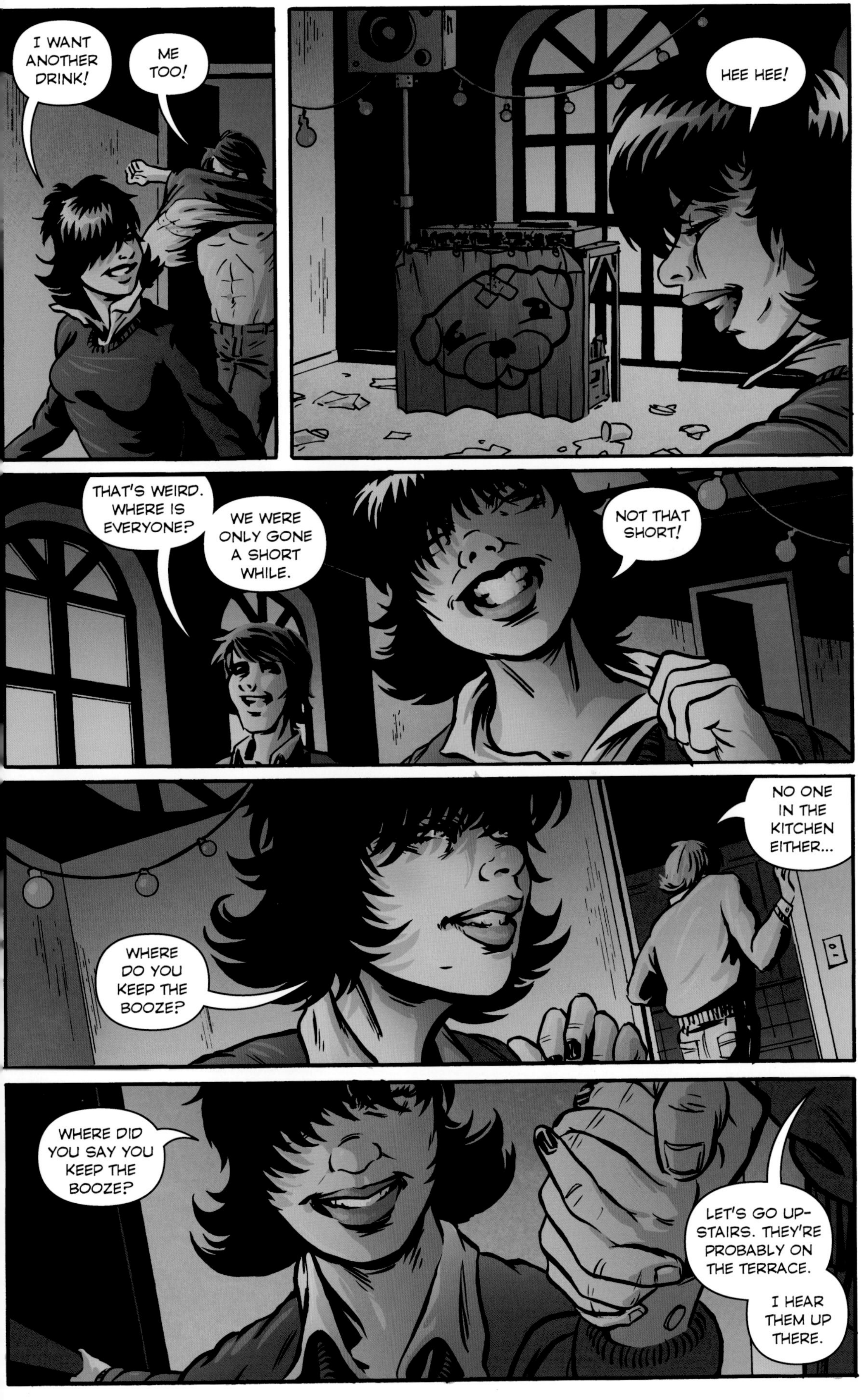

I WANT ANOTHER DRINK!
ME TOO!
HEE HEE!
THAT'S WEIRD. WHERE IS EVERYONE?
WE WERE ONLY GONE A SHORT WHILE.
NOT THAT SHORT!
NO ONE IN THE KITCHEN EITHER...
WHERE DO YOU KEEP THE BOOZE?
WHERE DID YOU SAY YOU KEEP THE BOOZE?
LET'S GO UP-STAIRS. THEY'RE PROBABLY ON THE TERRACE.
I HEAR THEM UP THERE.

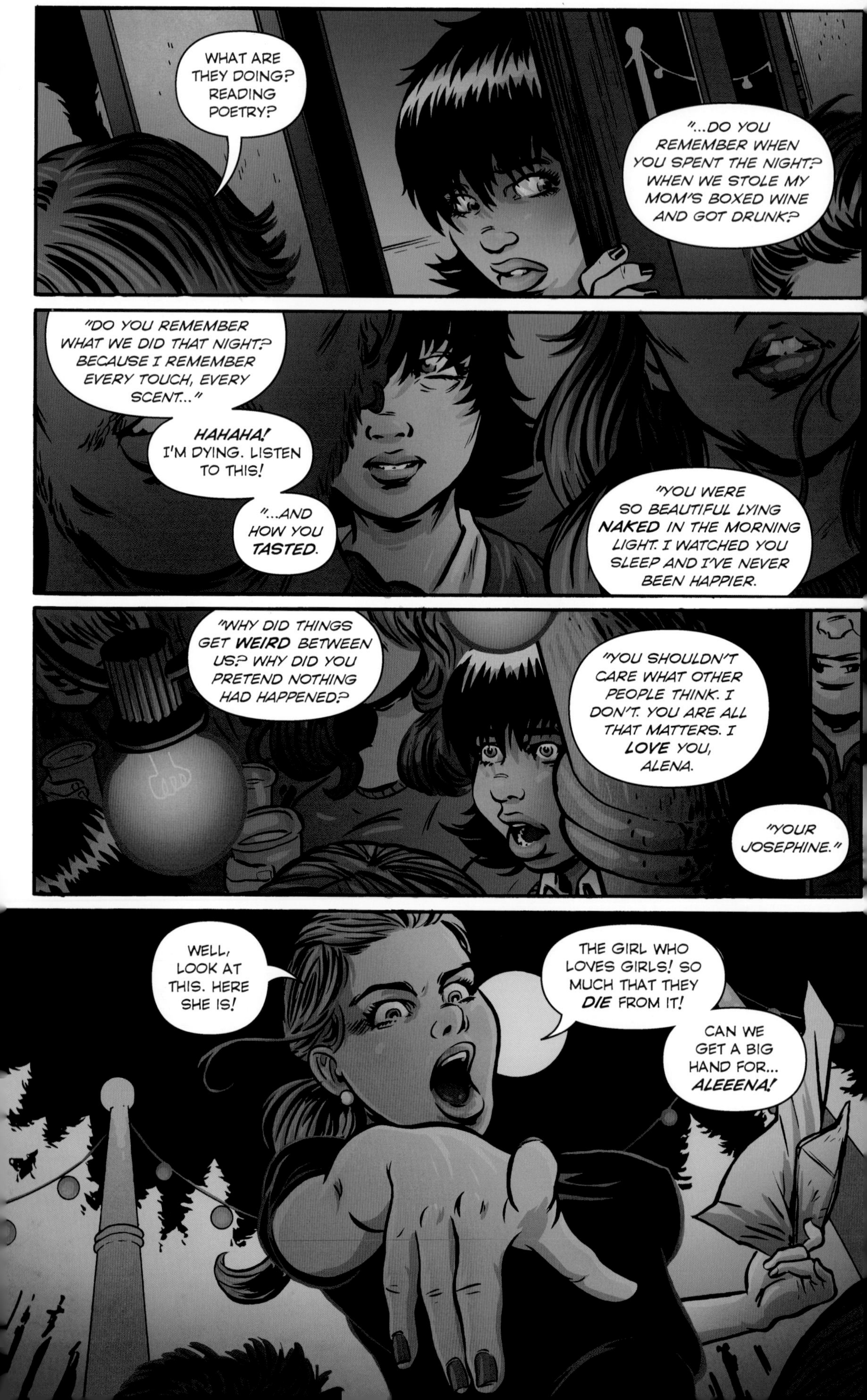
WHAT ARE THEY DOING? READING POETRY?
"...DO YOU REMEMBER WHEN YOU SPENT THE NIGHT? WHEN WE STOLE MY MOM'S BOXED WINE AND GOT DRUNK?
"DO YOU REMEMBER WHAT WE DID THAT NIGHT? BECAUSE I REMEMBER EVERY TOUCH, EVERY SCENT..."
HAHAHA! I'M DYING. LISTEN TO THIS!
"...AND HOW YOU TASTED.
"YOU WERE SO BEAUTIFUL LYING NAKED IN THE MORNING LIGHT. I WATCHED YOU SLEEP AND I'VE NEVER BEEN HAPPIER.
"WHY DID THINGS GET WEIRD BETWEEN US? WHY DID YOU PRETEND NOTHING HAD HAPPENED?
"YOU SHOULDN'T CARE WHAT OTHER PEOPLE THINK. I DON'T. YOU ARE ALL THAT MATTERS. I LOVE YOU, ALENA.
"YOUR JOSEPHINE."
WELL, LOOK AT THIS. HERE SHE IS!
THE GIRL WHO LOVES GIRLS! SO MUCH THAT THEY DIE FROM IT!
CAN WE GET A BIG HAND FOR... ALEEENA!

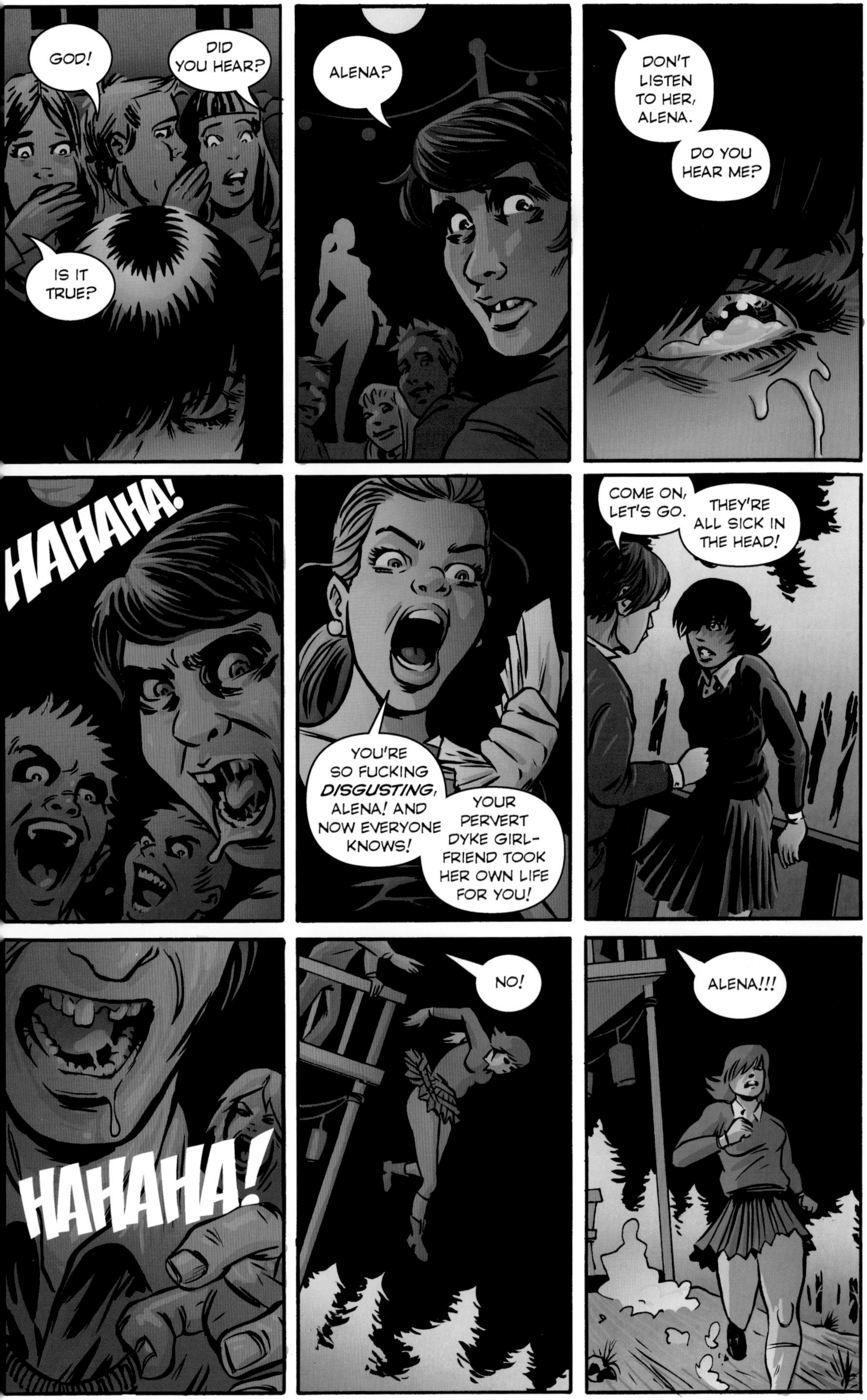
GOD!
DID YOU HEAR?
IS IT TRUE?
ALENA?
DON'T LISTEN TO HER, ALENA.
DO YOU HEAR ME?
HAHAHA!
YOU'RE SO FUCKING *DISGUSTING*, ALENA! AND NOW EVERYONE KNOWS!
YOUR PERVERT DYKE GIRL-FRIEND TOOK HER OWN LIFE FOR YOU!
COME ON, LET'S GO.
THEY'RE ALL SICK IN THE HEAD!
HAHAHA!
NO!
ALENA!!!

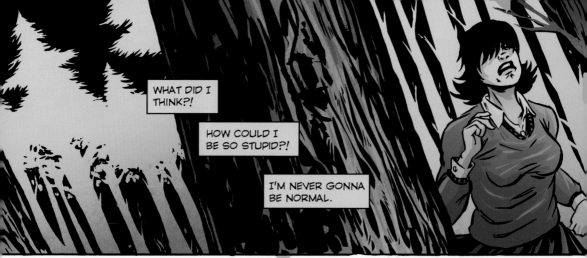

WHAT DID I THINK?!

HOW COULD I BE SO STUPID?!

I'M NEVER GONNA BE NORMAL.

IF ONLY I COULD BE LEFT ALONE.

I DON'T NEED ANYONE. I'M GONNA MAKE IT ON MY OWN.

WHEN SCHOOL'S OUT I'LL BE GONE FOREVER.

BUT HOW WILL I MAKE IT TILL THEN?

HERE YOU ARE!

EVERYONE'S LOOKING FOR YOU. BUT I FOUND YOU FIRST.

THIS IS FOR GETTING ME SUSPENDED FROM THE TEAM!

≥SOB≤

SHTOCK!

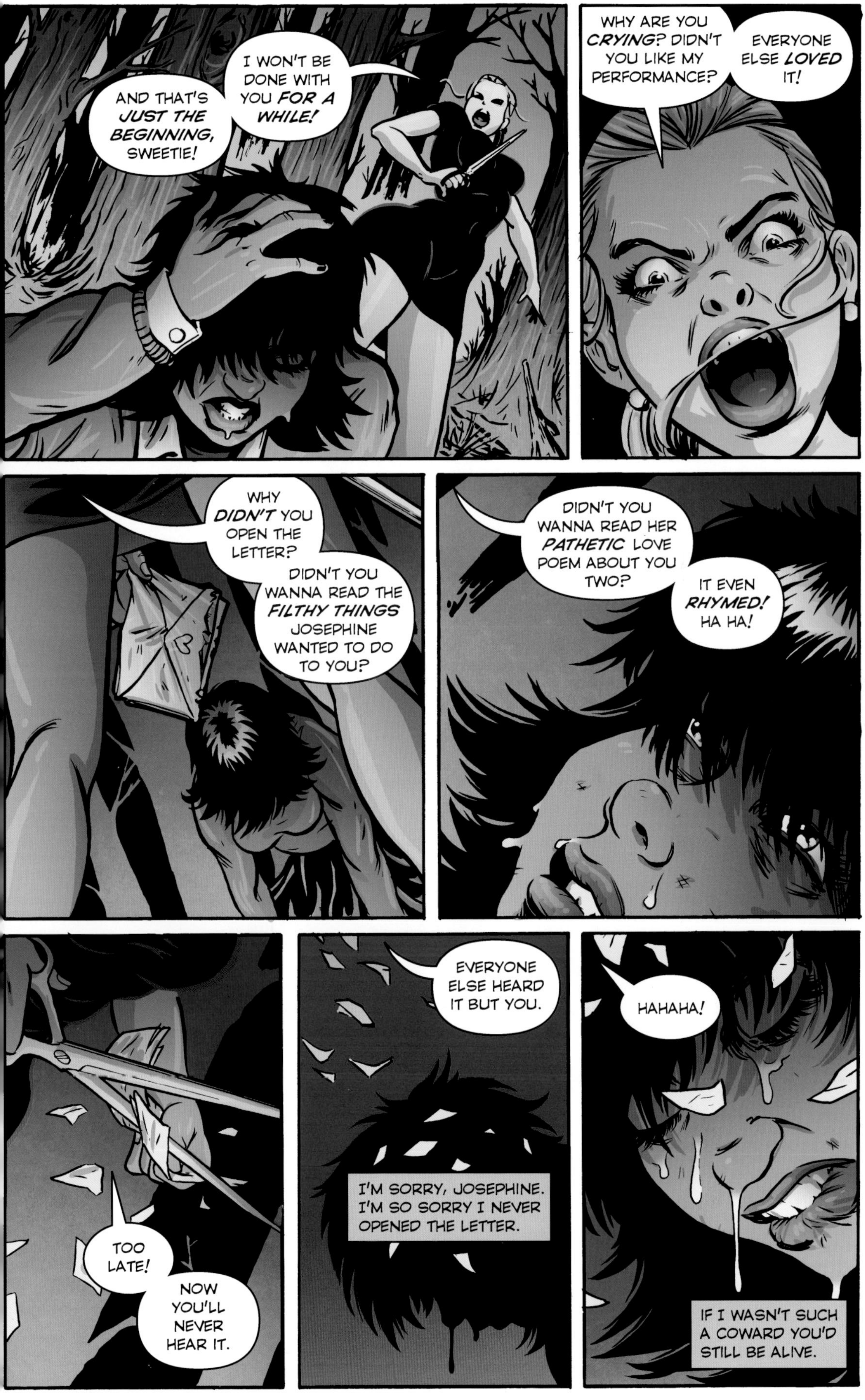
I WON'T BE DONE WITH YOU FOR A WHILE!
AND THAT'S JUST THE BEGINNING, SWEETIE!
WHY ARE YOU CRYING? DIDN'T YOU LIKE MY PERFORMANCE?
EVERYONE ELSE LOVED IT!
WHY DIDN'T YOU OPEN THE LETTER?
DIDN'T YOU WANNA READ THE FILTHY THINGS JOSEPHINE WANTED TO DO TO YOU?
DIDN'T YOU WANNA READ HER PATHETIC LOVE POEM ABOUT YOU TWO?
IT EVEN RHYMED! HA HA!
TOO LATE!
NOW YOU'LL NEVER HEAR IT.
EVERYONE ELSE HEARD IT BUT YOU.
I'M SORRY, JOSEPHINE. I'M SO SORRY I NEVER OPENED THE LETTER.
HAHAHA!
IF I WASN'T SUCH A COWARD YOU'D STILL BE ALIVE.

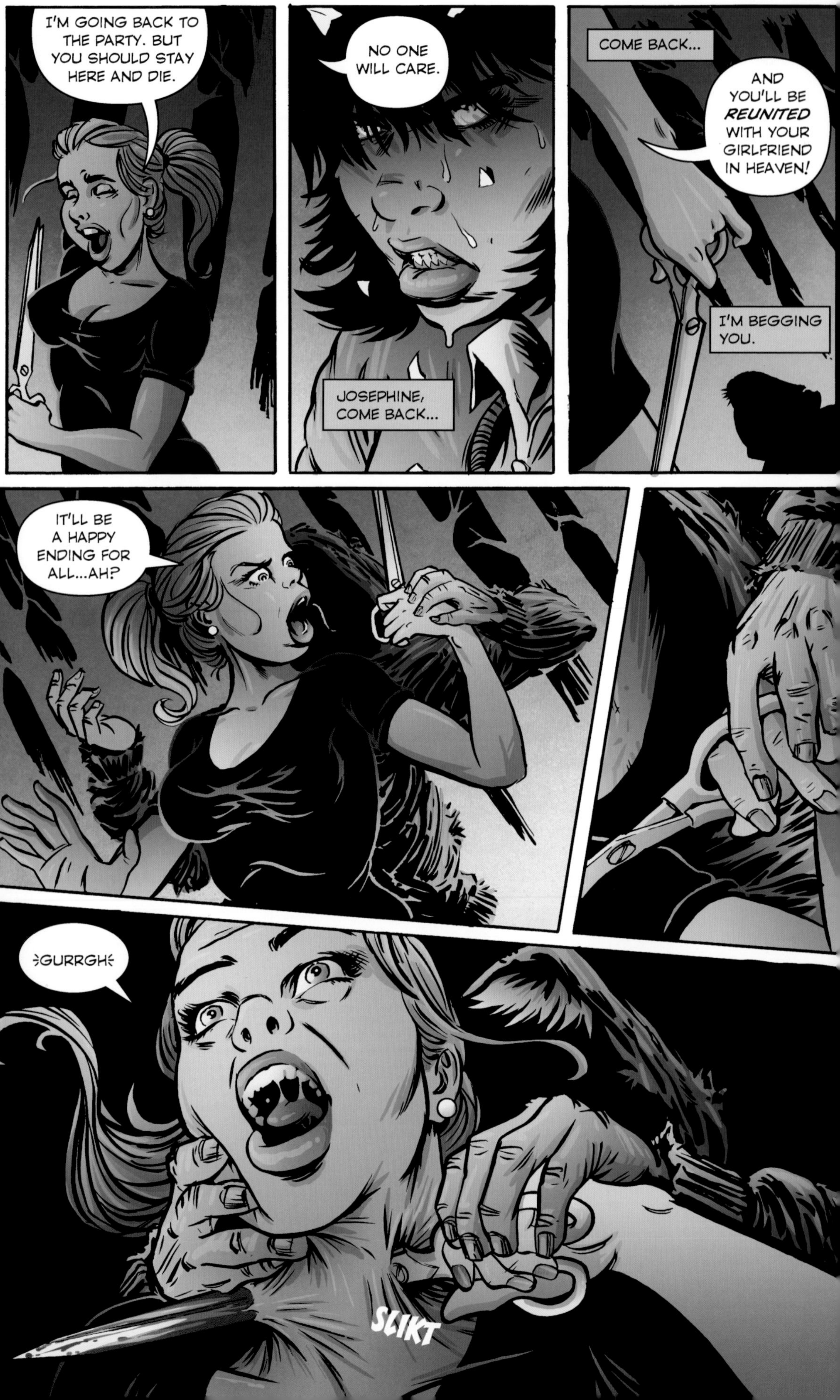
I'M GOING BACK TO THE PARTY. BUT YOU SHOULD STAY HERE AND DIE.
NO ONE WILL CARE.
JOSEPHINE, COME BACK...
COME BACK...
AND YOU'LL BE *REUNITED* WITH YOUR GIRLFRIEND IN HEAVEN!
I'M BEGGING YOU.
IT'LL BE A HAPPY ENDING FOR ALL...AH?
GURRGH
SLIKT

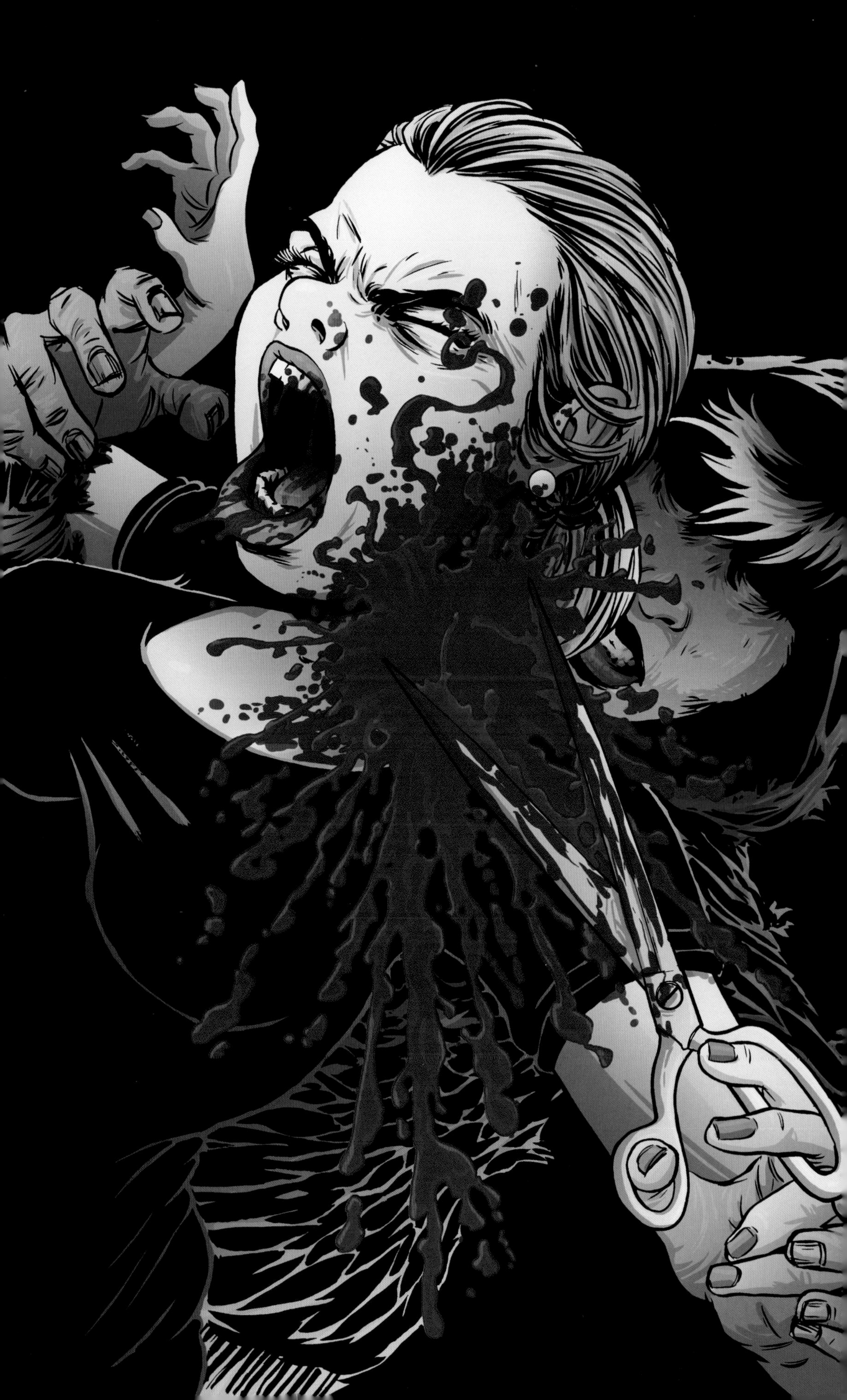

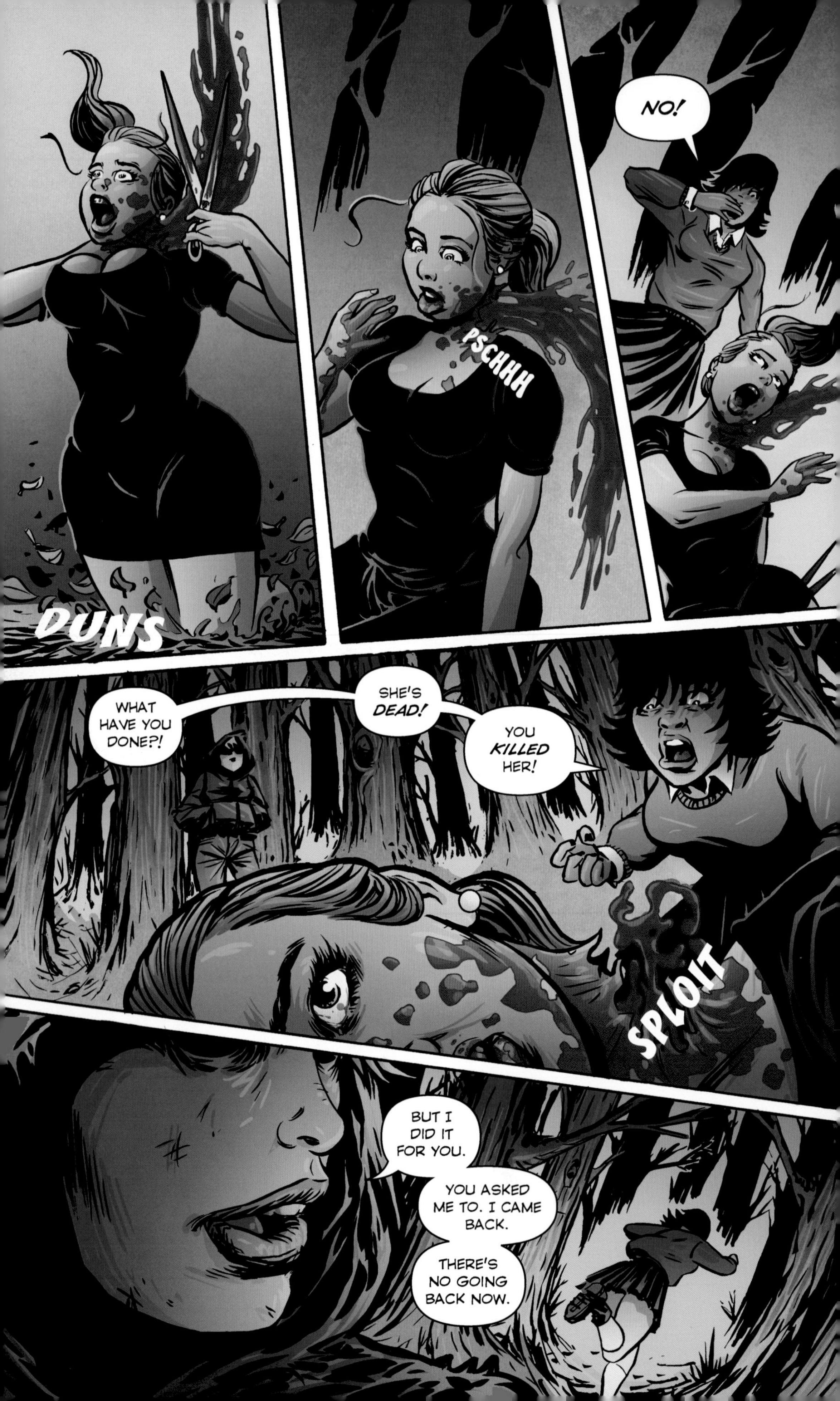
DUNS
PSCHHH
NO!
WHAT HAVE YOU DONE?!
SHE'S DEAD!
YOU KILLED HER!
SPLOIT
BUT I DID IT FOR YOU.
YOU ASKED ME TO. I CAME BACK.
THERE'S NO GOING BACK NOW.

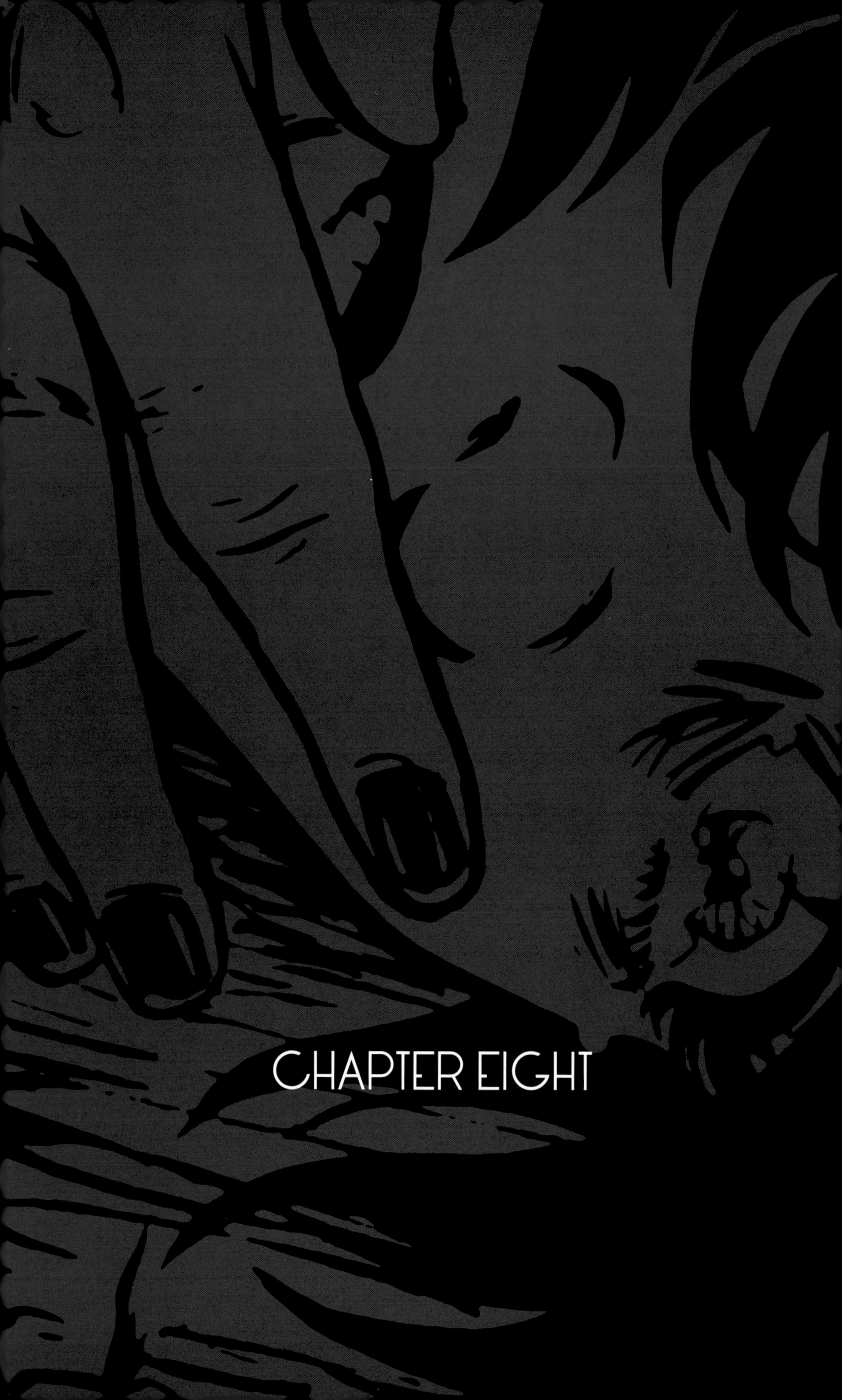

# CHAPTER EIGHT

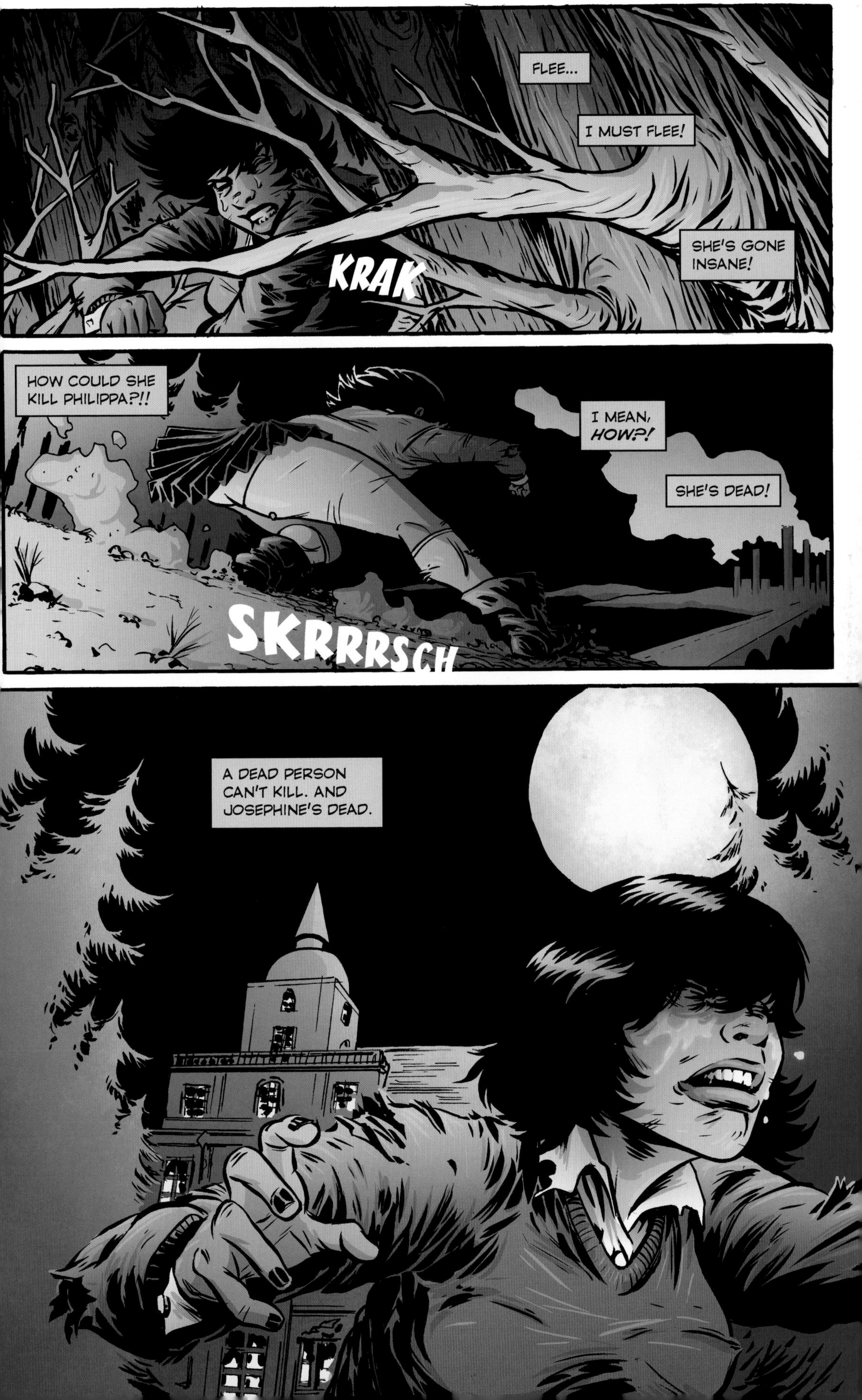
FLEE...
I MUST FLEE!
SHE'S GONE INSANE!
KRAK
HOW COULD SHE KILL PHILIPPA?!!
I MEAN, HOW?!
SHE'S DEAD!
SKRRRRSCH
A DEAD PERSON CAN'T KILL. AND JOSEPHINE'S DEAD.

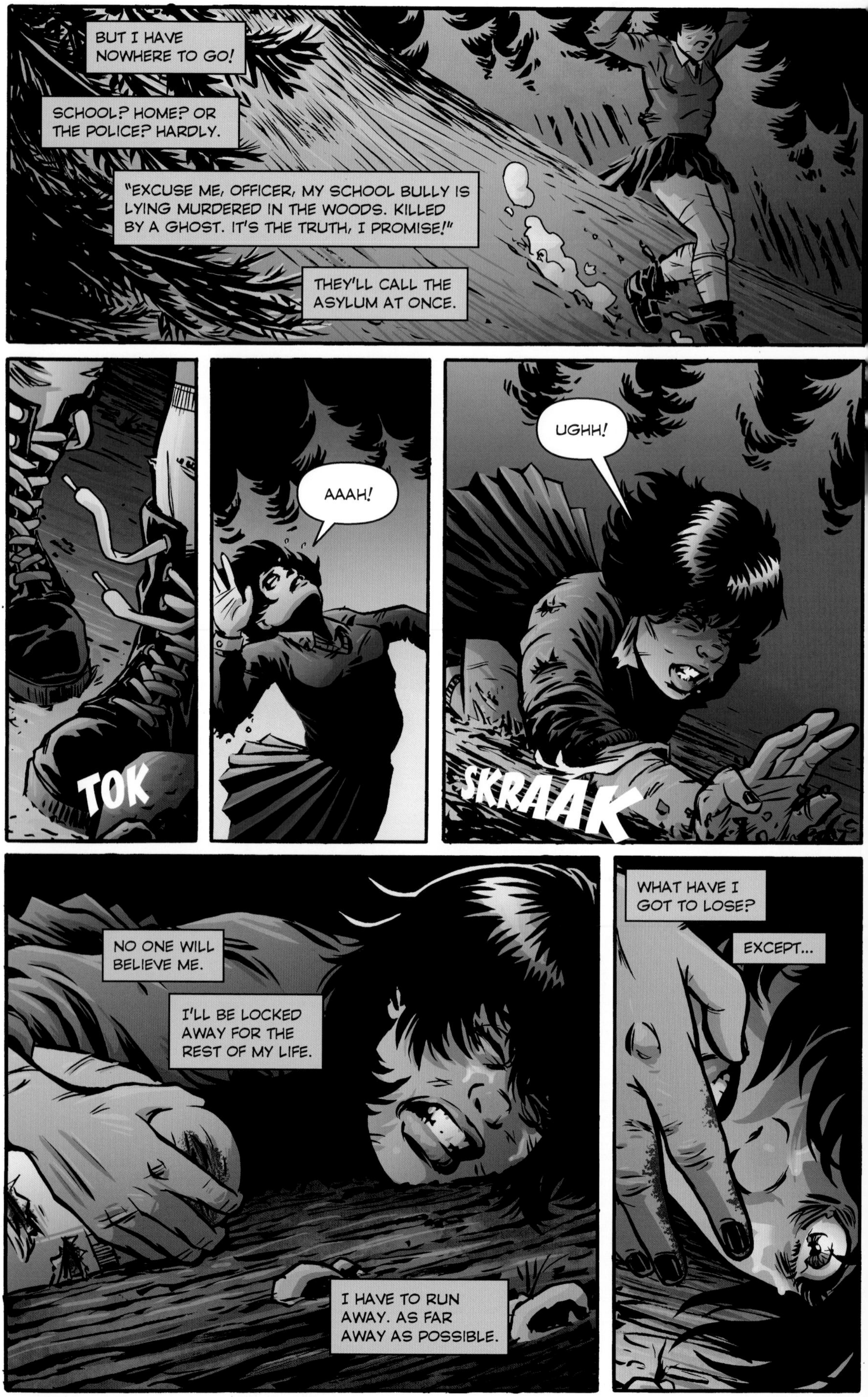
BUT I HAVE NOWHERE TO GO!
SCHOOL? HOME? OR THE POLICE? HARDLY.
"EXCUSE ME, OFFICER, MY SCHOOL BULLY IS LYING MURDERED IN THE WOODS. KILLED BY A GHOST. IT'S THE TRUTH, I PROMISE!"
THEY'LL CALL THE ASYLUM AT ONCE.
TOK
AAAH!
UGHH!
SKRAAK
NO ONE WILL BELIEVE ME.
I'LL BE LOCKED AWAY FOR THE REST OF MY LIFE.
I HAVE TO RUN AWAY. AS FAR AWAY AS POSSIBLE.
WHAT HAVE I GOT TO LOSE?
EXCEPT...

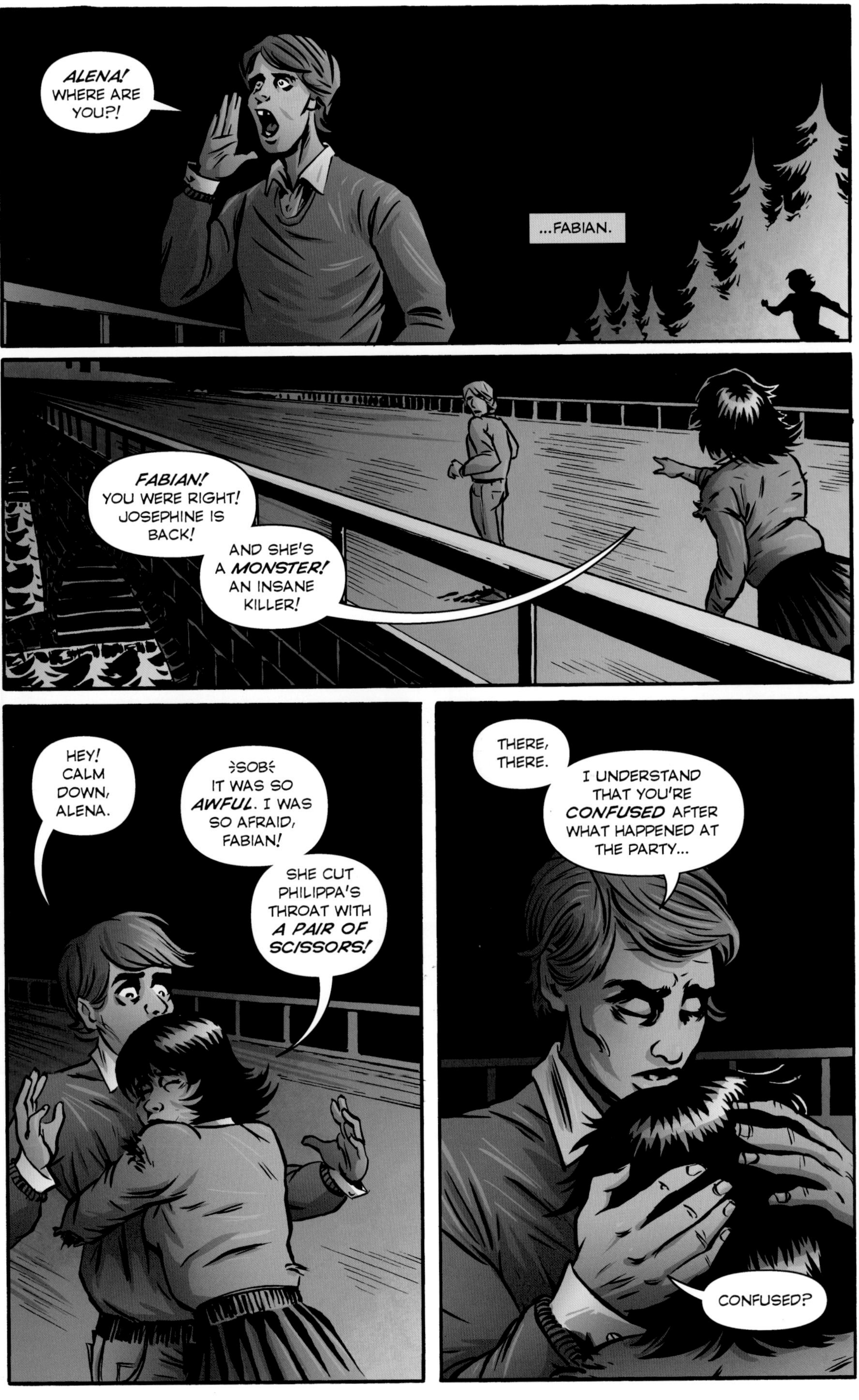

ALENA! WHERE ARE YOU?!
...FABIAN.
FABIAN! YOU WERE RIGHT! JOSEPHINE IS BACK!
AND SHE'S A MONSTER! AN INSANE KILLER!
HEY! CALM DOWN, ALENA.
SOB IT WAS SO AWFUL. I WAS SO AFRAID, FABIAN!
SHE CUT PHILIPPA'S THROAT WITH A PAIR OF SCISSORS!
THERE, THERE.
I UNDERSTAND THAT YOU'RE CONFUSED AFTER WHAT HAPPENED AT THE PARTY...
CONFUSED?

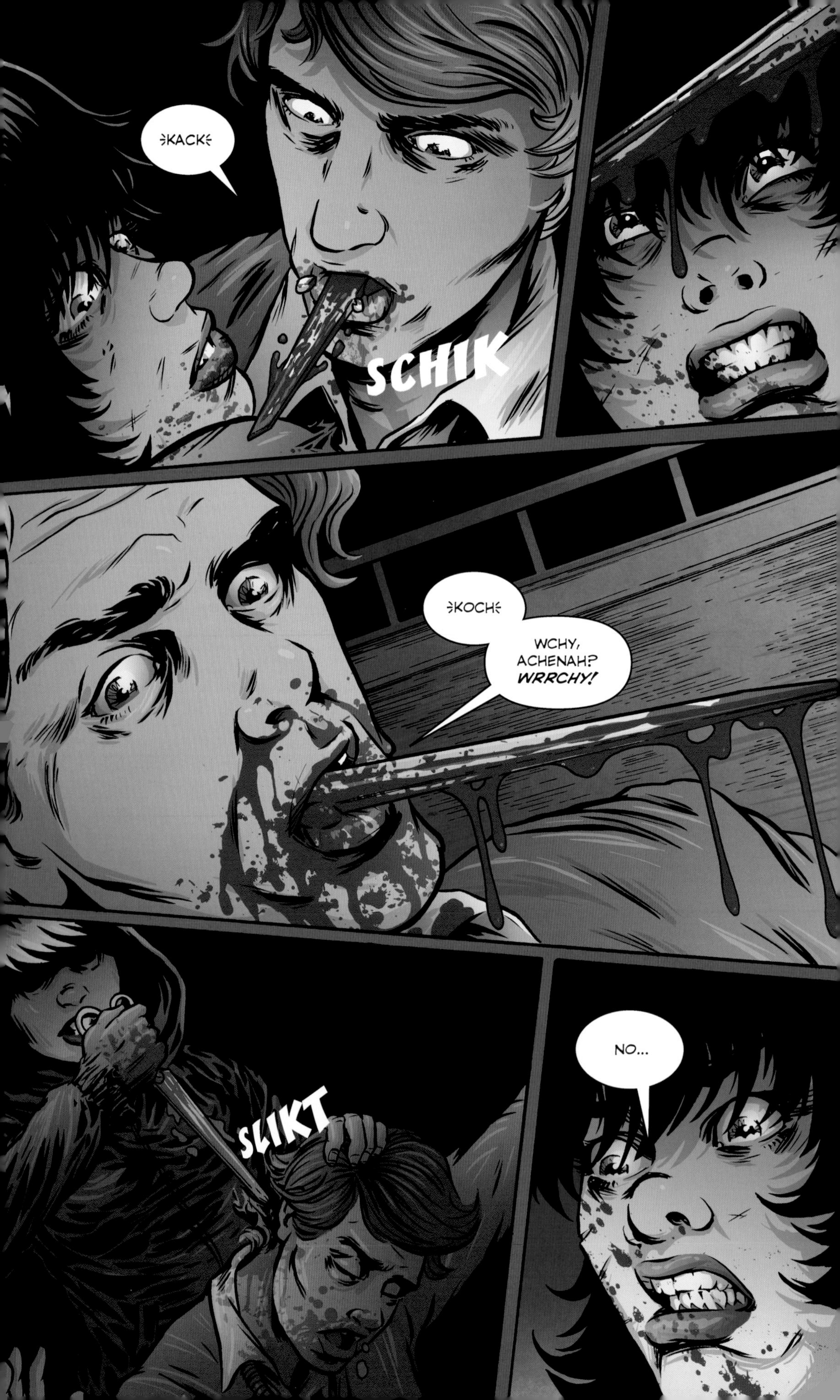
KACK
SCHIK
KOCH
WCHY, ACHENAH? WRRCHY!
SLIKT
NO...

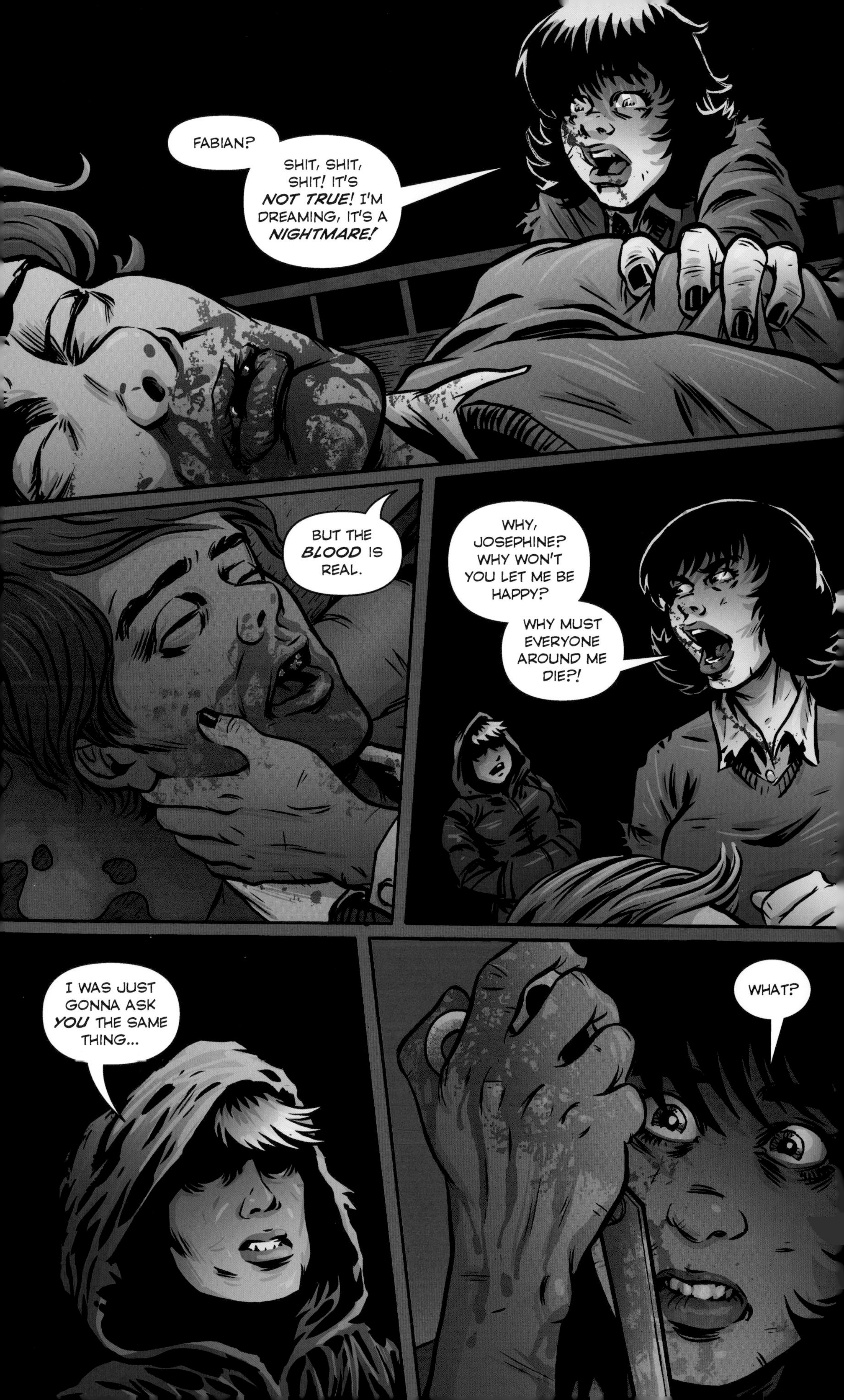
FABIAN?
SHIT, SHIT, SHIT! IT'S *NOT TRUE!* I'M DREAMING, IT'S A *NIGHTMARE!*
BUT THE *BLOOD* IS REAL.
WHY, JOSEPHINE? WHY WON'T YOU LET ME BE HAPPY?
WHY MUST EVERYONE AROUND ME DIE?!
I WAS JUST GONNA ASK *YOU* THE SAME THING...
WHAT?

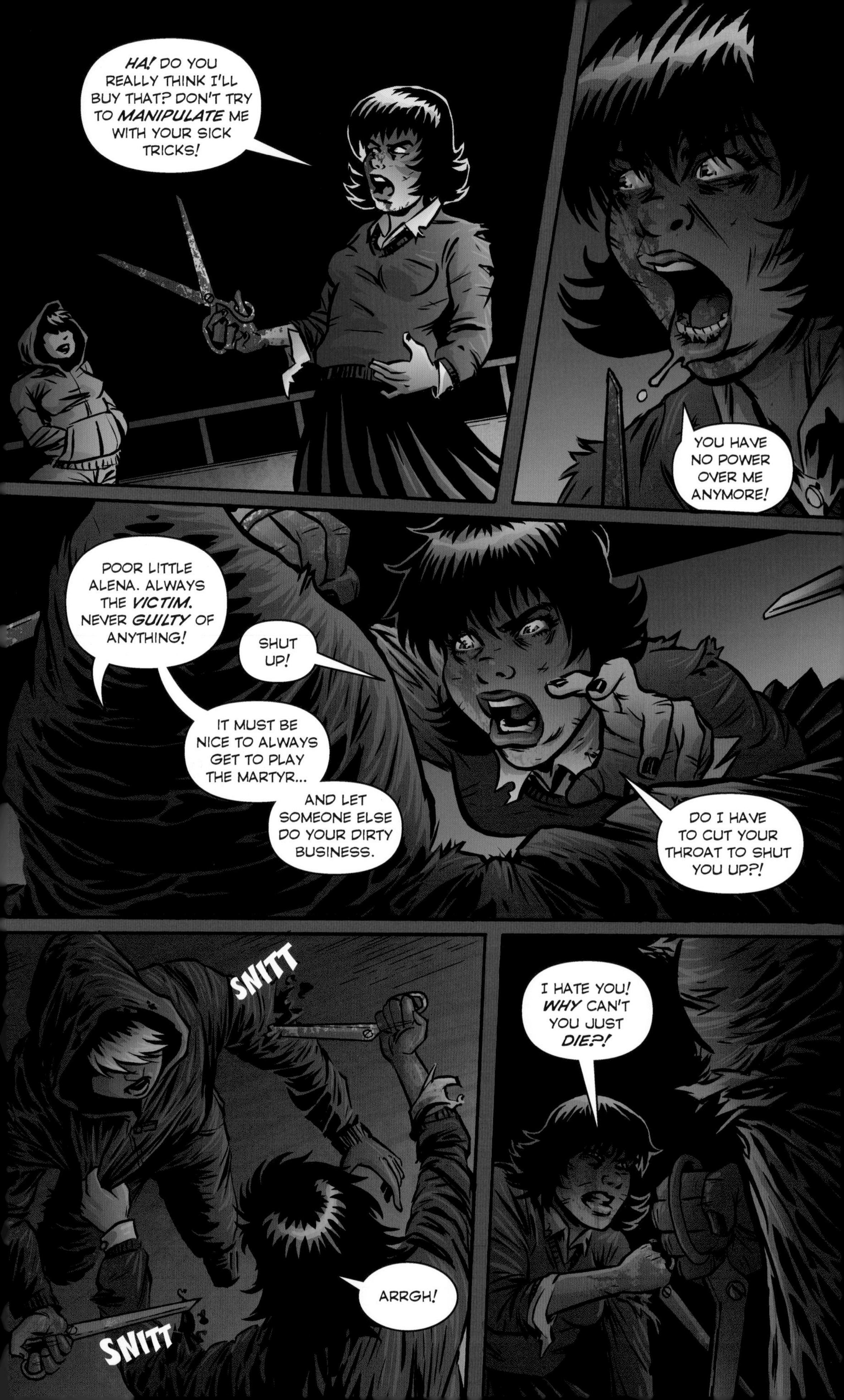
HA! DO YOU REALLY THINK I'LL BUY THAT? DON'T TRY TO MANIPULATE ME WITH YOUR SICK TRICKS!
YOU HAVE NO POWER OVER ME ANYMORE!
POOR LITTLE ALENA. ALWAYS THE VICTIM. NEVER GUILTY OF ANYTHING!
SHUT UP!
IT MUST BE NICE TO ALWAYS GET TO PLAY THE MARTYR...
AND LET SOMEONE ELSE DO YOUR DIRTY BUSINESS.
DO I HAVE TO CUT YOUR THROAT TO SHUT YOU UP?!
SNITT
ARRGH!
SNITT
I HATE YOU! WHY CAN'T YOU JUST DIE?!

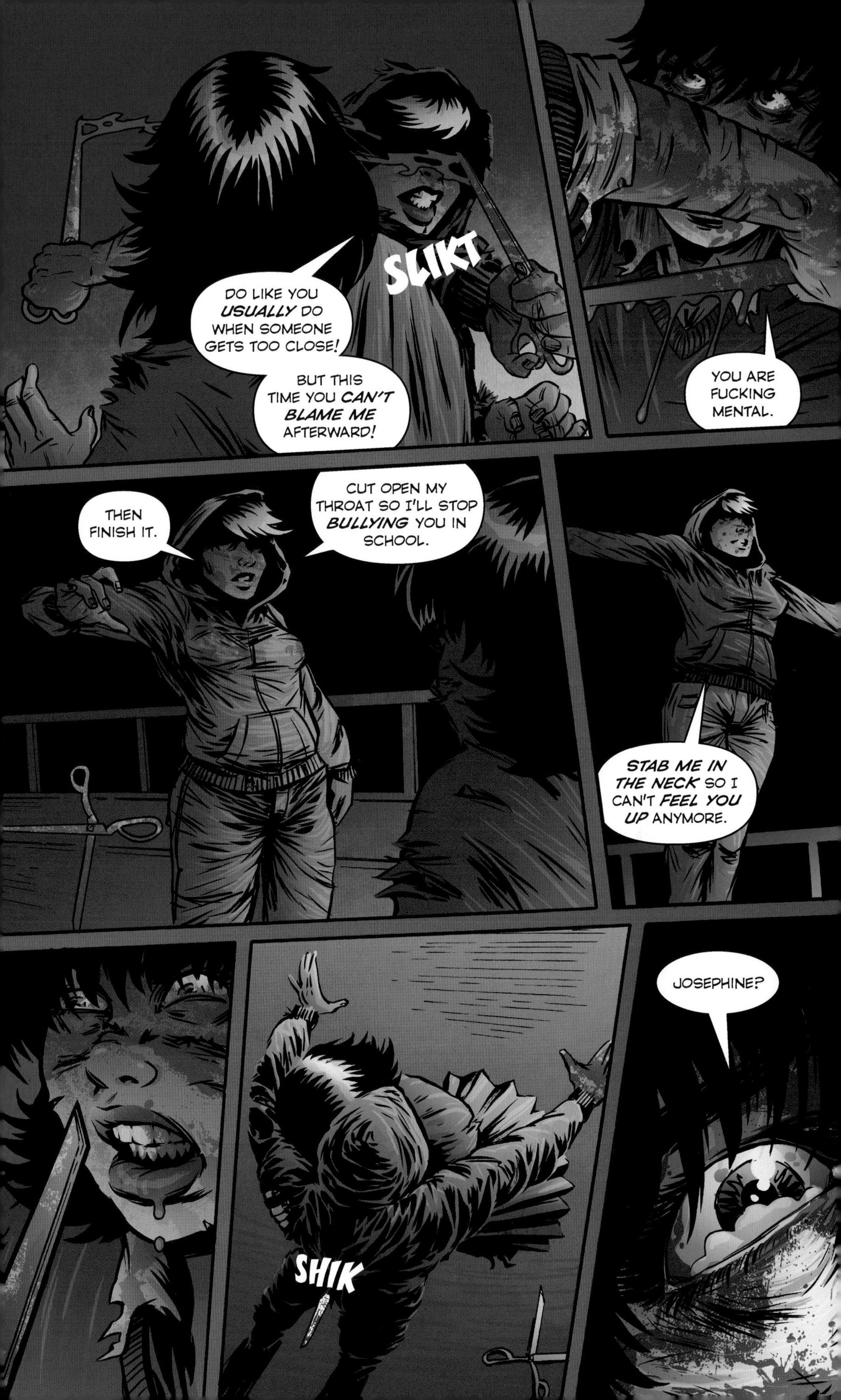

DO LIKE YOU *USUALLY* DO WHEN SOMEONE GETS TOO CLOSE!
SLIKT
BUT THIS TIME YOU *CAN'T BLAME ME* AFTERWARD!
YOU ARE FUCKING MENTAL.
THEN FINISH IT.
CUT OPEN MY THROAT SO I'LL STOP *BULLYING* YOU IN SCHOOL.
*STAB ME IN THE NECK* SO I CAN'T *FEEL YOU UP* ANYMORE.
SHIK
JOSEPHINE?

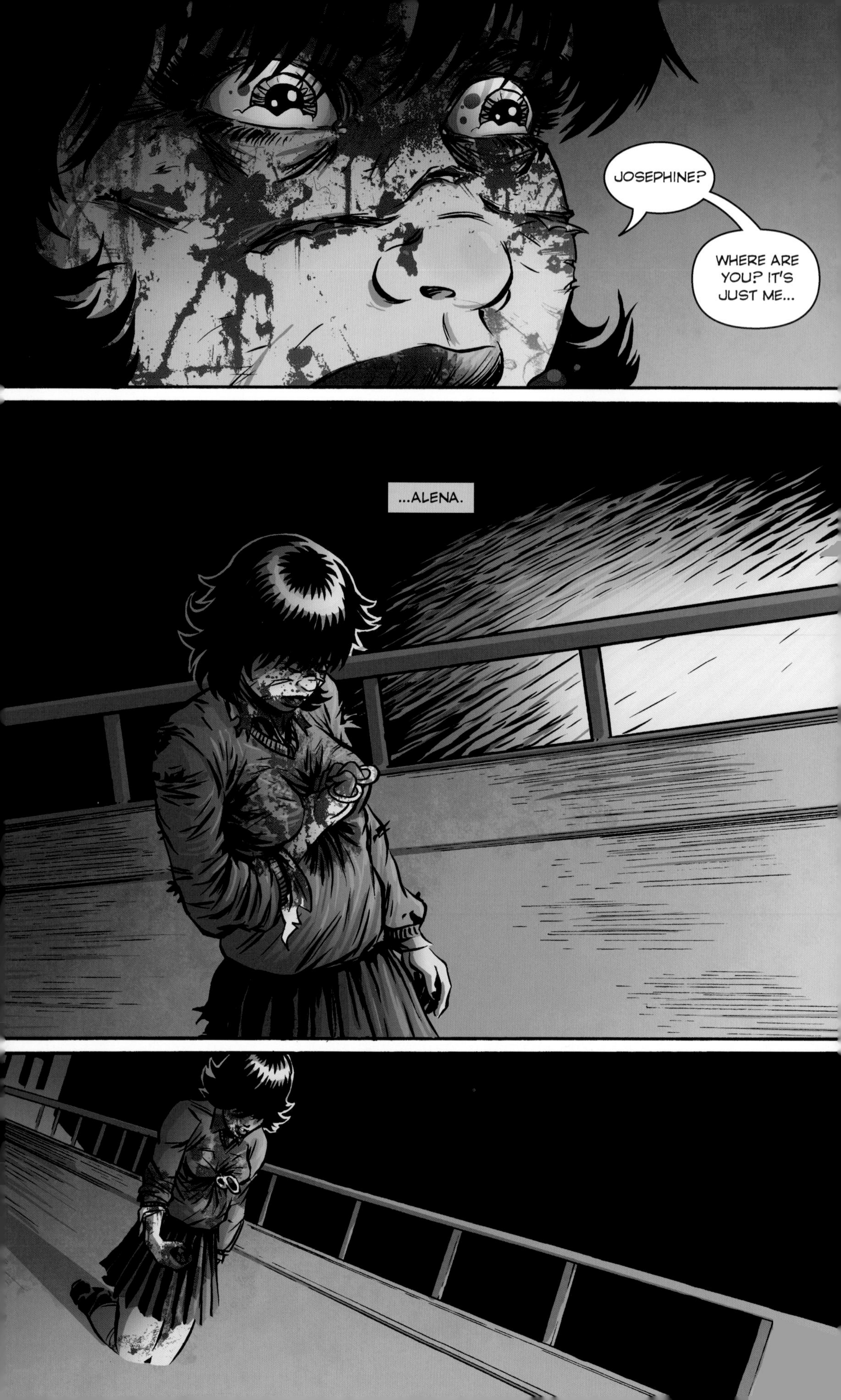
JOSEPHINE?
WHERE ARE YOU? IT'S JUST ME...
...ALENA.

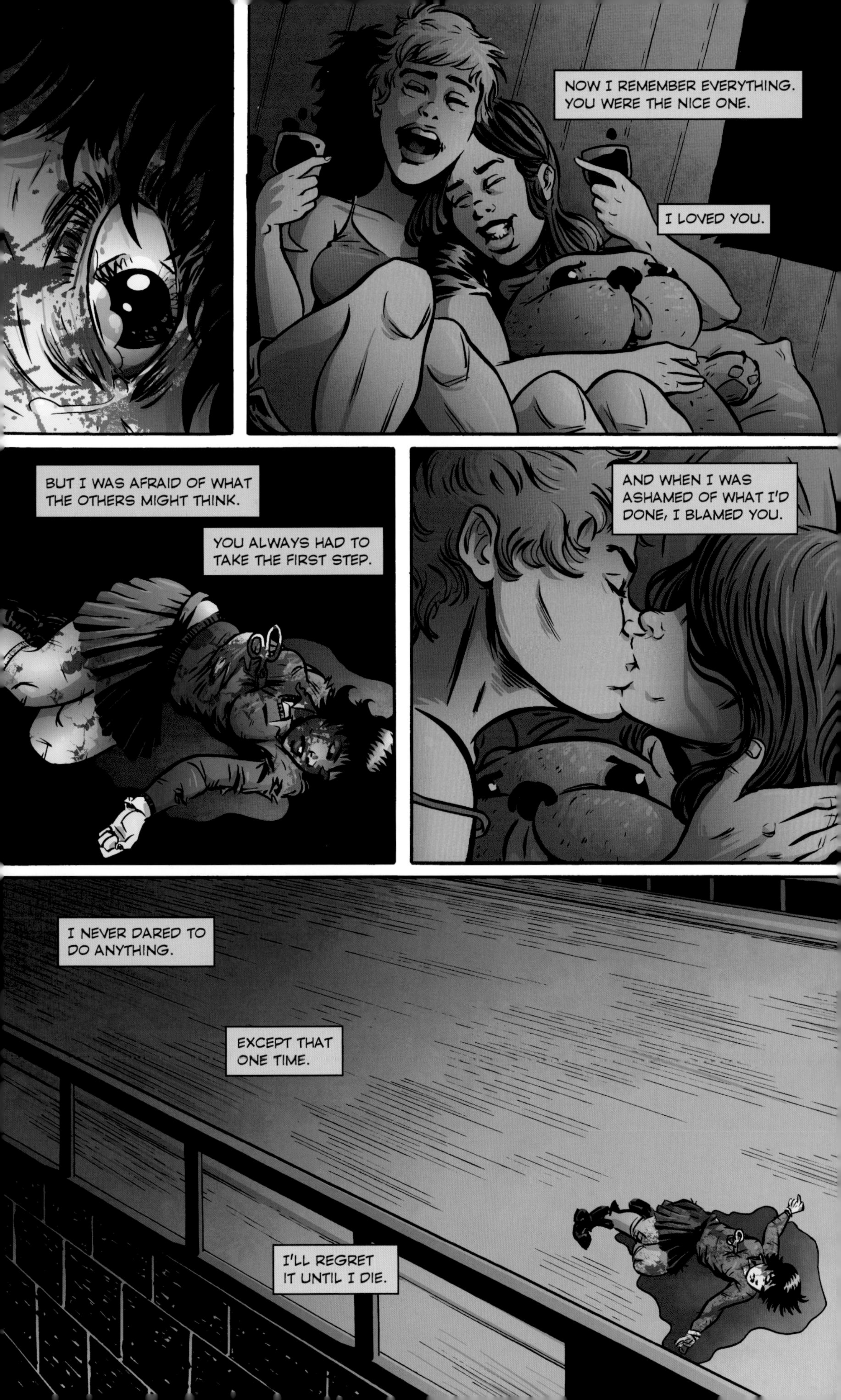
NOW I REMEMBER EVERYTHING. YOU WERE THE NICE ONE.
I LOVED YOU.
BUT I WAS AFRAID OF WHAT THE OTHERS MIGHT THINK.
YOU ALWAYS HAD TO TAKE THE FIRST STEP.
AND WHEN I WAS ASHAMED OF WHAT I'D DONE, I BLAMED YOU.
I NEVER DARED TO DO ANYTHING.
EXCEPT THAT ONE TIME.
I'LL REGRET IT UNTIL I DIE.

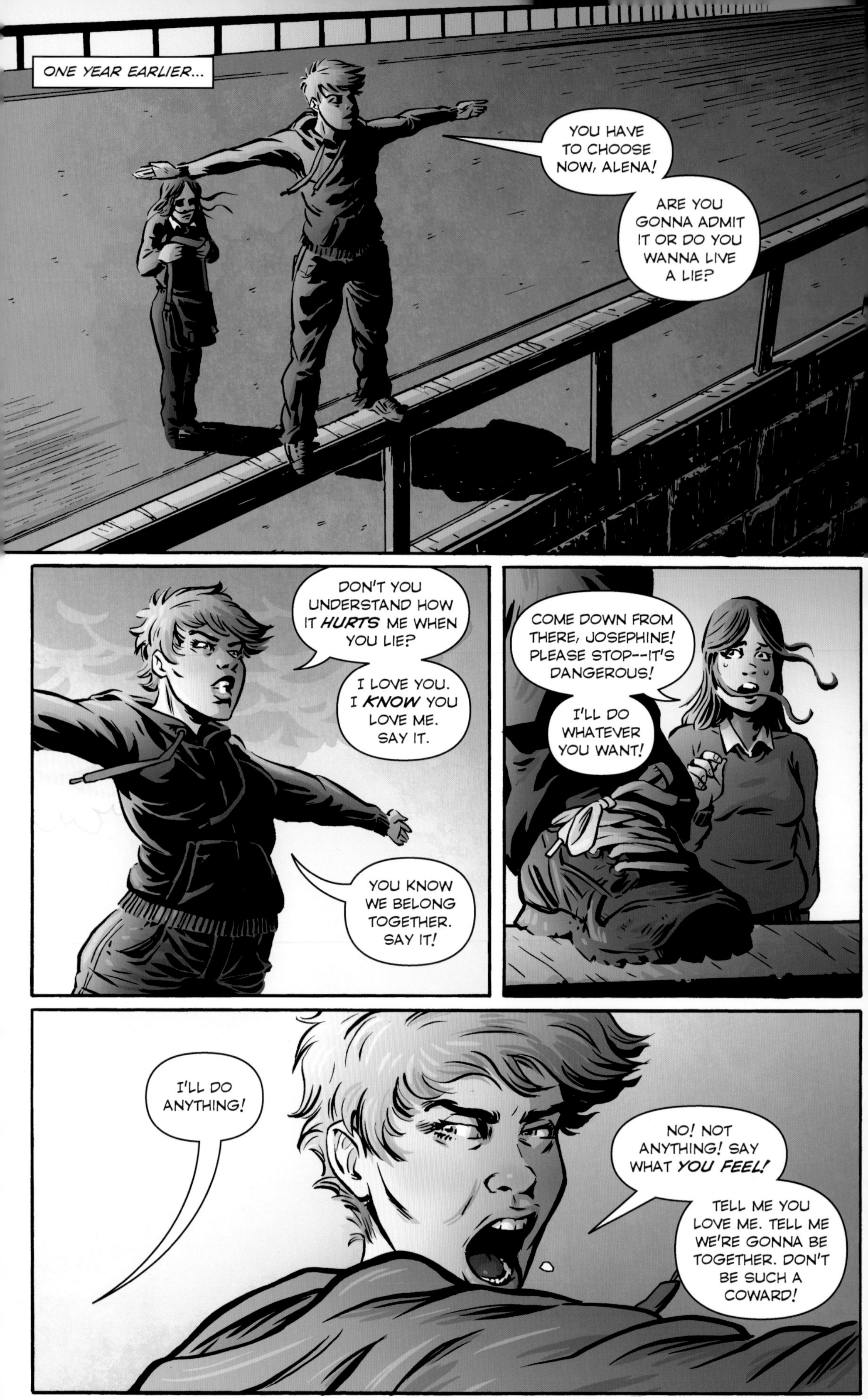
ONE YEAR EARLIER...
YOU HAVE TO CHOOSE NOW, ALENA!
ARE YOU GONNA ADMIT IT OR DO YOU WANNA LIVE A LIE?
DON'T YOU UNDERSTAND HOW IT *HURTS* ME WHEN YOU LIE?
I LOVE YOU. I *KNOW* YOU LOVE ME. SAY IT.
YOU KNOW WE BELONG TOGETHER. SAY IT!
COME DOWN FROM THERE, JOSEPHINE! PLEASE STOP--IT'S DANGEROUS!
I'LL DO WHATEVER YOU WANT!
I'LL DO ANYTHING!
NO! NOT ANYTHING! SAY WHAT *YOU FEEL!*
TELL ME YOU LOVE ME. TELL ME WE'RE GONNA BE TOGETHER. DON'T BE SUCH A COWARD!

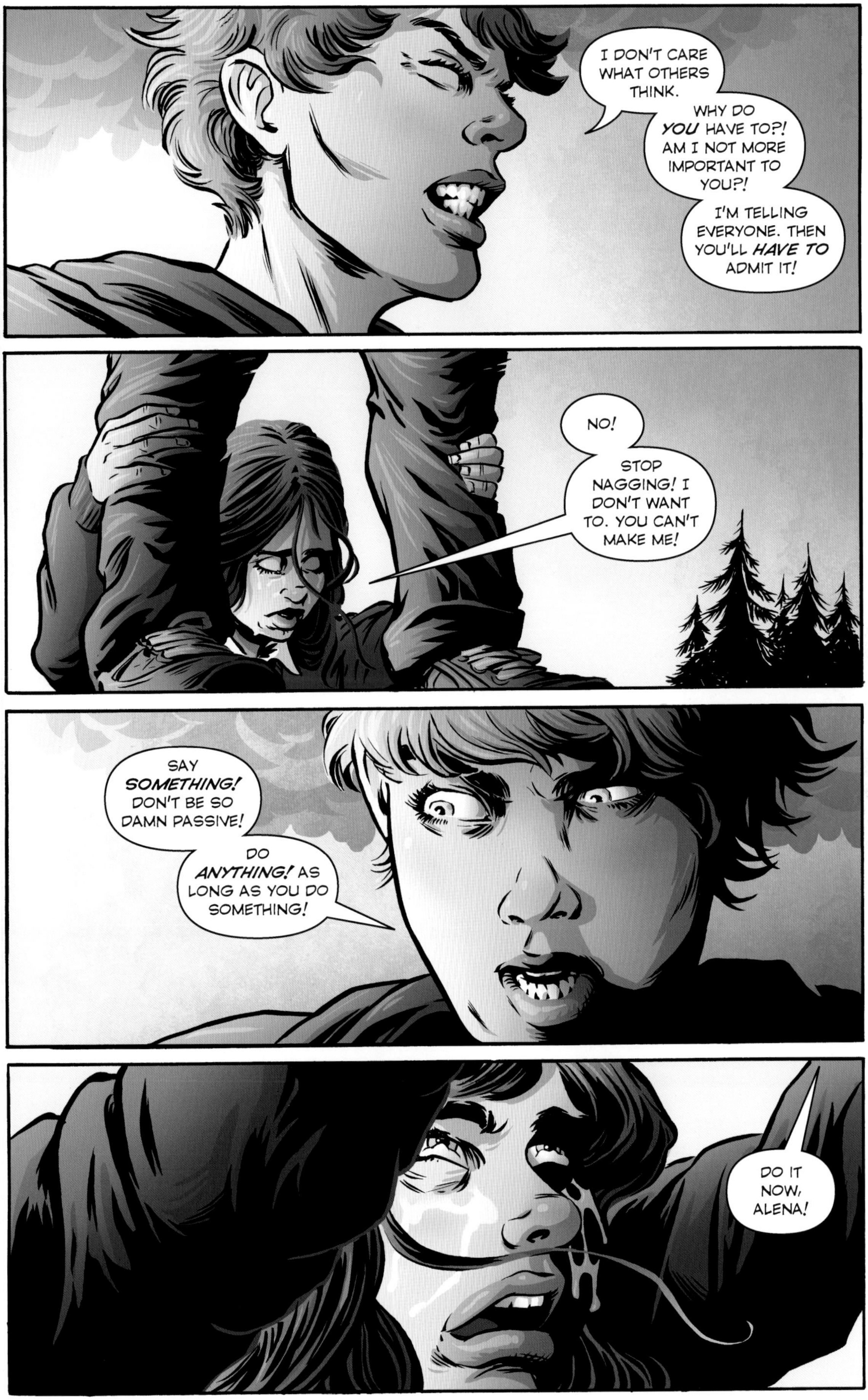
I DON'T CARE WHAT OTHERS THINK.
WHY DO YOU HAVE TO?! AM I NOT MORE IMPORTANT TO YOU?!
I'M TELLING EVERYONE. THEN YOU'LL HAVE TO ADMIT IT!
NO!
STOP NAGGING! I DON'T WANT TO. YOU CAN'T MAKE ME!
SAY SOMETHING! DON'T BE SO DAMN PASSIVE!
DO ANYTHING! AS LONG AS YOU DO SOMETHING!
DO IT NOW, ALENA!

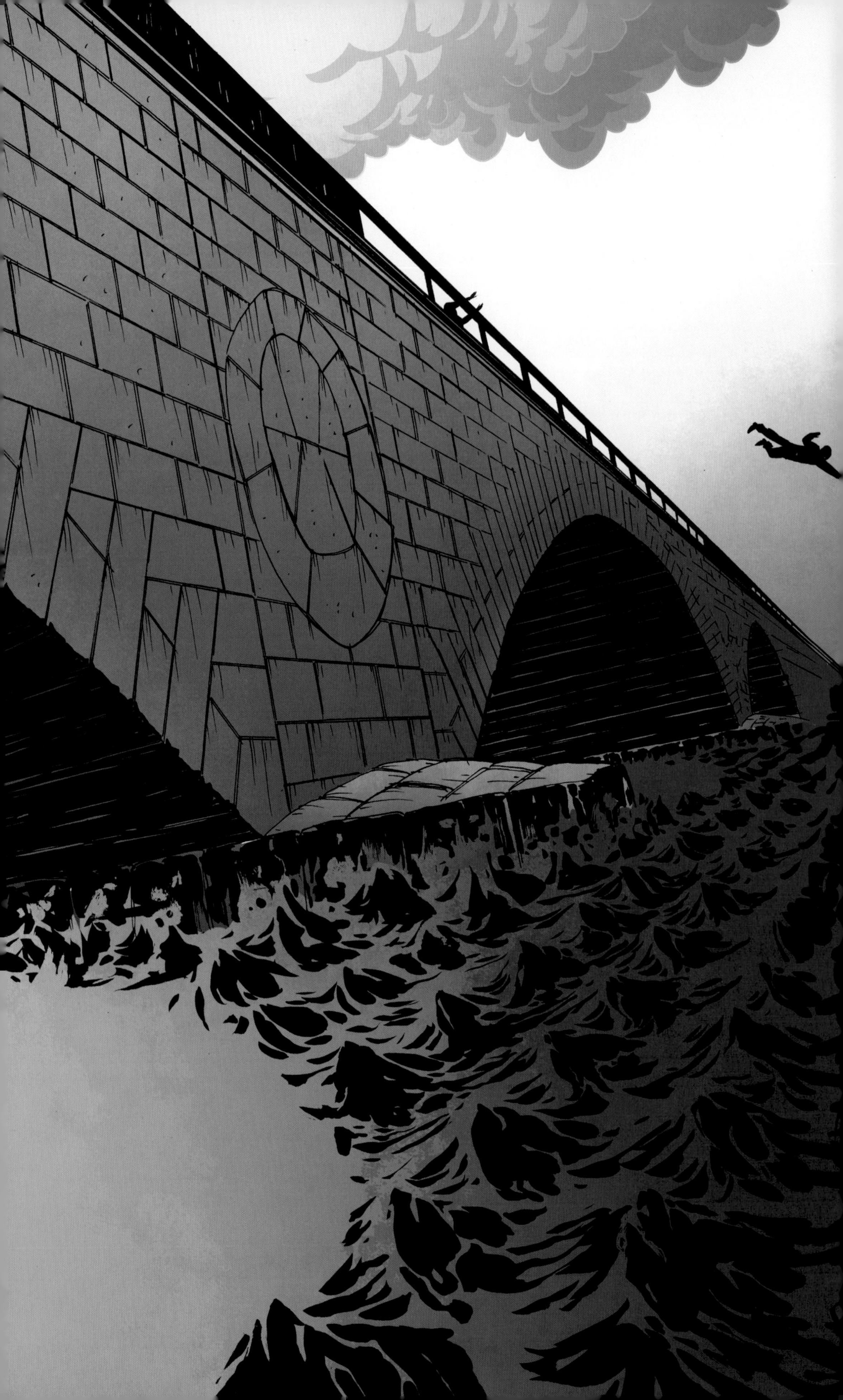

# ALENA THE MOVIE

## Afterword by director Daniel di Grado...

I first came in contact with *Alena* one autumn evening almost four years ago. My friend Mike had asked me if I wanted to participate in a horror movie quiz at the Swedish Film Institute in Stockholm. I said sure and then asked who else would be on our team. Mike said, among others, a comic book artist, Kim W. Andersson.

After the quiz, I searched for Kim's comics, and I immediately loved what I found. There was a dark, romantic vein in everything he had done that appealed to me deeply. Especially the humor in his black depictions of love in *The Complete Love Hurts*. There was a tone in the comics that played on and referenced the films and books that I loved when I was younger. And the fact that he is an amazing artist did not make the reading any less enjoyable.

That's when I found Kim's graphic novel *Alena*, with its confused and strong "heroine." It was so liberating to be swallowed up by this story which balanced the fantastic with the everyday evil that always exists in our surroundings. It was filled with pain and sudden death, but also maturity, responsibility, and love. It was impossible not to fall in love with—and be horrified by—Alena's story.

About six months later, Kim and I ran into each other again at a party and started talking about how great it would be if we could make a movie of the book, and we began to dream. But not much more happened. As it often goes when you sit and dream, other things intervened. But *Alena* refused to let go of me. Then one spring day I called Kim and asked if we could make it happen. To my delight, he said yes.

After that everything went very fast. The screenplay was written, funding was secured, and roles were added. Suddenly we had a film. It was something different, a sort of independent twin of the comic, which is often the case when transferring one art form to another.

But I think we were faithful to the original. It has the same story and theme. I'm delighted to hear that Dark Horse Comics is publishing the graphic novel in the US.

When someone tells me that they have not seen the movie *Jaws*, I am envious of what they have ahead of them: a treasure that one would like to have unseen in order to be abducted again into its wonderful imagination. I feel the same way about *Alena*.

I hope and believe that Alena's time here with us is not over and that she speaks to many out there. So with this release, I hope more people discover Alena and take her home. Just as I once did.

So to all of you who are reading *Alena* for the first time, I can only say I'm jealous and congratulations!

And, if you are curious, we finished third in the horror movie quiz.

DANIEL DI GRADO
JUNE 2015

Daniel di Grado directs Amalia Holm as our heroine Alena and Rebecka Nyman as her best friend Josephine.

# . . . But the last word is mine.

I created this comic book, I made up all the characters, I let them suffer the happiness and sadness, love and heartbreak, joy and fear—and I love them all. Then someone came along who wanted to borrow it all to make a movie. To surrender your story in this way requires great confidence.

Confidence is exactly what I had in director Daniel di Grado and producer Alexander Rönnberg. Since day one they have worked hard—first to get to make this film and then even harder when it actually happened.

I had the privilege to be involved all the way—when we worked on the script, chose actors, picked out the costumes, makeup, and locations. I knew all the stages of the process from making my comics, but this time I got to build the world with a collection of incredibly talented people.

When it was time to begin filming, I took a step back to let Daniel realize his vision, but he allowed me to look over his shoulder. Of course I had to drive out to the set a few times and perhaps make a small cameo. Yes, I am the shopkeeper who runs after Josephine at the beginning of the film.

It takes an incredible number of people to make a movie, and everyone involved was absolutely amazing. When you see the movie, promise to stay seated and watch the credits and spare a thought for each person in the long list. They were indispensable in making this film as beautiful, sad, and scary as it is.

Here and on the following pages are pictures from the set with commentary by me and a few collages of photos from behind the scenes.

KIM W. ANDERSSON
JUNE 2015

Ekensberg, the magical place where our romantic horror drama unfolds. In reality, it is Skokloster Castle, and it's absolutely magical in the autumn.

I remember the amazing feeling when Amalia Holm first stood in front of me as Alena. A character I'd created several years earlier was now real, made of flesh and blood.

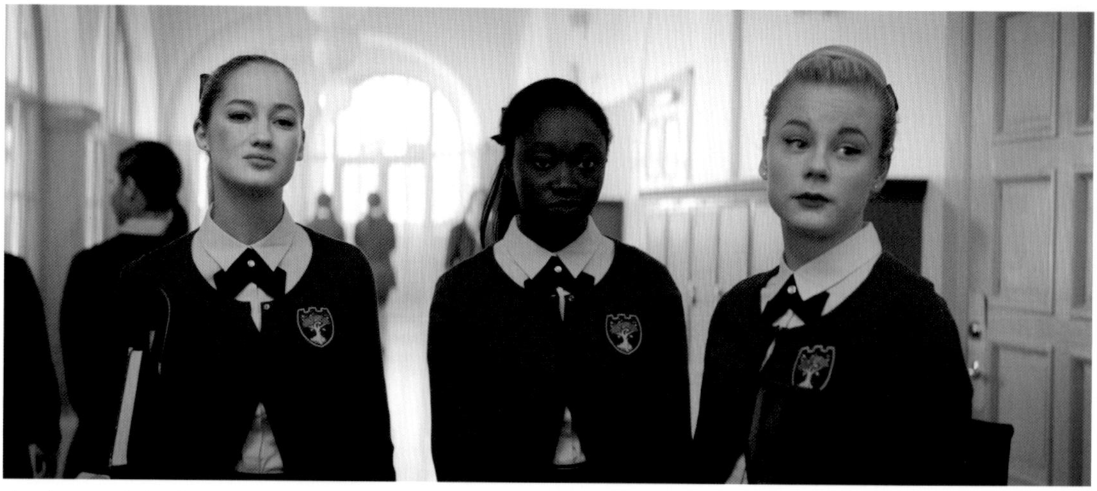

Ekensberg is ruled with an iron fist by the lacrosse girls, who are as beautiful as they are dangerous. Fanny Klefelt as Cecilia, Marie Senghore as Tessan, and Molly Nutley as Alena's main tormentor Philippa.

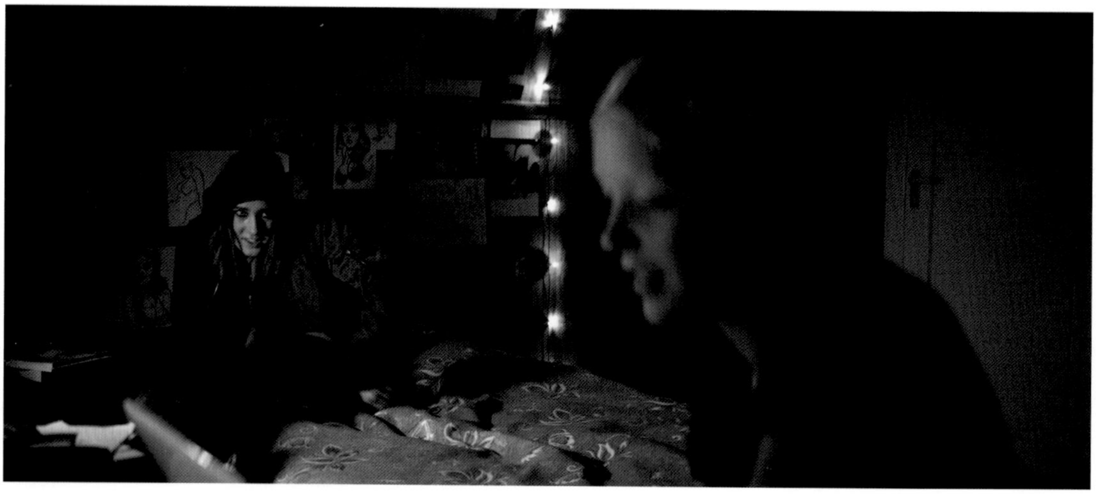

Rebecka Nyman as Josephine, Alena's best friend in life and in death. Rebecka is perhaps the one that suffered the most during filming—everything from getting made up into a monster for hours to being suspended from a crane over a bridge.

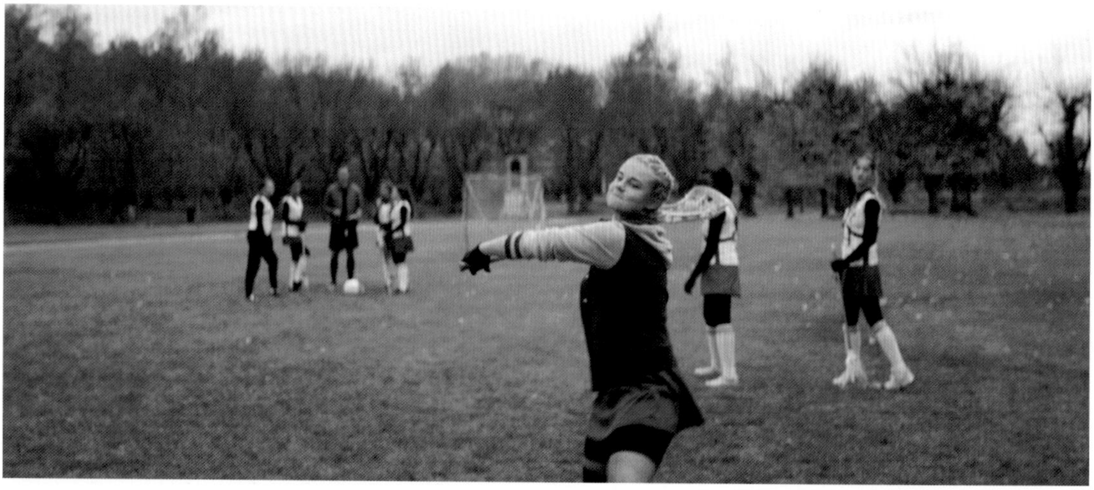

The reason the girls play lacrosse in the book is just that I think it looks cool. It's a tough sport with stylish uniforms. Before filming began, we had the actors train with the national lacrosse team and learn to play for real. But Molly had played earlier when she went to school in England and thus had a head start.

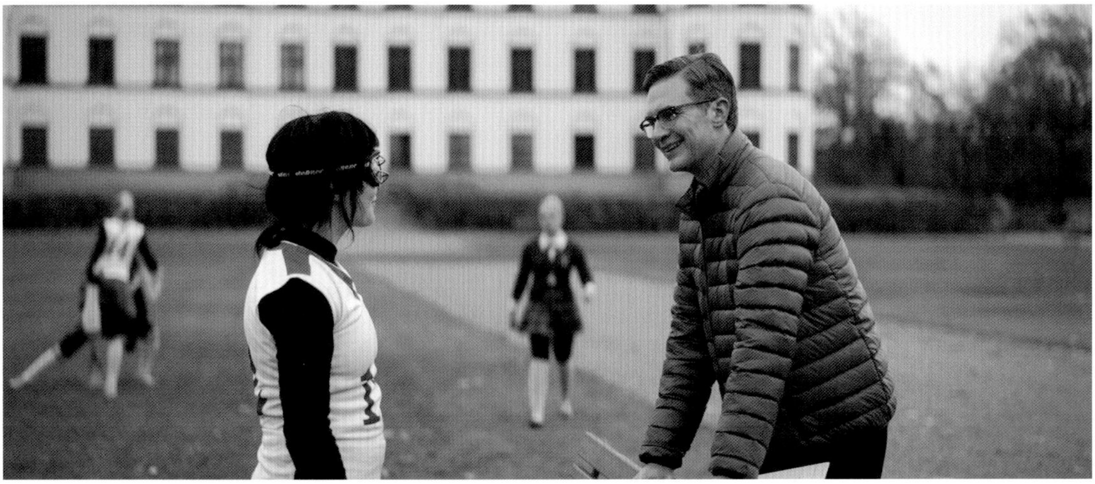

The only male in the entire school is the lacrosse coach, played by the great Johan Ehn. Being alone among all these mean girls, he is unsure how he should behave, but he likes Alena immediately.

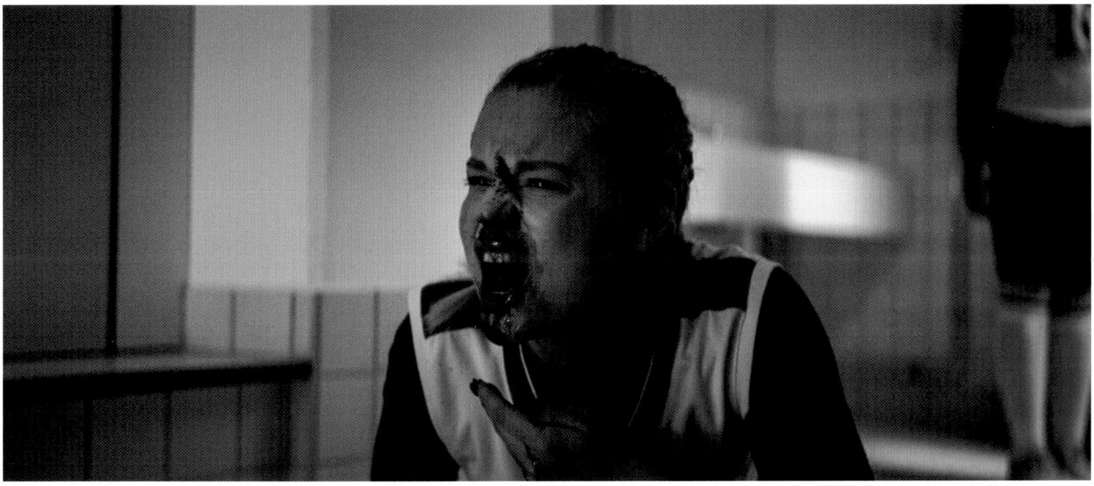

I can go on forever about how awesome it is to see your comic panels come to life. It is so easy to draw the worst thing you can imagine, especially when you have the idea that someone should have to suffer. Here is a clear example of my idea coming to real life; compare to the end of chapter 3 (*pages 44–48*).

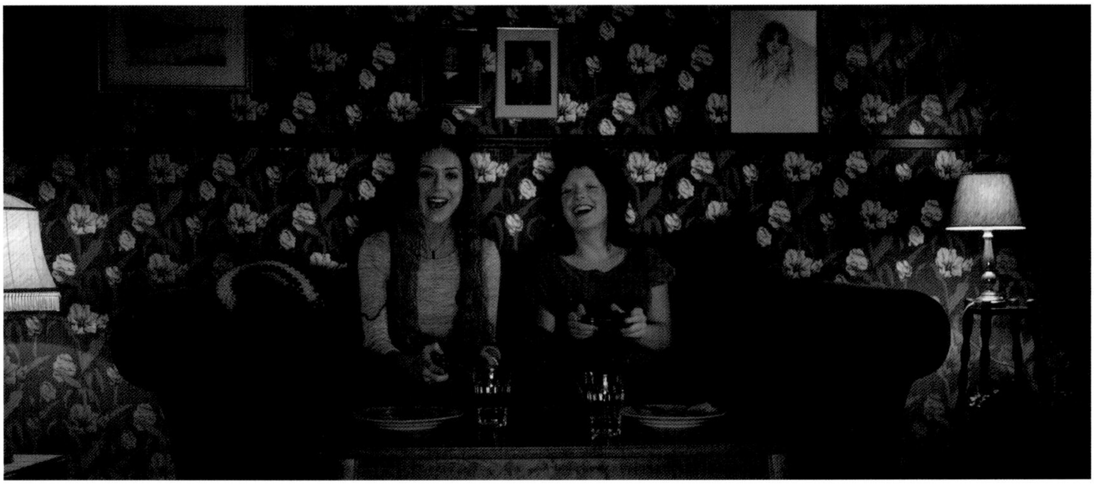

One of the biggest changes we made from the graphic novel for the film was to make Ekensberg an all-girls school, and with it we turned Fabian into Fabienne, played by Felice Jankell. It felt very obvious when the suggestion was made, a natural update of the story.

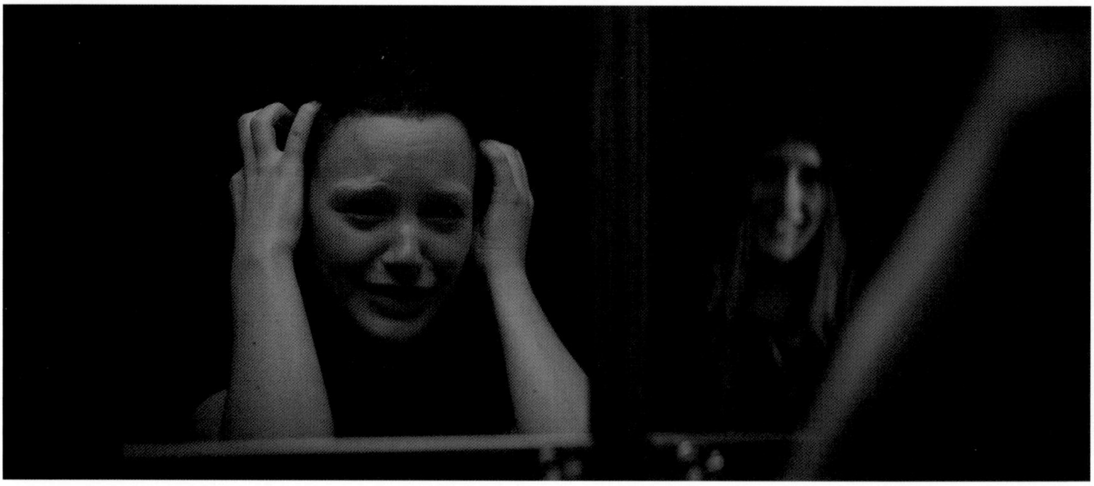

It is not easy for anyone to be a teenager, but I still think that Alena is a little worse off than most of us. She suffers hell in school every day and only has one friend to lean on for support. One single friend . . . who is dead.

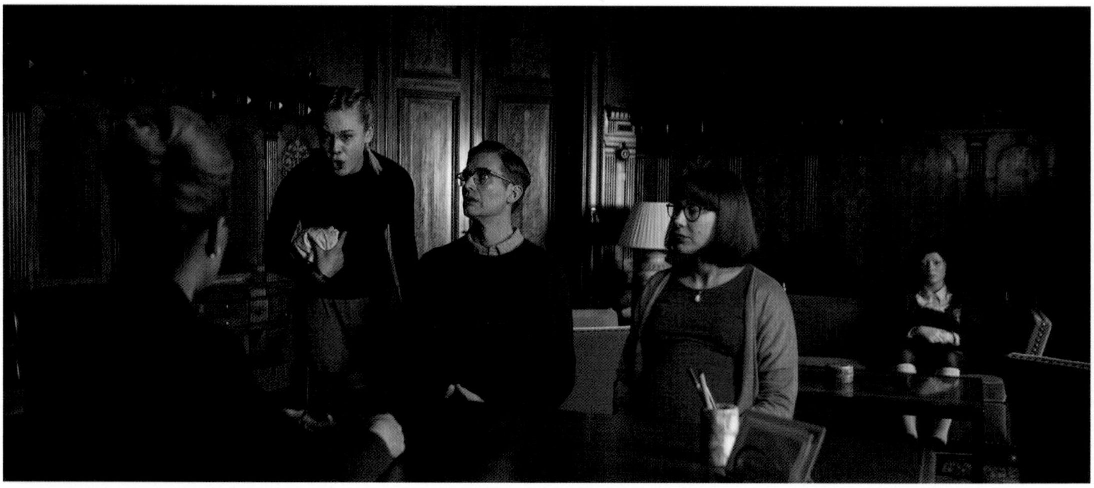

From the left we have the headmistress, played by Helena af Sandeberg, Molly, Johan, and the counselor, portrayed by Ulrika Ellemark. I am particularly pleased with how Ulrika embodied the counselor; she is nearly identical to the comic original.

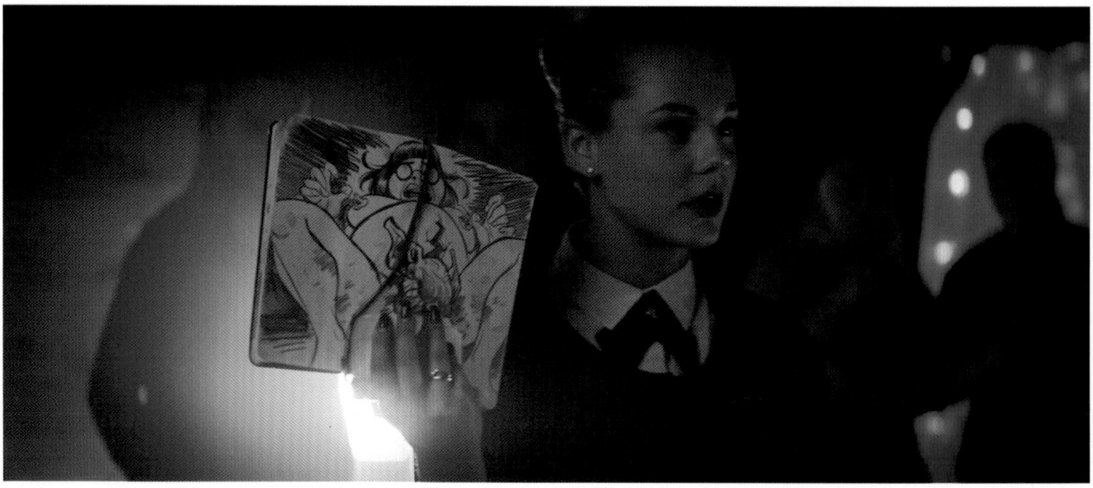

It was very exciting to see Daniel using colors in a way similar to the graphic novel, which is evident in this scene. See chapter 7 for comparison. Here you can also see one of Alena's drawings from her sketchbook, a caricature of the poor counselor giving birth to a monstrous creature. Of course I got to draw all the artwork in the film.

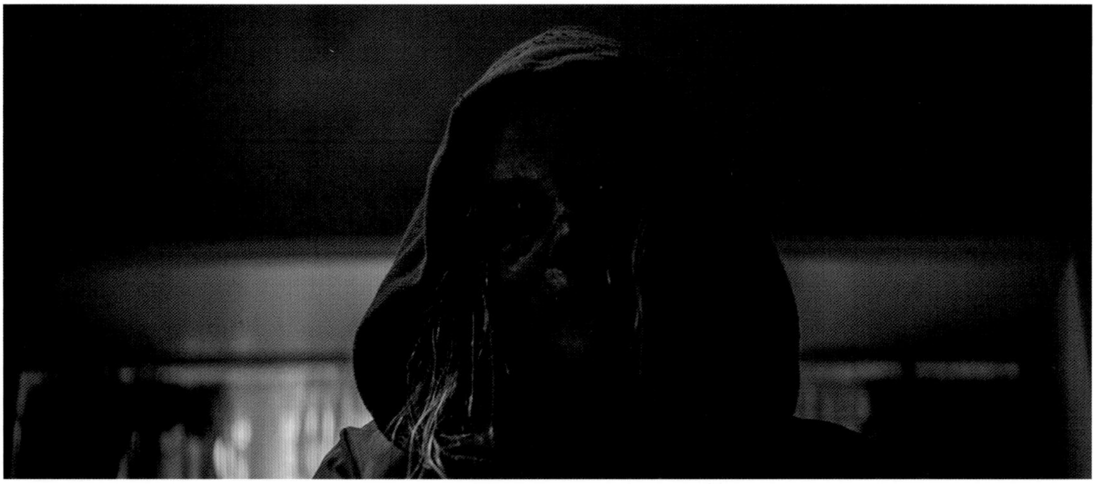

Josephine's death mask was designed by the Oscar-nominated Love Larson, one of Sweden's top artists when it comes to makeup effects. There were many talented people who wanted to be involved in the making of *Alena*. Real horror is not often done in Swedish cinema.

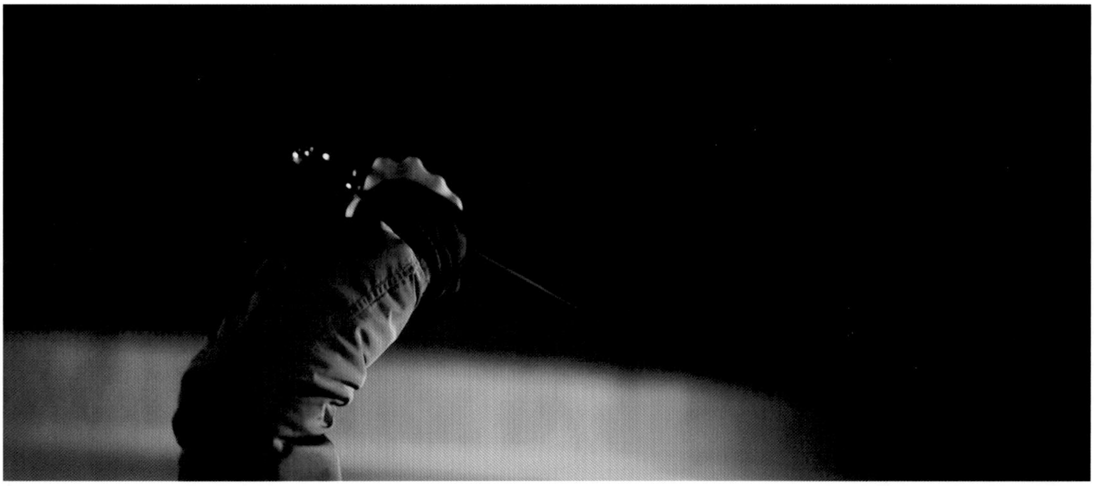

Some images from the film are very similar to the panels in the graphic novel. No one is happier about this than I am. For example, compare this image with the end of chapter 5 (*page 73*).

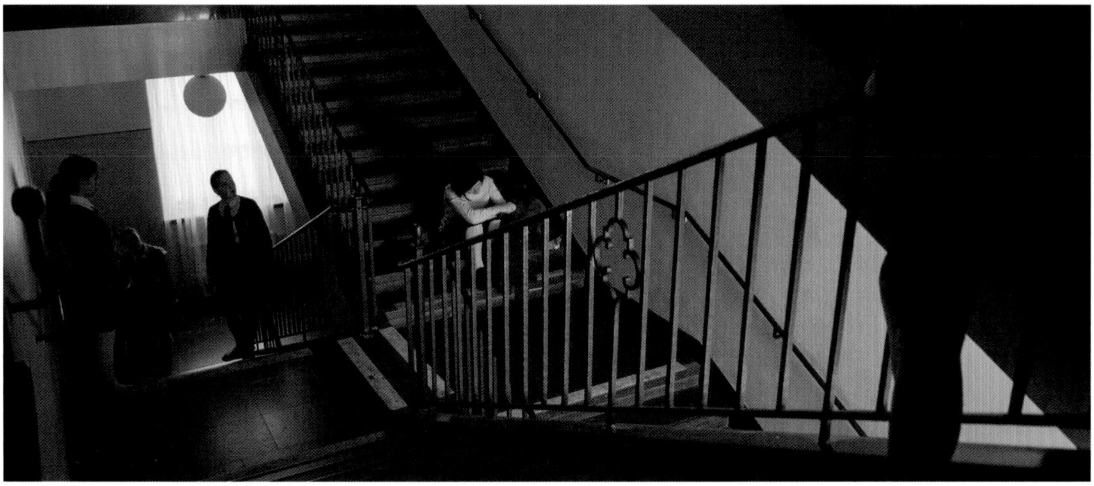

The set was filled with amazing environments like this. Daniel and cinematographer Simon Olsson utilized them fully and created wonderful compositions. Then we filled our school with talented extras in school uniforms—clearly a winning concept.

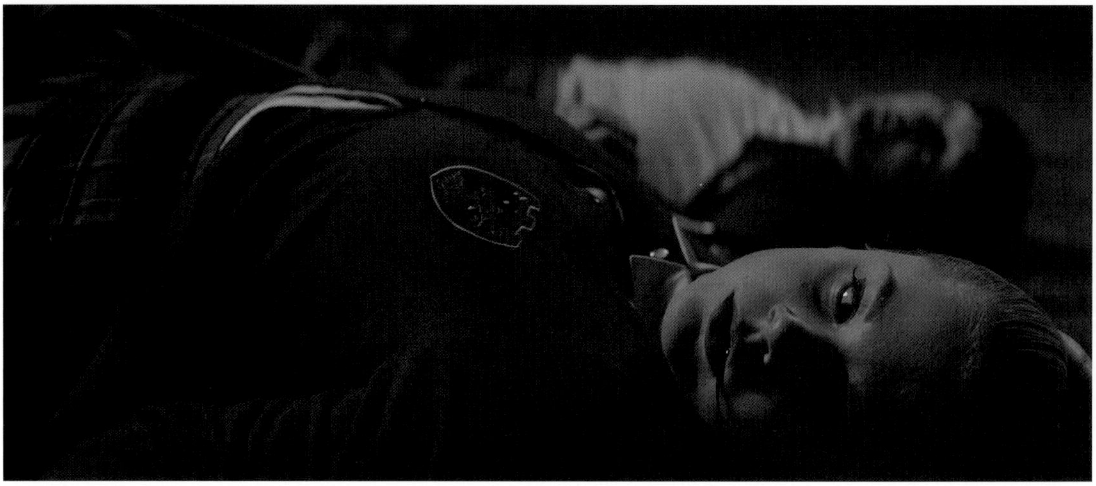

Not many of the girls stay with us until the end of our story. One by one they are killed, in various ways. Here we see Philippa, who has suffered from a pair of scissors used in an unconventional way. Two Polish experts in mechanical special effects helped us with this, Janusz Stpiczynski and Waldemar Zachoszcz from the studio Złudzenia i Marzenia.

They built a rig that allowed the scissors to slide in a precise orbit and splash blood in a glorious way. This created the illusion of the brutal murder.

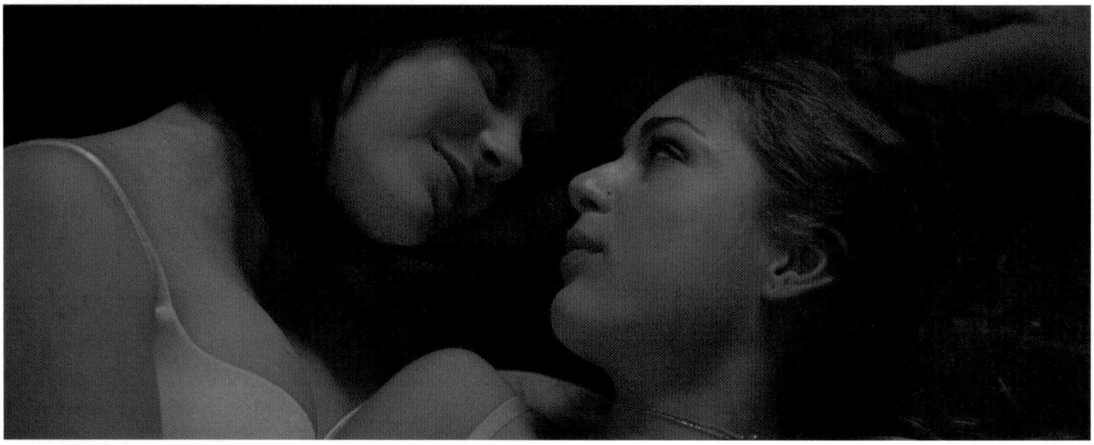

You have to weigh the terrible things with love and romance. How else do you cope with all the blood and violence? But true romance never ends happily; true love always hurts terribly. In my comics, in any case.

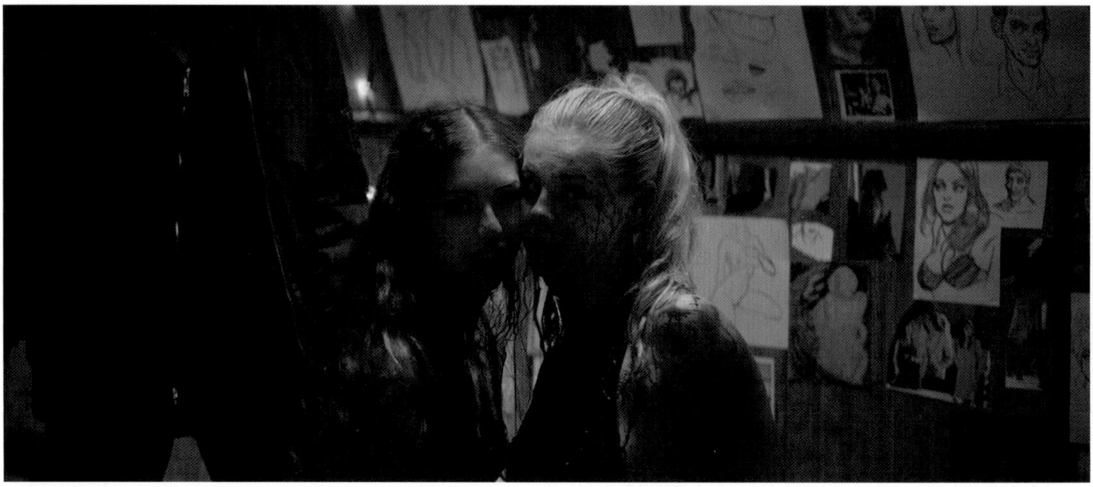

The dream sequence at the end of chapter 4 was what I looked forward to most when making the film. Here it was something completely new, but still the same—which one can say about the whole film, actually. A new, updated version of my beloved graphic novel with real blood instead of ink.

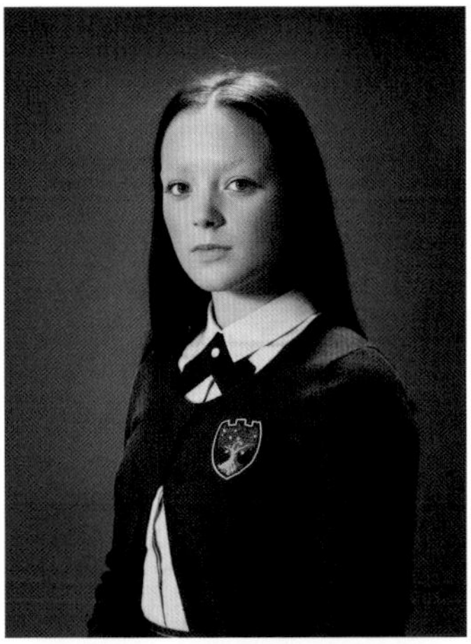
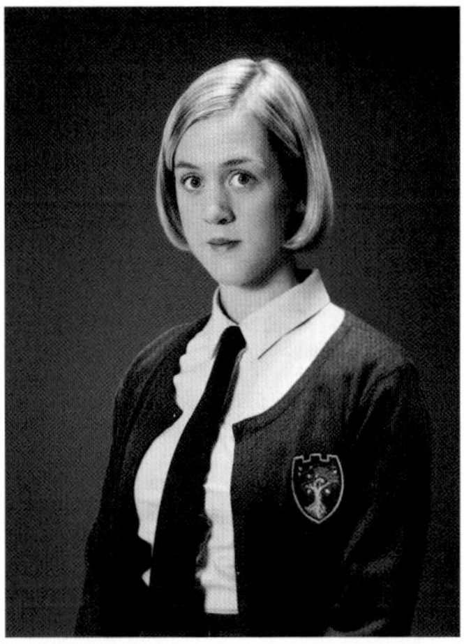
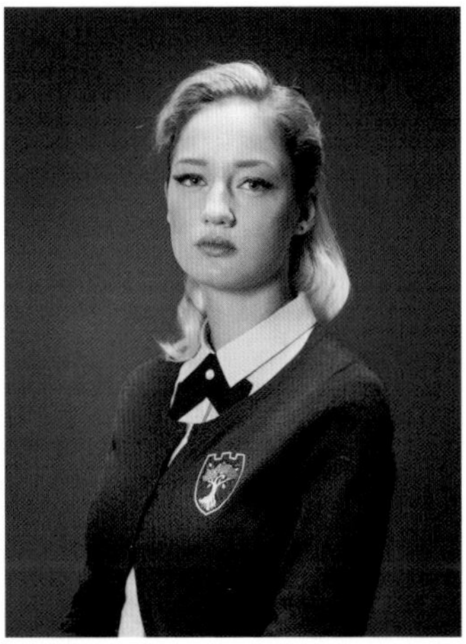
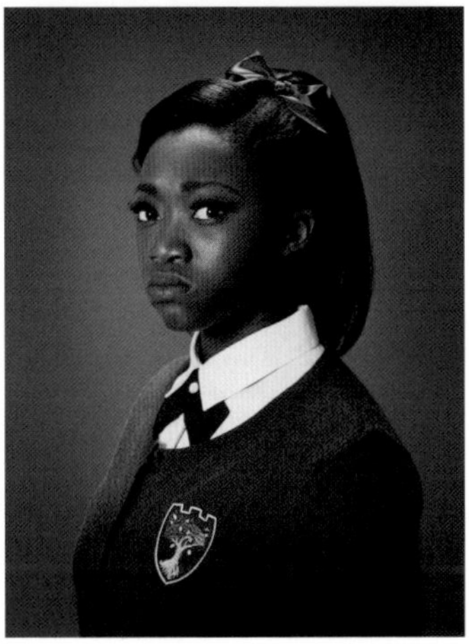
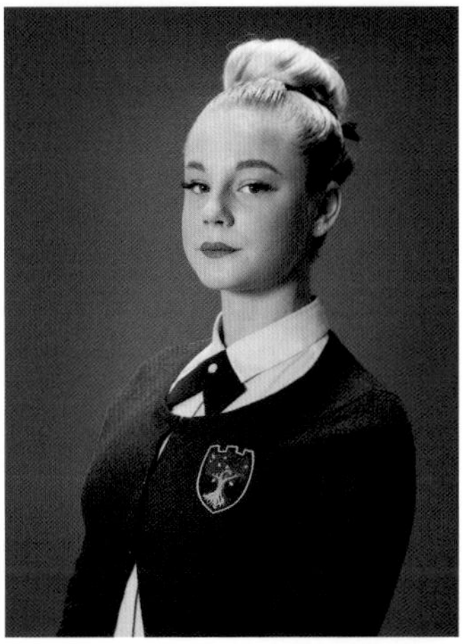
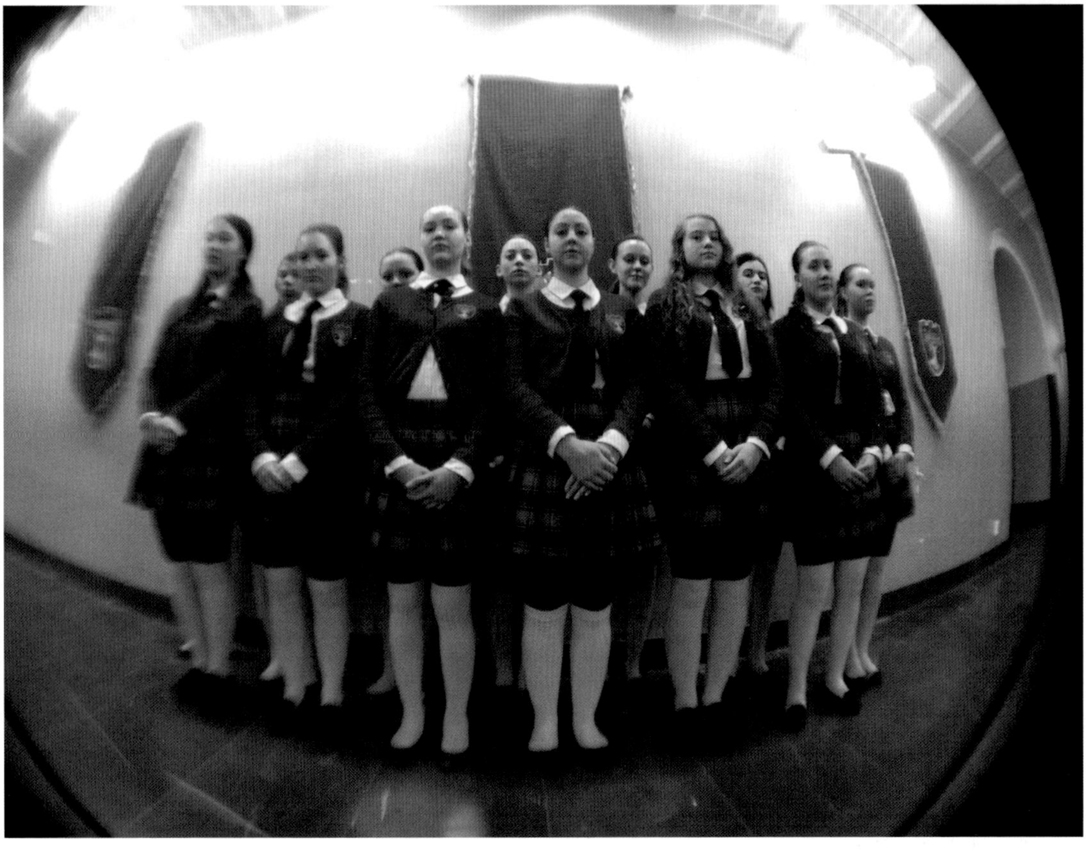

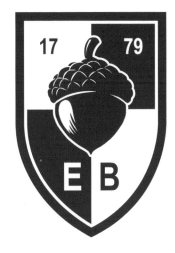

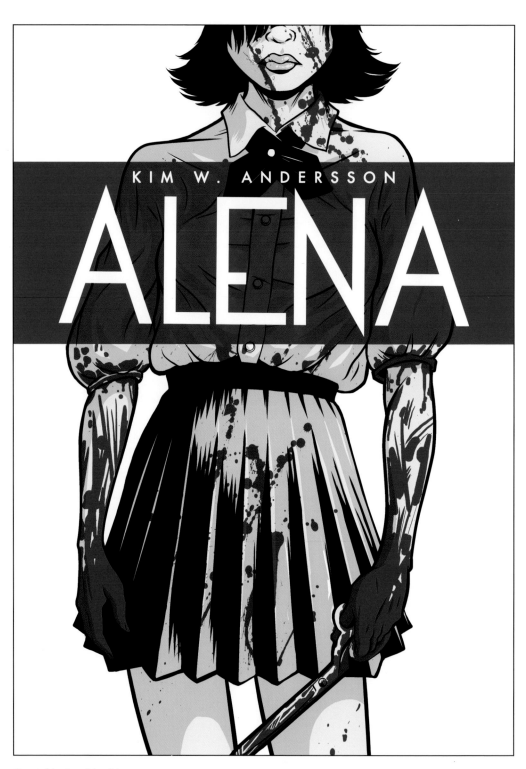

Cover of the Swedish edition.

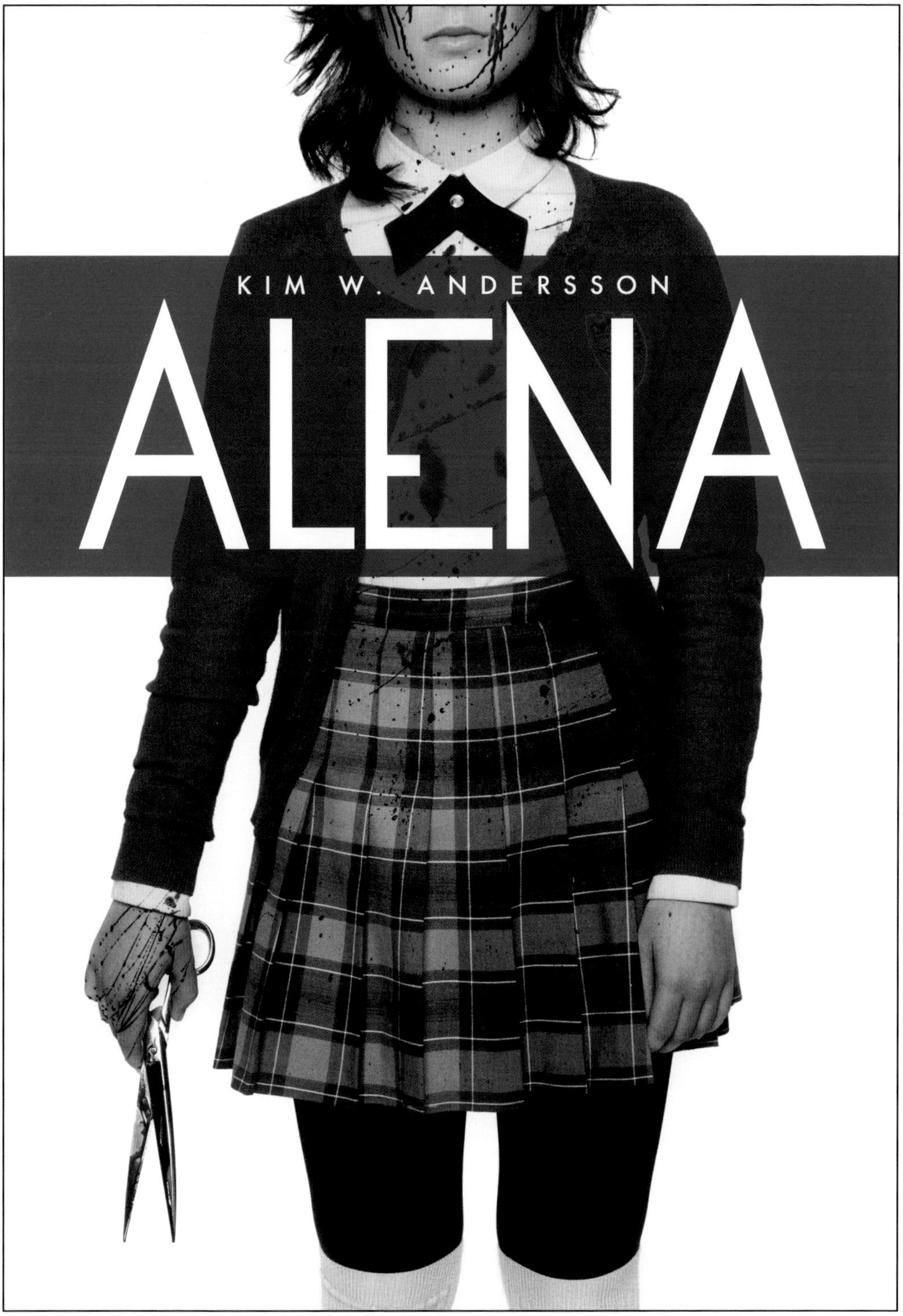
KIM W. ANDERSSON
ALENA

ALEXA

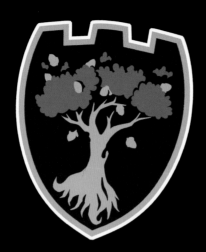

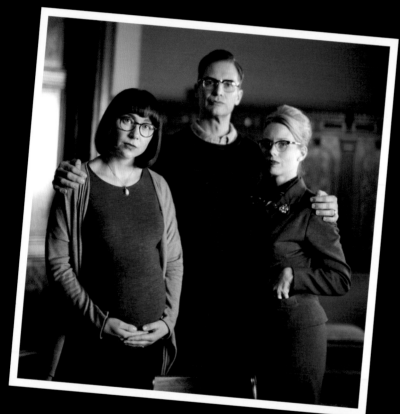

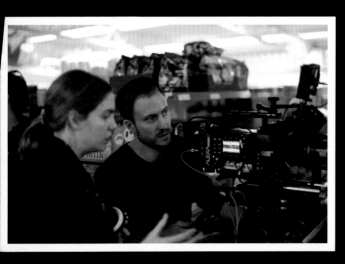

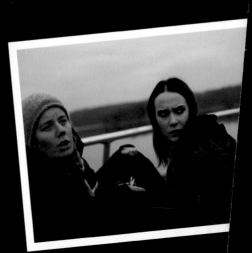

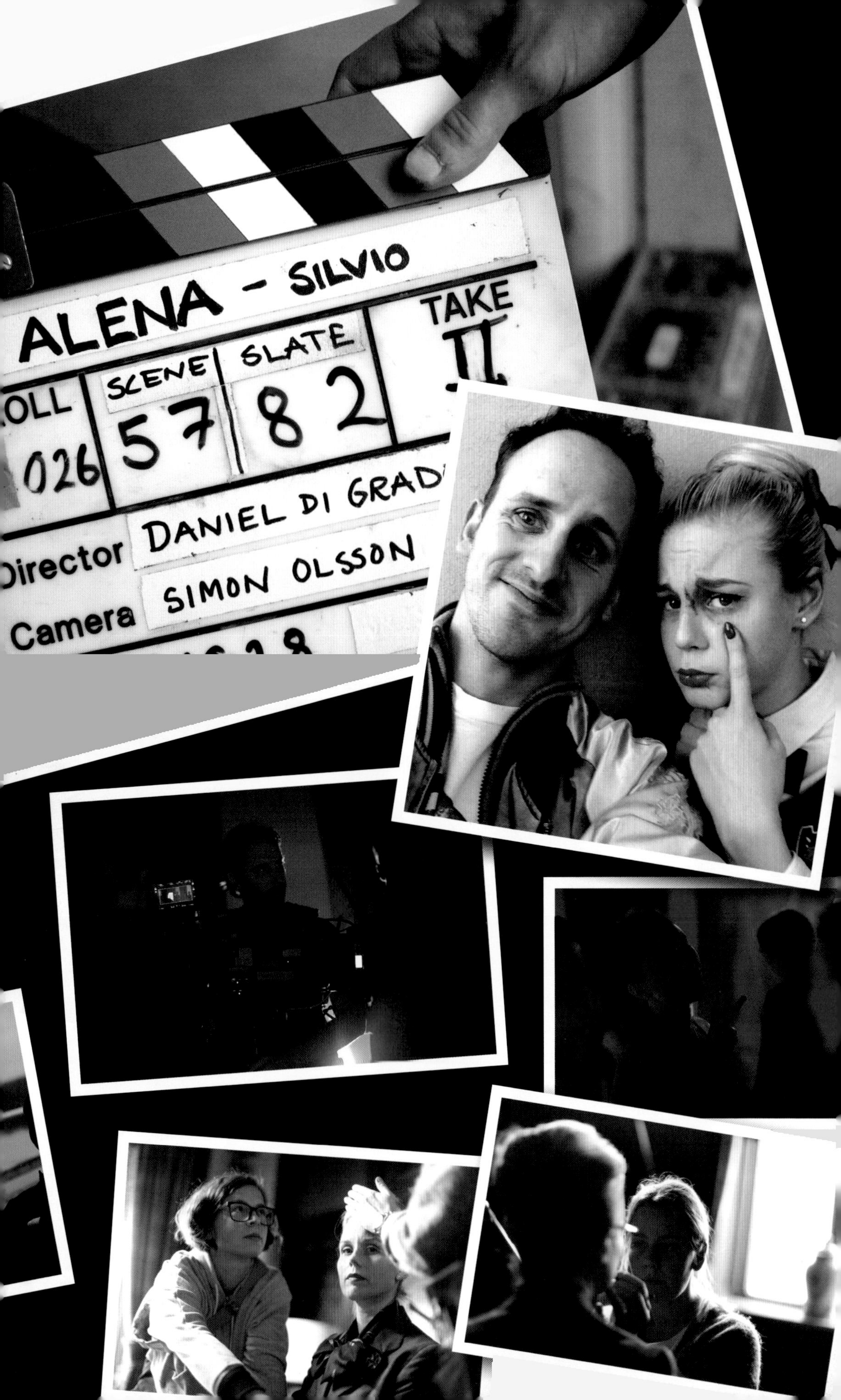
ALENA - SILVIO
TAKE
SCENE
SLATE
OLL
026
57
82
DANIEL DI GRAD
Director
SIMON OLSSON
Camera

ALENA

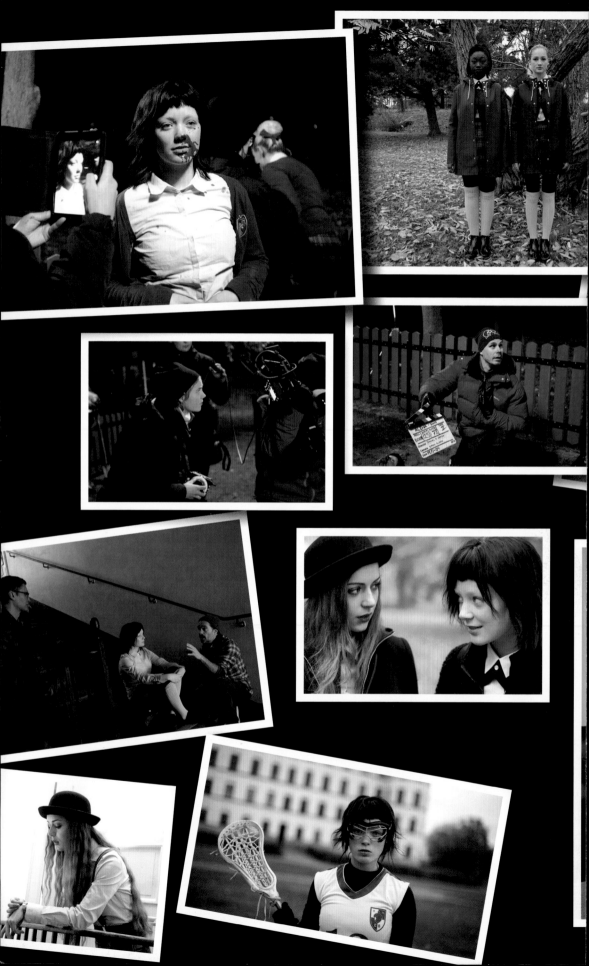

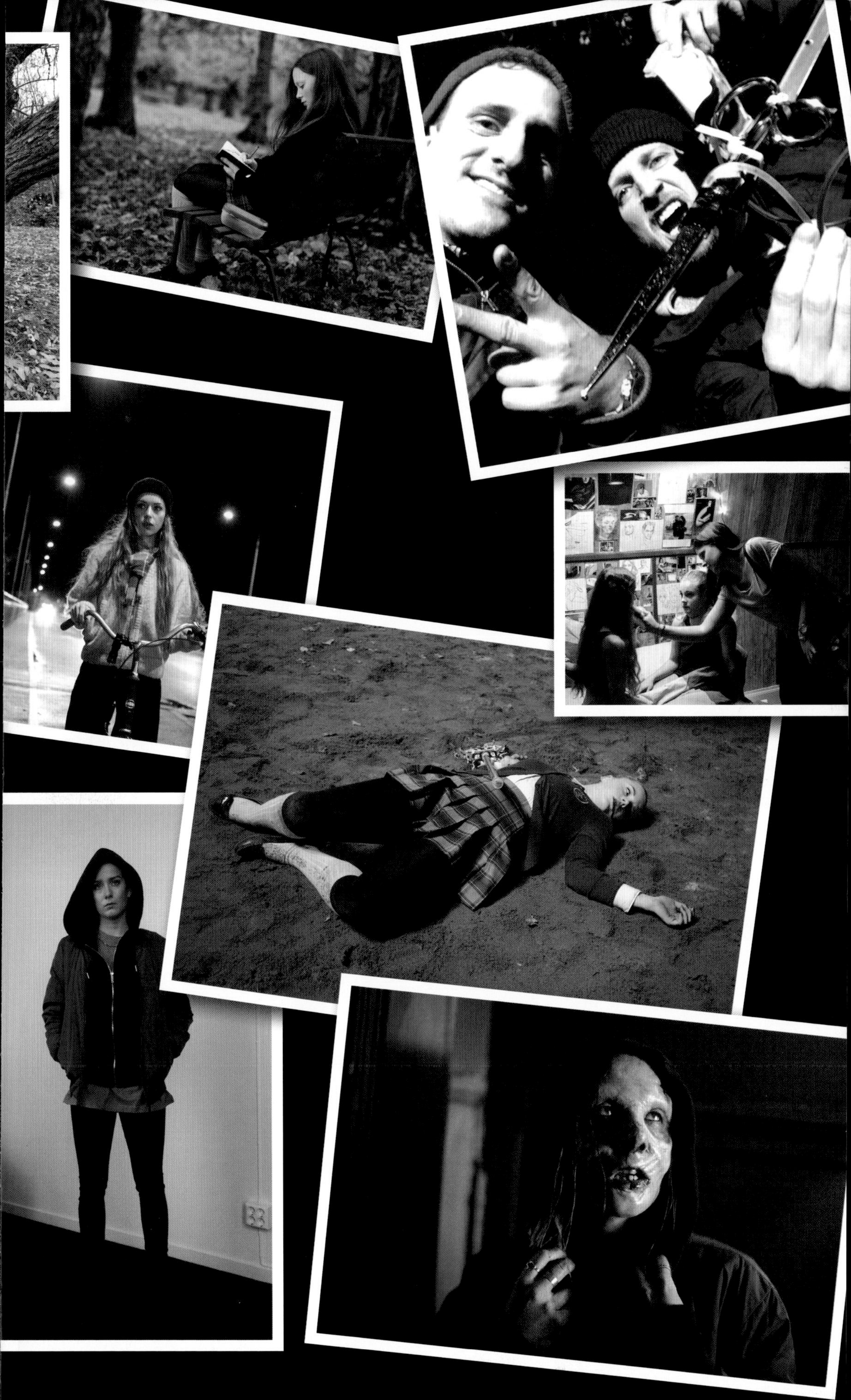

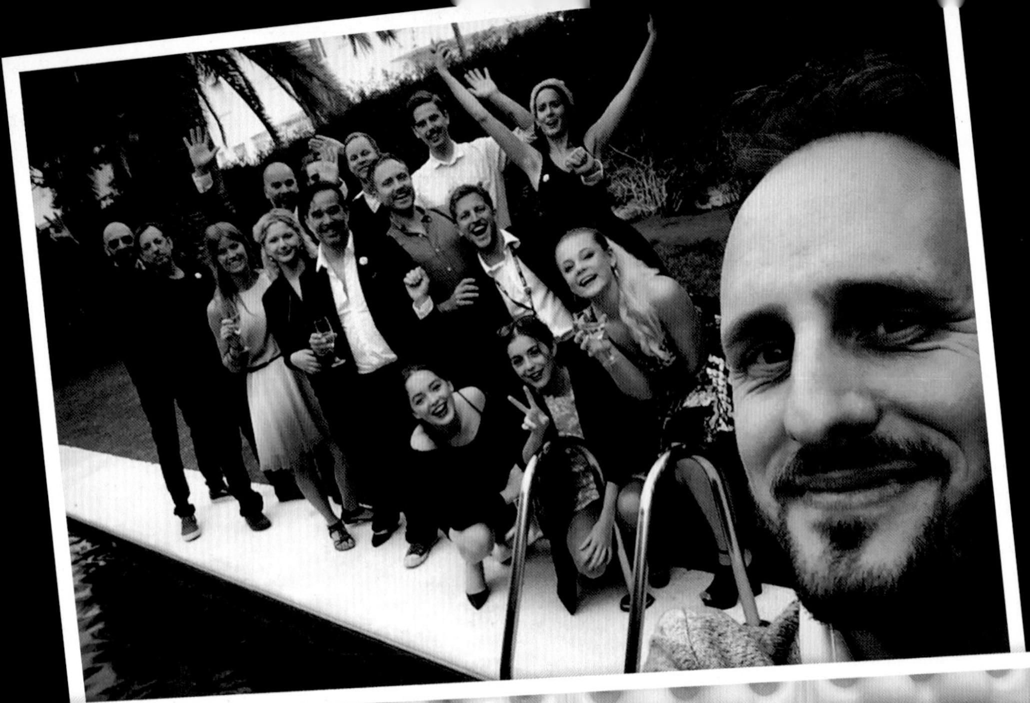

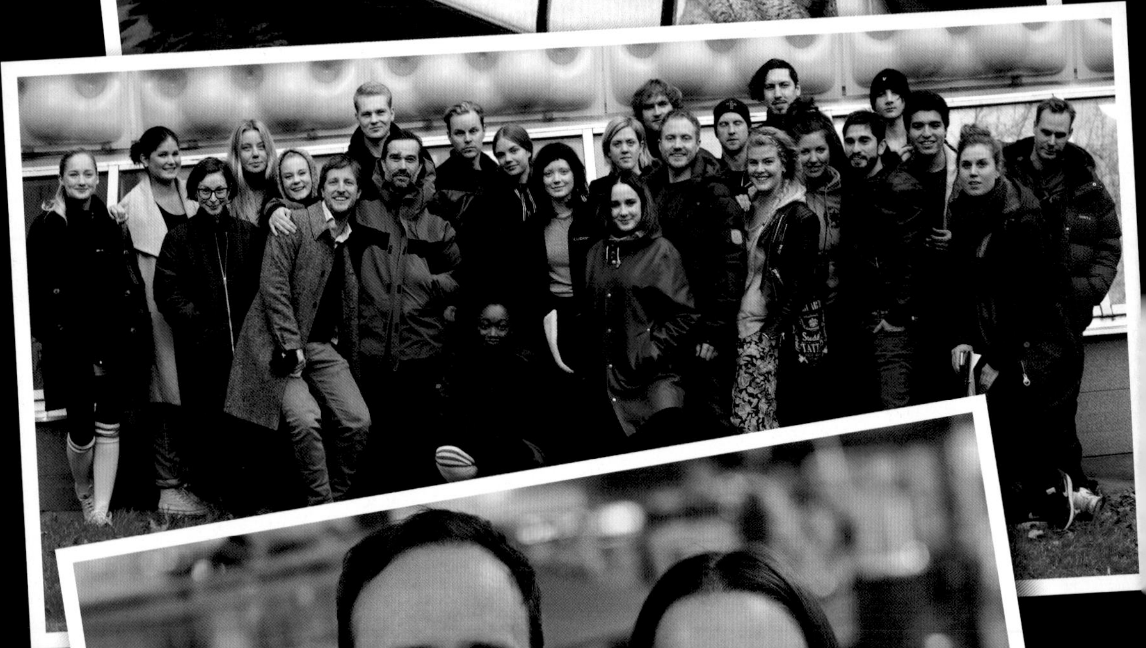

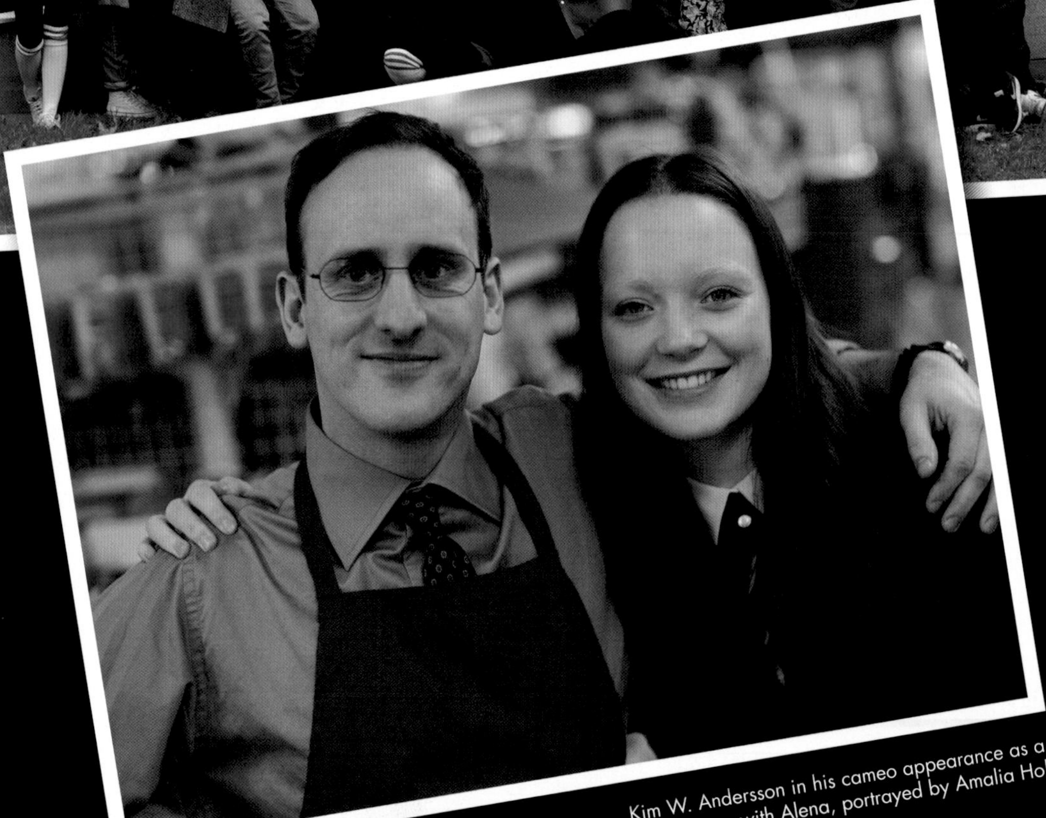

Kim W. Andersson in his cameo appearance as a shopkeeper, with Alena, portrayed by Amalia Holm.

KIM W. ANDERSSON
SANDY TANAKA

Digital Art Technician
CHRISTINA McKENZIE

Neil Hankerson Executive Vice President • Tom Weddle Chief Financial Officer • Randy Stradley Vice President of Publishing • Michael Martens Vice President of Book Trade Sales • Matt Parkinson Vice President of Marketing • David Scroggy Vice President of Product Development • Dale LaFountain Vice President of Information Technology • Cara Niece Vice President of Production and Scheduling • Nick McWhorter Vice President of Media Licensing • Ken Lizzi General Counsel • Dave Marshall Editor in Chief • Davey Estrada Editorial Director • Scott Allie Executive Senior Editor • Chris Warner Senior Books Editor • Cary Grazzini Director of Print and Development • Lia Ribacchi Art Director • Mark Bernardi Director of Digital Publishing • Michael Gombos Director of International Publishing and Licensing

Published by Dark Horse Books
A division of Dark Horse Comics, Inc.
10956 SE Main Street
Milwaukie, OR 97222

DarkHorse.com
International Licensing: 503-905-2377

To find a comics shop in your area, call the Comic Shop Locator Service toll-free at (888) 266-4226.

First Dark Horse edition: August 2016
ISBN 978-1-50670-215-5

1 3 5 7 9 10 8 6 4 2
Printed in China

Alena

Alena was originally published in Sweden by Kolik Förlag.

Library of Congress Cataloging-in-Publication Data

Names: Andersson, Kim, author, illustrator.
Title: Alena / Kim Andersson.
Description: Milwaukie, OR : Dark Horse Books, 2016.
Identifiers: LCCN 2016011511 | ISBN 9781506702155 (paperback)
Subjects: LCSH: Comic books, strips, etc. | BISAC: COMICS & GRAPHIC NOVELS / Manga / Media Tie-In. | COMICS & GRAPHIC NOVELS / Horror. | COMICS & GRAPHIC NOVELS / Crime & Mystery.
Classification: LCC PN6790.S883 A4713 2016 | DDC 741.5/9485–dc23
LC record available at http://lccn.loc.gov/2016011511

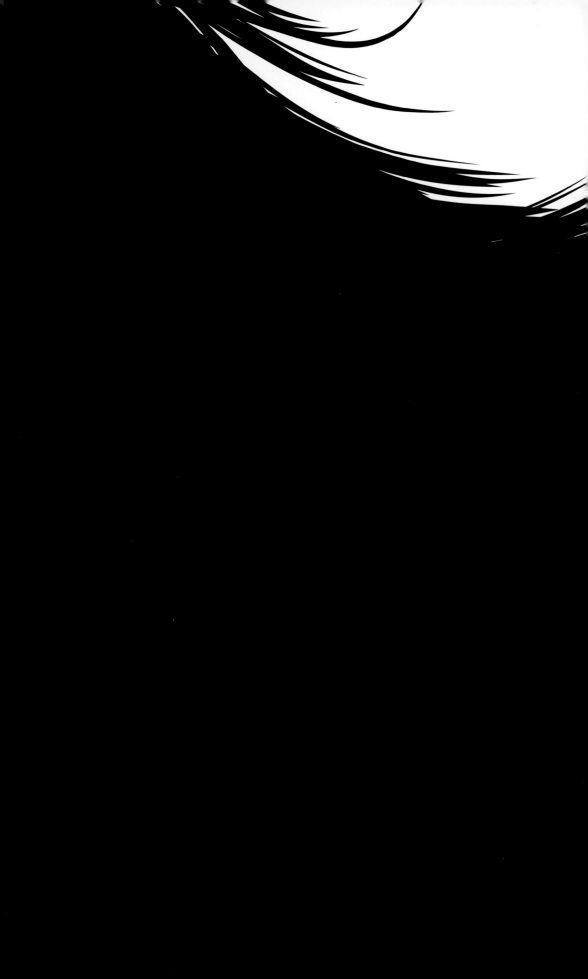

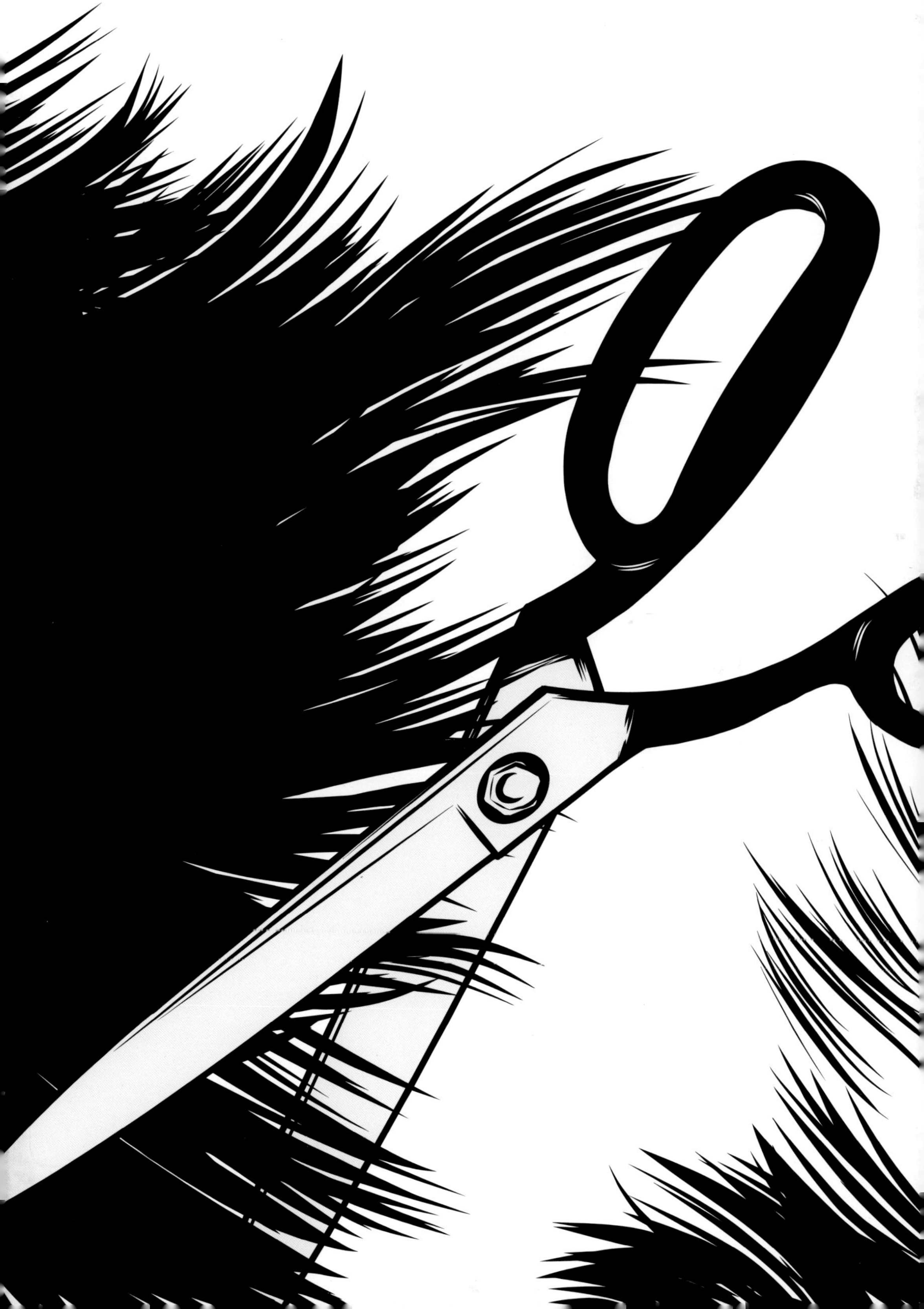

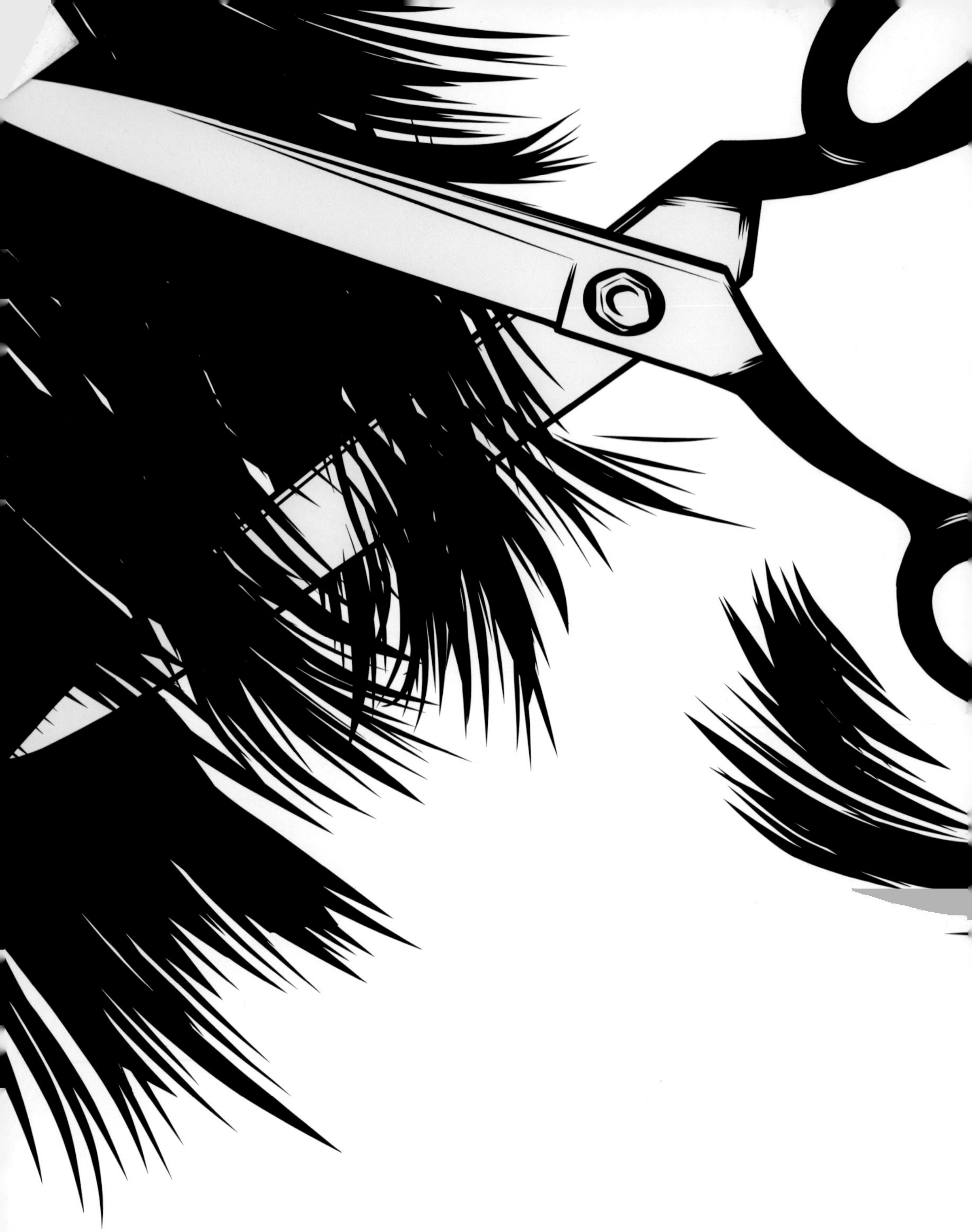